FOR ENGLISH LEARNERS

Language Development Practice

English Language Development

Mc
Graw
Hill
Education

www.mheonline.com/readingwonders

Table of Contents

Sentences and Sentence Fragments............1
Run-on Sentences............ 4
Types of Sentences I 7
Types of Sentences II 10
Simple and Complete Subject............13
Simple and Complete Predicate............16
Compound Subjects............19
Compound Predicates 22
Simple Sentences............25
Compound Sentences............28
Complex Sentences I............31
Complex Sentences II............34
Relative Pronouns in Complex Sentences............37
Relative Adverbs in Complex Sentences 40
Common and Proper Nouns 43
Concrete and Abstract Nouns 46
Countable and Uncountable Nouns 49
Nouns Derived from Other Words 52
Singular and Plural Nouns I 55
Singular and Plural Nouns II 58
Irregular Plural Nouns............61
Other Irregular Nouns/Collective Nouns............64
Singular Possessive Nouns............67
Plural Possessive Nouns 70
Noun Phrases............73
Expanding Noun Phrases............76
Appositives 79
Appositive Phrases 82
Verbs: Main Verb 85
Verbs: Helping Verb 88
Action Verbs: Present, Past, Future I 91
Action Verbs: Present, Past, Future II 94
Action Verbs and Direct Objects............97
Action Verbs and Indirect Objects............ 100
Progressive Form/Subject-Verb Agreement 103
Timeless Present............106
Past and Future Tenses............109
Future Progressive............112
Avoiding Shifts in Verb Tense I............115
Avoiding Shifts in Verb Tense II............118
Present Perfect Tense 121
Past and Future Perfect Tenses............124
Helping Verbs and Tenses............127
Special Helping Verbs: *can, may*............130

Auxiliary Verbs: *ought, will, shall*............133
Auxiliary Verbs: *prefer to, would rather*............136
Linking Verbs I............139
Linking Verbs II............142
Predicate Nouns............145
Predicate Adjectives............148
Tense and Agreement of Linking Verbs I............151
Tense and Agreement of Linking Verbs II............154
Present Tense of Regular Verbs............157
Past Tense of Regular Verbs............160
Present Tense of Irregular Verbs............163
Past Tense of Irregular Verbs............166
More Irregular Past Tenses I............169
More Irregular Past Tenses II............172
Active and Passive Voice 175
Conditional Tense............178
Progressive/Future/Conditional Perfect I............181
Progressive/Future/Conditional Perfect II............184
Phrasal Verbs I............187
Phrasal Verbs II............190
Phrasal Verbs with Multiple Meanings I............193
Phrasal Verbs with Multiple Meanings II............196
Singular and Plural Personal Pronouns............199
Avoiding Vague Pronoun References............ 202
Subject Pronouns 205
Object Pronouns 208
Relative Pronouns: *that, which*............211
Relative Pronouns: *who, whom, whose*............214
Interrogative Pronouns............217
Indefinite Pronouns............ 220
Reflexive Pronouns............223
Intensive Pronouns............226
Reciprocal Pronouns............229
Possessive Pronouns 232
Pronoun-Antecedent Agreement I............235
Pronoun-Antecedent Agreement II 238
Pronoun-Verb Agreement I............241
Pronoun-Verb Agreement II............244
Pronoun-Verb Contractions............247
Pronouns and Homophones............250
Adjectives: Placement in a Sentence............253
Order of Adjectives in a Sentence............256
Proper Adjectives............259
Articles............262

Concrete Descriptive Adjectives.................................265
Ordinal Numbers..268
Demonstrative Adjectives and Pronouns..................271
Comparing with *More* and *Most*............................274
Comparative and Superlative Adjectives I.............277
Comparative and Superlative Adjectives II...........280
Comparative with *As _ As/Too* + Adjective..........283
Adjectives with *–ish* or *–y*....................................286
Nouns to Adjectives I..289
Nouns to Adjectives II...292
Adverbs/Position/Ending in *–ly*................................295
Adverbs: When/Where/How/To What Extent....298
Adverbs to Describe Frequency.................................301
Intensifiers..304
Relative Adverbs..307
Adverbs that Modify Adjectives.................................310
Comparing with Adverbs...313
Comparing with Irregular Adverbs.............................316
Negatives: Correcting Double Negatives.................319
Negatives with Helping Verbs....................................322
Specialized Adverbs..325
Conjunctive Adverbs..328
Prepositions...331
Prepositional Phrases...334
Prepositions Indicating Time.....................................337
Prepositions Indicating Place....................................340
Prepositions Indicating Movement...........................343
Prepositions Indicating Direction..............................346
Prepositions Indicating Location...............................349
Prepositions as Quantifiers..352
Prepositions as Sentence Connectors.....................355
Specialized Prepositions..358
Preposition Combinations I..361
Preposition Combinations II.......................................364
Coordinating Conjunctions I......................................367
Coordinating Conjunctions II.....................................370
Correlative Conjunctions I..373
Correlative Conjunctions II...376
Subordinating Conjunctions I....................................379
Subordinating Conjunctions II...................................382
Conjunctive Adverbs I...385
Conjunctive Adverbs II..388
Transitional Words and Expressions I.......................391
Transitional Words and Expressions II......................394
Present, Past, and Future Questions I......................397

Present, Past, and Future Questions II.....................400
Statements and Questions I..403
Statements and Questions II.......................................406
Use *Can* to Show Ability...409
Use *Did, Do,* and *Does* to Ask Questions.................412
Compound Sentences I...415
Compound Sentences II..418
Complex Sentences I...421
Complex Sentences II..424
Compound Subject Nouns and Predicates...............427
Adjectives/Adverbs/Prepositional Phrases.............430
Combining with Correlative Conjunctions...............433
Combining Sentences: Appositives............................436
Expanding Sentences: Noun Phrases I.....................439
Expanding Sentences: Noun Phrases II....................442
Expanding with Adjectives/Adjective Phrases......445
Expanding with Adjectives/Adjective Phrases......448
Expanding Sentences: Adverbs..................................451
Expanding Sentences: Adverb Phrases....................454
Expanding with Prepositional Phrases I...................457
Expanding with Prepositional Phrases II..................460
Condensing Sentences I..463
Condensing Sentences II...466
Antonyms..469
Synonyms..472
Shades of Meaning..475
Multiple Meaning Words..478
Homophones...481
Homographs..484
Idioms/Adages/Proverbs I..487
Idioms/Adages/Proverbs II...490
Figurative Language I..493
Figurative Language II...496
Connotation and Denotation I....................................499
Connotation and Denotation II...................................502
Nominalizations I...505
Nominalizations II..508
Prefixes: *un-, mis-, dis-, bi-, re-*...............................511
Prefixes: *im-, in-, pre-, mini-*...................................514
Suffixes: *-able, -ible, -er, -ful*..................................517
Suffixes: *-en, -ward, -less*..520
Time Words I...523
Time Words II..526
Cognates I...529
Cognates II..532

Name _____

> A **sentence** is a group of words that tells a complete thought. A complete sentence has a subject and a predicate. If part of the sentence is missing, the word group is called a **sentence fragment.**
>
> **Sentence:**   William and David walked to school.
>
> **Sentence Fragment:**   William and David.

Circle the word that correctly describes each item.

1.   We rode horses at the farm.

   sentence   fragment

2.   One very tall white horse.

   sentence   fragment

3.   Held on tightly to the saddle.

   sentence   fragment

4.   Ate apples from our hands.

   sentence   fragment

5.   Mr. Hansen gives riding lessons.

   sentence   fragment

6.   My little sister Marie.

   sentence   fragment

TEACHER: Read the directions and questions to students. Guide students to complete the exercise, providing support as needed.

Grades 4-6   1

Name _____

A **sentence** is a group of words that tells a complete thought. A complete sentence has a subject and a predicate. If part of the sentence is missing, the word group is called a **sentence fragment.**

Sentence: William and David walked to school.

Sentence Fragment: William and David.

Correct each fragment by adding words from the box. Use each set of words just once. Then write the sentence correctly.

One white horse	Mr. Hansen	costs $20
The red barn	fits on the horse's back	

1. _____ has stalls for six horses.

   _____

2. That brown saddle _____.

   _____

3. _____ gave us riding lessons.

   _____

4. _____ ate apples from our hands.

   _____

5. Each lesson _____.

   _____

TEACHER: Read the directions and questions to students. Guide students to complete the exercise, providing support as needed.

Name _____

> A **sentence** is a group of words that tells a complete thought. A complete sentence has a subject and a predicate. If part of the sentence is missing, the word group is called a **sentence fragment**.

Read the passage. Underline each sentence fragment. Then add words to make complete sentences and rewrite the passage correctly on the lines below.

1. Mr. Hansen gives riding lessons. *Chose a tall white horse. Ate apples from my hand. The brown saddle. Rode around the track.*

_____

_____

_____

_____

_____

Name _____

A **run-on sentence** is two or more complete sentences that run together. Break run-on sentences into two separate complete sentences or add the correct punctuation.

> **Run-on sentence:** Dave went to the library he got a new book.

> **Corrected sentences:** Dave went to the library. He got a new book.

A. Draw a line between the two complete thoughts in each run-on sentence.

1. Cal is running he is very fast.

2. He ran in a race it was last week.

3. Cal nearly won an older boy beat him.

B. Rewrite each run-on sentence from Part A as two separate sentences.

1. _____ _____

2. _____ _____

3. _____ _____

4 Grades 4-6

TEACHER: Read the directions and questions in Part A and Part B to students. Guide students to complete each exercise, providing support as needed.

Name _____

> A **run-on sentence** is two or more complete sentences that run together. Break run-on sentences into two separate complete sentences or add the correct punctuation.
>
> **Run-on sentence:** Dave went to the library he got a new book.
>
> **Corrected sentences:** Dave went to the library. He got a new book.

A. Circle the correct sentences. Place an _X_ over run-on sentences.

1. **a.** Cal is a fast runner.

    b. He loves running he runs every day.

    c. Now he is training for a race.

2. **a.** Cal ran in a race last week.

    b. Many children raced around the track.

    c. Cal nearly won an older boy beat him.

B. Rewrite the run-on sentences from above as two single sentences.

1. _____

    _____

2. _____

    _____

TEACHER: Read the directions and questions in Part A and Part B to students. Guide students to complete each exercise, providing support as needed.

Name _____

> A **run-on sentence** is two or more complete sentences that run together. Break run-on sentences into two separate complete sentences or add the correct punctuation.

Break each run-on sentence into two sentences. Write the new sentences on the lines.

1. Cal is the best runner in our school he runs very fast.

   _____

   _____

2. Last week Cal ran in a race many children raced around the track.

   _____

   _____

3. Cal nearly came in first one older boy beat him by inches.

   _____

   _____

TEACHER: Read the directions and questions to students. Guide students to complete the exercise, providing support as needed.

Name _____

A sentence is a group of words that contains a complete thought. There are different types of sentences.

Statements are sentences that tell something. They end with a period.

Donna tries on a dress.   The dress is red.

Questions are sentences that ask something. They end with a question mark (?).

Is that a nice color?   Does the dress fit?

Add the correct end mark to each sentence. Write _S_ next to each statement. Write _Q_ next to each question.

1. The stores opened at ten o'clock _____

2. Can you see the dress shop _____

3. How much does this one cost _____

4. This blue dress is my favorite _____

5. Where is the price tag _____

TEACHER: Read the directions and questions to students. Guide students to complete the exercise, providing support as needed.

Name _____

> A sentence is a group of words that contains a complete thought. There are different types of sentences.
>
> **Statements** are sentences that tell something. They end with a period.
>
> > Donna tries on a dress.
>
> **Questions** are sentences that ask something. They end with a question mark (?).
>
> > Is that a nice color?

A. Add the correct end mark to each sentence.

1. **a.** Have the stores opened yet _____
   b. The dress shop opens at ten o'clock _____

2. **a.** This blue dress is on sale _____
   b. How much does the dress cost _____

3. **a.** Did you try on the red dress _____
   b. Red is my favorite color _____

B. Decide if the sentence is a statement or a question. Write your answer on the line. Then rewrite the sentence correctly.

1. which dress did Mai choose _____

   _____

2. she can wear it to my party _____

   _____

3. who paid for the new dress _____

   _____

TEACHER: Read the directions and questions in Part A and Part B to students. Guide students to complete each exercise, providing support as needed.

Name _____

A sentence is a group of words that contains a complete thought. There are different types of sentences.

Statements are sentences that tell something. They end with a period.

Questions are sentences that ask something. They end with a question mark (?).

Read the passage. Then rewrite the passage correctly on the lines below. Add end marks where they are needed.

1. Mai needed a dress for a party Would she be able to find the right dress She and her mother drove to the mall They looked at many nice dresses Which one would Mai choose

_____

_____

_____

_____

_____

Name _____

> **Commands** are sentences that ask or order you to do something. They end with a period.
>
> Please taste this.   Stir the soup.
>
> **Exclamations** are sentences that show strong feeling. They end with an exclamation point (!).
>
> How delicious that is!   What a strong flavor it has!
>
> **Interjections** are words that show strong feelings. Follow an interjection with an exclamation point.
>
> Ouch!   Wow!

Write C next to each command. Write E next to each exclamation. Write I next to each interjection.

1. Your mother is such a great cook! _____

2. Cut the carrots carefully. _____

3. Great! _____

4. Please hand me the spoon. _____

5. What good soup we made! _____

TEACHER: Read the directions and questions to students. Guide students to complete the exercise, providing support as needed.

Name _____

> **Commands** are sentences that ask or order you to do something. They end with a period.
>
> **Exclamations** are sentences that show strong feeling. They end with an exclamation point (!).
>
> **Interjections** are words that show strong feelings. Follow an interjection with an exclamation point.

A. Add the correct end mark to each sentence or word.

1. **a.** Try this vegetable soup _____

    b. Excellent _____

2. **a.** Please add those sliced carrots _____

    b. You did such a great job _____

3. **a.** What wonderful soup we made _____

    b. Yum _____

B. Decide if the sentence is a command or an exclamation. Write your answer on the line. Then rewrite the sentence correctly.

1. how colorful the soup is _____

    _____

2. mix in the other vegetables _____

    _____

3. what a tasty treat this will be _____

    _____

TEACHER: Read the directions and questions in Part A and Part B to students. Guide students to complete each exercise, providing support as needed.

Name _____

> **Commands** are sentences that ask or order you to do something. They end with a period.
>
> **Exclamations** are sentences that show strong feeling. They end with an exclamation point (!).
>
> **Interjections** are words that show strong feelings. Follow an interjection with an exclamation point.

Read the passage. Then rewrite the passage correctly on the lines below. Add end marks where they are needed.

1. Help Mom make a pot of soup Find the carrots and corn What bright colors they have Mix them into the pot Nice work

_____

_____

_____

_____

_____

TEACHER: Read the directions and questions to students. Guide students to complete the exercise, providing support as needed.

Name _____

> A **complete subject** is all the words that are in the subject part of a sentence. The **simple subject** is the main word or words in the complete subject.
>
> The noisy train ran on the tracks nearby.
>
> **Complete Subject** = the noisy train   **Simple Subject** = train

Underline the complete subject. Circle the simple subject.

1. That map tells about the trains.

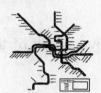

2. These long trains run underground.

3. A driver sits in the front of the train.

4. Some passengers look for seats.

5. The long trip goes quickly.

TEACHER: Read the directions and questions to students. Guide students to complete the exercise, providing support as needed.

Name _____

A **complete subject** is all the words that are in the subject part of a sentence. The **simple subject** is the main word or words in the complete subject.

The noisy train ran on the tracks nearby.

Complete Subject = the noisy train   **Simple Subject** = train

A. Underline the complete subject. Circle the simple subject.

1. That map shows us all of the subway stops.

2. The first stop is near the park.

3. My oldest cousin will meet us there.

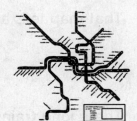

B. Add a subject to each sentence. Circle your simple subject.

1. _____ rode on the subway.

2. _____ found a seat.

3. _____ looked out the window.

4. _____ stopped suddenly.

TEACHER: Read the directions and questions in Part A and Part B to students. Guide students to complete each exercise, providing support as needed.

Name _____

> A **complete subject** is all the words that are in the subject part of a sentence. The **simple subject** is the main word or words in the complete subject.

A. Underline the complete subject in each sentence. Write the simple subject on the line.

1. My father rides the subway to work. _____

2. His office is far downtown. _____

3. He leaves for the train at seven o'clock. _____

4. The number 3 train stops near his building. _____

5. Many passengers get off at that stop. _____

B. Choose three of the simple subjects that you wrote above. Use them in three new sentences. Write the sentences on the lines.

1. _____

_____

2. _____

_____

3. _____

_____

Name _____

A **complete predicate** is all the words in a sentence that tell what the subject does or is. The **simple predicate** is the verb in the complete predicate.

A few drops of rain fell on my head.

Complete Predicate: fell on my head

Simple Predicate: fell

Read each sentence. Underline the complete predicate. Circle the simple predicate.

1. A dark cloud covered the sun.

2. A flash of lightning lit the sky.

3. I opened my new umbrella.

4. The rain splashed on the sidewalk.

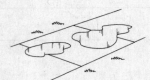

5. My feet felt warm and dry.

TEACHER: Read the directions and questions to students. Guide students to complete the exercise, providing support as needed.

Name _____

> A **complete predicate** is all the words in a sentence that tell what the subject does or is. The **simple predicate** is the verb in the complete predicate.
>
> A few drops of rain fell on my head.
>
> **Complete Predicate:** fell on my head
>
> **Simple Predicate:** fell

A. Underline the complete predicate. Circle the simple predicate.

1. Bright lightning lit my whole room.

2. All of us heard the rumble of thunder.

3. The storm brought wind and heavy rain.

B. Add a predicate to each sentence. Circle your simple predicate.

1. My new umbrella _____.

2. The pouring rain _____.

3. Puddles on the sidewalk _____.

4. A loud boom of thunder _____.

TEACHER: Read the directions and questions in Part A and Part B to students. Guide students to complete each exercise, providing support as needed.

Name _____

> A **complete predicate** is all the words in a sentence that tell what the subject does or is. The **simple predicate** is the verb in the complete predicate.

A. Underline the complete predicate in each sentence. Write the simple predicate on the line.

1. Thunderstorms scare some people. _____

2. Today's storm was no problem for me. _____

3. My mother listened to the weather report. _____

4. I carried a big black umbrella. _____

5. Tall rubber boots protected my feet. _____

B. Choose three of the simple predicates that you wrote above. Use them in three new sentences. Write the sentences on the lines.

1. _____

_____

2. _____

_____

3. _____

_____

TEACHER: Read the directions and questions in Part A and Part B to students. Guide students to complete each exercise, providing support as needed.

Name _____

A sentence may have more than one subject. The word *and* is often used to link two or more complete subjects to make a **compound subject**.

The cat **and** her kittens lay in the box.

A. Write *S* if the sentence has a single subject. Write *C* if the sentence has a compound subject.

1. The little black kitten played with its toys. _____

2. My sister and I took care of the kittens. _____

3. A ball and some yarn are their favorite toys. _____

4. They play with each other all day long. _____

B. Underline the two subjects in each sentence.

1. The gray kitten and the white one play.

2. The mother cat and I watch them carefully.

3. Their teeth and tiny claws are so sharp!

4. Tina and our father named the little one "Tiger."

TEACHER: Read the directions and questions in Part A and Part B to students. Guide students to complete each exercise, providing support as needed.

Name _____

> A sentence may have more than one subject. The word *and* is often used to link two or more complete subjects to make a **compound subject**.
>
> <u>The cat</u> **and** <u>her kittens</u> lay in the box.

A. Read each sentence. Underline the two complete subjects in each compound subject.

1. Lola and the kittens are sound asleep.

2. My sister Tina and I take care of them.

3. Milk and a warm bed are important.

4. The black kitten and her brothers will grow fast.

B. Add complete subjects to each sentence to form a compound subject.

1. _____ and _____ are so cute!

2. _____ and _____ play with them.

3. _____ and _____ make great pets.

4. _____ and _____ are good toys for cats.

TEACHER: Read the directions and questions in Part A and Part B to students. Guide students to complete each exercise, providing support as needed.

Name _____

A sentence may have more than one subject. The word *and* is often used to link two or more complete subjects to make a **compound subject**.

A. Combine sentences to make one sentence with a compound subject. Write the new sentence on the line.

1. Lola slept in the box. Her babies slept in the box.

   _____

2. The littlest kitten ran around. Her brothers ran around.

   _____

3. My sister Tina held the tiny kitten. I held the tiny kitten.

   _____

B. Underline all of the complete subjects in each sentence.

1. Fish, milk, and dry food are good for cats.

2. My father, my sister, and I visit the pet shop.

3. A parrot, two turtles, and a cat are in the window.

TEACHER: Read the directions and questions in Part A and Part B to students. Guide students to complete each exercise, providing support as needed.

Name _____

> A sentence may have more than one predicate. The word *and* is often used to link complete predicates to make a **compound predicate**.
>
> Ben <u>bends down</u> **and** <u>rolls the ball</u>.

A. Write *S* if the sentence has a single predicate. Write *C* if the sentence has a compound predicate.

1. The ball hits and knocks down the pins. _____

2. Ben's ball hit nine of the pins. _____

3. Ben jumps up and cheers loudly. _____

4. He may hit the last pin this time. _____

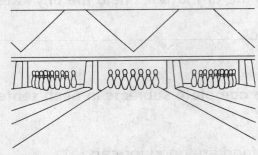

B. Read each sentence. Underline all the complete predicates in each sentence.

1. Jake stands up and chooses a ball.

2. He steps forward and drops the ball.

3. The heavy ball spins and rolls slowly.

4. Two white pins wobble and fall over.

TEACHER: Read the directions and questions in Part A and Part B to students. Guide students to complete each exercise, providing support as needed.

Name _____

> A sentence may have more than one predicate. The word *and* is often used to link complete predicates to make a **compound predicate**.
>
> Ben <u>bends down</u> **and** <u>rolls the ball</u>.

A. Underline the two complete predicates in each sentence.

1. Ben searches for a ball and picks a blue one.

2. He leans forward and swings his arm back.

3. The blue ball hits the lane and rolls quickly.

4. The ten white pins crash and spin away.

B. Add complete predicates to each sentence to form a compound predicate.

1. The children _____ and _____.

2. My heavy ball _____ and _____.

3. One player _____ and _____.

4. Bowling _____ and _____.

TEACHER: Read the directions and questions in Part A and Part B to students. Guide students to complete each exercise, providing support as needed.

Name _____

A sentence may have more than one predicate. The word *and* is often used to link complete predicates to make a **compound predicate**.

A. Combine sentences to make one new sentence with a compound predicate. Write the new sentence on the line.

1. The ball is heavy. The ball has three holes.

   _____

2. Ben lifted the ball. Ben leaned forward.

   _____

3. The white pins shook. The white pins fell down.

   _____

B. Underline all of the complete predicates in each sentence.

1. Ben aimed, pulled his arm back, and let go.

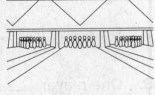
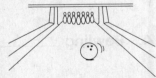

2. The ball dropped, spun, and rolled down the lane.

3. Ben's friends jumped up, pounded Ben's back, and cheered.

TEACHER: Read the directions and questions in Part A and Part B to students. Guide students to complete each exercise, providing support as needed.

Name _____

> A **simple sentence** has one subject or compound subject and one predicate or compound predicate.
>
> This tray / holds my lunch.
>
> Milk and juice / come in cartons.
>
> I / filled my tray and paid for my lunch.

Draw one line to divide the complete subject from the complete predicate in each simple sentence.

1. This sandwich smells delicious.

2. Bananas and apples are tasty.

3. My tray holds one bowl of soup.

4. My whole lunch cost less than two dollars.

5. The lunch lady smiled and gave me change.

TEACHER: Read the directions and questions to students. Guide students to complete the exercise, providing support as needed.

Name _____

A **simple sentence** has one subject or compound subject and one predicate or compound predicate.

This tray / holds my lunch.

Complete each simple sentence by adding a subject or predicate from the box below. Use each set of words just once. Then write the simple sentence correctly.

smells delicious	bananas and apples	sat with Kyle
the lunch lady	opened and drank his milk	

1. _____ are in the fruit bowl.

   _____

2. The onion soup _____.

   _____

3. _____ smiled and took my money.

   _____

4. Lucy and I _____.

   _____

5. My friend Kyle _____.

   _____

TEACHER: Read the directions and questions to students. Guide students to complete the exercise, providing support as needed.

Name _____

> A **simple sentence** has one subject or compound subject and one predicate or compound predicate.
>
> This tray holds my lunch.

Find the complete subjects and predicates in each simple sentence. Write them on the lines provided.

1. Bananas and apples fill the fruit bowl.

   subject _____ predicate _____

2. The onion soup smells delicious.

   subject _____ predicate _____

3. The friendly lunch lady smiled and took my money.

   subject _____ predicate _____

4. Lucy and Fred sat at the table near the door.

   subject _____ predicate _____

5. My friend Kyle opened and drank his milk.

   subject _____ predicate _____

TEACHER: Read the directions and questions to students. Guide students to complete the exercise, providing support as needed.

Name _____

> A **compound sentence** may be made of two or more simple sentences. The sentences may be joined by the word *and, or,* or *but*. A comma divides the sentences.
>
> Cam/planted a garden, and flowers/grow there.

A. Write *S* if the sentence is simple. Write *C* if the sentence is compound.

1. Daisies and poppies grow in the garden. _____

2. Daisies are white, but poppies are red. _____

3. Cam built a fence, and rabbits cannot get in. _____

4. The rabbits hop around and peek inside. _____

B. Draw lines to divide the subjects from the predicates in each compound sentence.

1. The garden is lovely, and everyone likes it.

2. Cam weeds the garden, or she picks flowers.

3. The daisies are pretty, but they have no smell.

4. Roses smell better, but their thorns are sharp.

TEACHER: Read the directions and questions in Part A and Part B to students. Guide students to complete each exercise, providing support as needed.

Name _____

> A **compound sentence** may be made of two or more simple sentences. The sentences may be joined by the word *and, or,* or *but*. A comma divides the sentences.
>
> Cam / planted a garden, and flowers / grow there.

Draw lines to separate subjects from predicates. Write *S* if the sentence is simple. Write *C* if the sentence is compound.

1. White daisies and red poppies grow here. _____

2. Cam built a fence, and the rabbits stay outside. _____

3. One rabbit hops around and peeks inside. _____

4. Cam waters the flowers, or she weeds them. _____

5. Roses are lovely, but lilacs smell even better. _____

6. Poppies, roses, or tulips may be red. _____

Name _____

A **compound sentence** may be made of two or more simple sentences. The sentences may be joined by the word *and, or,* or *but*. A comma divides the sentences.

Cam planted a garden, and flowers grow there.

Cam's Garden

Cam planted a beautiful garden.

Poppies and large white daisies grow there.

She built a fence and the rabbits cannot get in.

Cam waters the garden daily or she weeds the flowerbeds.

The poppies grow tall and shine brightly.

Cam's roses have a nice smell but her lilacs smell even better.

She picks a bouquet and brings it inside.

The garden is lovely and everyone likes it.

A. Circle the compound sentences in the passage above.

B. Add commas where they belong in the compound sentences above.

TEACHER: Read the directions and questions to students. Guide students to complete the exercise, providing support as needed.

Name _____

> A **complex sentence** is made of an independent clause and one or more dependent clauses. A subordinating conjunction often begins a dependent clause. Subordinating conjunctions include
>
> after   although   as   because   before   if   since   until   while

A. **Write *C* next to each complex sentence. Write *S* next to each simple sentence.**

1. The lions paced as the people watched. _____

2. The sun shines on the children while they play. _____

3. The kitten plays with yarn. _____

4. The girl reads because she loves stories. _____

B. **Write the subordinating conjunctions from the sentences above on the lines below.**

1. _____

2. _____

3. _____

Name _____

> A **complex sentence** is made of an independent clause and one or more dependent clauses. A subordinating conjunction, such as *because, since, while, before, after, although, as, if,* or *until,* often begins a dependent clause.

A. Circle the complex sentences. Underline each dependent clause. Place an X over simple sentences.

1. **a.** The lions paced as the people watched.

   b. The lions are hungry because it is time for their dinner.

   c. Visitors enjoy seeing the lions.

2. **a.** The sun shines on the children while they play.

   b. When one player kicks the ball, another player blocks it.

   c. The children play soccer as the sun shines.

B. Write the subordinating conjunction that begins each dependent clause on the lines provided.

1. Sarita bakes a cake because it is her mother's birthday. _____

2. We plan to visit the beach while it is still summer. _____

3. If you want to have a picnic, pack some food in a basket. _____

TEACHER: Read the directions and questions in Part A and Part B to students. Guide students to complete each exercise, providing support as needed.

Name _____

> A **complex sentence** is made of an independent clause and one or more dependent clauses. A subordinating conjunction, such as *because, since, while, before, after, although, as, if,* or *until,* often begins a dependent clause.

A. Circle the independent clause in each complex sentence. Underline each dependent clause.

1. The puppy whined because he wanted Kate to throw the ball.

2. We went swimming while we were camping.

3. After the sun went down, we sang songs.

B. List the subordinating conjunctions from the sentences above on the lines below.

1. _____

2. _____

3. _____

Name _____

A **complex sentence** is made of an independent clause and one or more dependent clauses. A subordinating conjunction often begins a dependent clause. Subordinating conjunctions include

after   although   as   because   before   if   since   until   while

Write the subordinating conjunction that completes each complex sentence correctly.

1. Rory fell asleep (because/until) _____ he was tired.

2. We stayed up (before/until) _____ the sun went down.

3. (If/After) _____ the sun went down, we sang songs.

4. I will put out the fire (if/while) _____ you will help.

5. (Before/As) _____ we ate dinner, we washed our hands.

TEACHER: Read the directions and questions to students. Guide students to complete the exercise, providing support as needed.

Name _____

> A **complex sentence** is made of an independent clause and one or more dependent clauses. A subordinating conjunction, such as *because, since, while, before, after, although, as, if,* or *until,* often begins a dependent clause.

Complete each complex sentence by using an appropriate subordinating conjunction.

1. Some campers went to sleep early _____ they were tired.

2. We stayed up _____ the moon rose.

3. _____ we watched the moon rise, we roasted marshmallows.

4. _____ the sun went down, we sang songs.

5. A raccoon came into the campsite _____ he smelled food.

6. I will put out the fire _____ you promise to help.

7. _____ the fire was out, we could see the stars.

8. _____ we went to our tents, we took a walk in the woods.

Name _____

> A **complex sentence** is made of an independent clause and one or
> more dependent clauses. A subordinating conjunction, such as *because,*
> *since, while, before, after, although, as, if,* or *until,* often begins a
> dependent clause.

A. **Combine the simple sentences to form a complex sentence.**
Use a subordinating conjunction to begin each dependent clause.

1. Jan went to bed. She was tired.

   _____

2. The movie ended. We walked home.

   _____

3. She waited in line. She played a game.

   _____

B. **Form a complex sentence by adding a dependent clause to each**
independent clause. Begin each dependent clause with a subordinating
conjunction.

1. The lions are hungry _____ .

   _____

2. The children play soccer _____ .

   _____

3. _____ , Max ate his sandwich.

   _____

TEACHER: Read the directions and questions in Part A and Part B to students. Guide
students to complete each exercise, providing support as needed.

Name _____

> A **relative pronoun** begins a dependent clause that gives more information about a noun. Relative pronouns include the words:
>
> that   which   who   whom   whose

A. Choose the relative pronoun that correctly completes each sentence.

1.   The musician _____ plays jazz is on stage.

     a. which   **b.** that   **c.** who   **d.** whose

2.   I live in the house _____ has the large porch.

     a. which   **b.** that   **c.** who   **d.** whom

3.   She wrote the novel *Wolf,* _____ became a best seller.

     a. which   **b.** that   **c.** who   **d.** whose

B. Choose the correct relative pronoun to complete each sentence.

1.   Paulina is the actress (who/whom) I like best.

2.   The baby (whom/whose) shirt is green is my little brother.

3.   Jules is the person with (which/whom) I worked at the cafe.

4.   I love the book (that/which) has a horse on its cover.

TEACHER: Read the directions and questions in Part A and Part B to students. Guide students to complete each exercise, providing support as needed.   Grades 4-6   **37**

Name _____

> A **relative pronoun** begins a dependent clause that gives more information about a noun. Relative pronouns include the words *that, which, who, whom,* and *whose.*

A. Choose the correct relative pronoun to complete each sentence.

1. Paulina is the singer (who/whom) also plays the violin.

2. He is playing the guitar (that/which) he used on the recording.

3. Jules is the drummer with (which/whom) I went to music camp.

4. The musician (who/whose) shirt is red plays the piano.

B. Write the relative pronoun that correctly completes each sentence.

1. I talked to the librarian _____ hair is curly.

2. I love the book _____ has a horse on its cover.

3. Mark Twain is the author _____ wrote *Tom Sawyer.*

4. She wrote the novel *Wolf,* _____ became a best seller.

TEACHER: Read the directions and questions in Part A and Part B to students. Guide students to complete each exercise, providing support as needed.

Name _____

> A **relative pronoun** begins a dependent clause that gives more information about a noun. Relative pronouns include the words *that, which, who, whom,* and *whose.*

A. Complete each sentence with the correct relative pronoun.

1. Mark Twain is the author _____ wrote the classic novel, *Tom Sawyer.*

2. He is playing the guitar _____ he used on the recording.

3. Jules is the drummer with _____ I went to music camp.

B. Read each sentence. Circle the sentences that correctly use relative pronouns.

1. The baby whose shirt is green is my little brother.

2. Jules is the person with who I worked at the cafe.

3. I love the book that has a horse on its cover.

TEACHER: Read the directions and questions in Part A and Part B to students. Guide students to complete each exercise, providing support as needed.

Name _____

A **relative adverb** can also be used to begin a dependent clause. Relative adverbs include:

when   where   why

A. Choose the relative adverb that correctly completes each sentence.

1. I do not remember the house _____ Anna lives.
    a. when   **b.** where   **c.** why

2. This long line is the reason _____ I am going home.
    a. when   **b.** where   **c.** why

3. Fall is the time _____ we usually go apple picking.
    a. when   **b.** where   **c.** why

B. Choose the correct relative adverb to complete each sentence.

1. This is the school (when/where) I went to
    Kindergarten.

2. The roller coasters are the reason (why/where)
    I enjoy amusement parks.

3. Six o'clock is the time (why/when) I usually wake up.

4. She went to the store (where/why) I bought my dress.

TEACHER: Read the directions and questions in Part A and Part B to students. Guide students to complete each exercise, providing support as needed.

Name _____

> A **relative adverb** can begin a dependent clause. Relative adverbs include the words *when, where,* and *why.*

A. Circle the correct relative adverb to complete each sentence.

1. This is the school (when/where) I went to Kindergarten.

2. The roller coasters are the reason (where/why) I enjoy amusement parks.

3. Six o'clock is the time (when/where) I usually wake up.

B. Rewrite each sentence. Replace the underlined word or words with an appropriate relative adverb.

1. I do not remember the house <u>at which</u> we had the meeting.

_____

2. This long line is the reason <u>that</u> I went home.

_____

3. Fall is the season <u>in which</u> we usually go apple picking.

_____

TEACHER: Read the directions and questions in Part A and Part B to students. Guide students to complete each exercise, providing support as needed.

Name _____

> A **relative adverb** can begin a dependent clause. Relative adverbs include the words *when, where,* and *why.*

A. Complete each sentence by writing the correct relative adverb.

1. This is the school _____ I went to Kindergarten.

2. The roller coasters are the reason _____ I enjoy amusement parks.

3. Six o'clock is the time _____ I usually wake up.

B. Read each short paragraph. Underline any relative adverbs.

1. We are meeting at Anna's house again. I do not remember the house where we had the meeting last time. I will call her on my phone!

2. I saw a preview for a new movie. It is the reason why I decided to go tonight. When I got to the theater, there was a long line.

3. Fall is the season when we usually go apple picking. This year, we did not have time to pick apples. I was disappointed.

TEACHER: Read the directions and questions in Part A and Part B to students. Guide students to complete each exercise, providing support as needed.

Name _____

> A **common noun** names a type of person, place, or thing. Common nouns are not capitalized.
>
> A **proper noun** names a specific person, place, or thing. Proper nouns are capitalized.
>
> city   teacher   park
>
> Los Angeles   Mr. Ropa   Wildwood Park

Read the underlined word. Then circle the word that shows what kind of noun it is.

1. We visited the <u>museum</u>.

   common   proper

2. The class went on a trip to <u>Chicago</u>.

   common   proper

3. <u>Viola</u> is the player who just scored.

   common   proper

4. My dog is afraid of <u>fireworks</u>.

   common   proper

5. You will need a <u>towel</u> at the beach.

   common   proper

6. We went camping at <u>Wilderness State Park</u>.

   common   proper

TEACHER: Read the directions and questions to students. Guide students to complete the exercise, providing support as needed.

Name _____

> A **common noun** names a type of person, place, or thing. Common nouns are not capitalized.
>
> A **proper noun** names a specific person, place, or thing. Proper nouns are capitalized.
>
> city   Los Angeles

A. Read each sentence. Write *C* if the underlined word is a common noun. Write *P* if the underlined word is a proper noun.

1. We visited the <u>museum</u> last week. _____

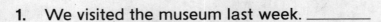

2. The class went on a field trip to <u>Chicago</u>. _____

3. <u>Viola</u> is the player who just scored a goal. _____

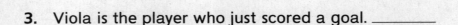

B. Read each sentence. Circle each common noun. Underline each proper noun.

1. Sammy, my dog, is afraid of fireworks.

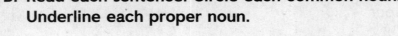

2. Bess sat on a towel at Silver Beach.

3. There are a lot of tents at Wilderness State Park.

TEACHER: Read the directions and questions in Part A and Part B to students. Guide students to complete each exercise, providing support as needed.

Name _____

> A **common noun** names a type of person, place, or thing. Common nouns are not capitalized.
>
> A **proper noun** names a specific person, place, or thing. Proper nouns are capitalized.

Find the common nouns and proper nouns in each sentence.
Write them on the lines.

1. We visited the museum when we went to New York City.

    common noun _____   proper noun _____

2. The students traveled to Chicago.

    common noun _____   proper noun _____

3. Viola just scored a goal.

    common noun _____   proper noun _____

4. Sammy is afraid of fireworks.

    common noun _____   proper noun _____

5. You will need a towel at Silver Beach.

    common noun _____   proper noun _____

6. We slept in a tent at Wilderness Park.

    common noun _____   proper noun _____

Name _____

A **concrete noun** names a person, place, or thing that you could see, hear, taste, smell, or touch. An **abstract noun** names something you cannot use your senses to see, hear, touch, taste, or smell.

Concrete Nouns: shoe, apple, paper

Abstract Nouns: happiness, courage, creativity

Read the underlined word. Then circle the word that shows what kind of noun it is.

1. The knight showed great <u>courage</u>.

    abstract   concrete

2. Children learn to sing in the <u>choir</u>.

    abstract   concrete

3. Suzie had great <u>love</u> for her new puppy.

    abstract   concrete

4. The <u>curiosity</u> of the students was obvious.

    abstract   concrete

5. Mr. Smith's class enjoyed the art <u>project</u>.

    abstract   concrete

6. We went to the store to buy some <u>eggs</u>.

    abstract   concrete

TEACHER: Read the directions and questions to students. Guide students to complete the exercise, providing support as needed.

Name _____

> A **concrete noun** names a person, place, or thing that you could see, hear, taste, smell, or touch. An **abstract noun** names something you cannot use your senses to see, hear, touch, taste, or smell.
>
> **Concrete Noun:** shoe   **Abstract Noun:** happiness

A. Read each sentence. Circle any concrete nouns.
Underline any abstract nouns.

1. The knight showed great courage as he fought the dragon.

2. Children learn to sing in the choir.

3. Suzie had great love for her new puppy.

4. The curiosity of the students was obvious.

5. Mr. Smith's class enjoyed the art project.

B. Circle the letter of the sentence that includes an abstract noun.

1. **a.** We bought eggs so we could make cookies.

   b. We used a recipe to make dough and frosting.

   c. We decorated the cookies with patience.

   d. We brought the cookies to the bake sale.

2. **a.** The rabbit was perfectly still.

   b. Its fear of the dog was clear.

   c. The dog sniffed near the trembling rabbit.

   d. The dog chased a squirrel.

Name _____

> A **concrete noun** names a person, place, or thing that you could see, hear, taste, smell, or touch. An **abstract noun** names something you cannot use your senses to see, hear, touch, taste, or smell.

A. Read each sentence. Circle any abstract nouns.

1. The knight showed courage as he fought the dragon.

2. Children learn to sing in the choir.

3. Suzie had great love for her new puppy.

4. The curiosity of the students was obvious.

5. The art project was filled with beauty.

B. Underline the concrete nouns in the sentences above. List them on the lines below.

1. _____   5. _____

2. _____   6. _____

3. _____   7. _____

4. _____   8. _____

TEACHER: Read the directions and questions in Part A and Part B to students. Guide students to complete each exercise, providing support as needed.

Name _____

> **Countable nouns** can be singular or plural: I have a <u>dollar</u>. I have two <u>dollars</u>.
>
> The adjectives *some, few,* and *many* can be used to tell more about count nouns: I have <u>few</u> dollars. I have <u>many</u> dollars.
>
> **Uncountable nouns** do not have singular or plural forms: I have <u>money</u>.
>
> The adjectives *some, little,* and *much* can be used to tell more about uncountable nouns: I have <u>some</u> money. I have <u>little</u> money. I don't have <u>much</u> money.

A. Choose the word that completes each sentence. Then write the word on the line.

1. We had _____ homework over the weekend.

   few   little

2. I made _____ cookies for the sale.

   many   much

3. Josie carried _____ baggage on the trip.

   few   little

4. Do you have _____ lemonade?

   many   much

B. Read each sentence. Circle the countable noun. Place an X on the uncountable noun.

1. I placed my homework in the backpack.

2. He poured water into the cup.

3. She made toast in the toaster.

Name _____

> **Countable nouns** can be singular or plural: I have a <u>dollar</u>. I have two <u>dollars</u>.
>
> The adjectives *some, few,* and *many* can be used to tell more about count nouns: I have <u>few</u> dollars. I have <u>many</u> dollars.
>
> **Uncountable nouns** do not have singular or plural forms: I have <u>money</u>.
>
> The adjectives *some, little,* and *much* can be used to tell more about uncountable nouns: I have <u>some</u> money. I have <u>little</u> money. I don't have <u>much</u> money.

A. Write *few, little, many,* or *much* to complete each sentence.

1. I made _____ cookies for the sale.

2. Josie carried _____ baggage on the trip.

3. I have _____ pages left to read in my book.

B. Circle the uncountable noun that correctly completes each sentence.

1. I like (pickles/mustard) on my sandwich.

2. The (snow/snowflakes) fell from the sky.

3. She made (bread/loaves) in the oven.

TEACHER: Read the directions and questions in Part A and Part B to students. Guide students to complete each exercise, providing support as needed.

Name _____

> **Countable nouns** can be singular or plural. The adjectives *some, few,* and *many* can be used to tell more about countable nouns. **Uncountable nouns** do not have singular or plural forms.
>
> The adjectives *some, little,* and *much* can be used to tell more about uncountable nouns.

A. Add *little, many, much,* or *few* to each sentence.
Write the new sentence on the line.

1. I made cookies for the sale.

   _____

2. Josie carried baggage on the trip.

   _____

3. Do you have bad weather where you live?

   _____

B. Circle each countable noun. Write an uncountable noun to complete the sentence.

1. I like _____ on my sandwich.

2. He poured _____ into the cup.

3. She made _____ in the toaster.

Name _____

> Gerunds are formed by adding *-ing* to the end of a verb. Gerunds function as nouns in a sentence.
>
> speak + *-ing* = speaking   walk + *-ing* = walking   sew + *-ing* = sewing

A. Underline the gerund in each sentence.

1. Running is one of my favorite sports.

2. His dancing was terrible.

3. Singing is one part of the competition.

4. My dog's only trick is sitting.

B. Write the verbs that are related to the gerunds you underlined above.

1. _____   3. _____

2. _____   4. _____

TEACHER: Read the directions and questions in Part A and Part B to students. Guide students to complete each exercise, providing support as needed.

Name _____

Gerunds are formed by adding *-ing* to the end of a verb. Gerunds function as nouns in a sentence.

speak + *-ing* = speaking

A. Read each word. Write the gerund of the word on the line.

1. run _____

2. dance _____

3. sing _____

B. Read each sentence. Change the verb from the sentence to a gerund, and use it in a new sentence.

1. My dog sits. _____

2. The birds fly. _____

3. The children play. _____

TEACHER: Read the directions and questions in Part A and Part B to students. Guide students to complete each exercise, providing support as needed.

Grades 4-6   **53**

Name _____

> Gerunds are formed by adding *-ing* to the end of a verb. Gerunds function as nouns in a sentence.

A. Read each sentence and underline the verb. Change the verb to a gerund, and use it in a new sentence.

1. My dog sits on the ground.

   _____

2. The birds fly in the air.

   _____

3. The children play inside.

   _____

B. Complete each sentence with a gerund formed from the verb in parentheses.

1. _____ is one of my favorite sports. (run)

2. His _____ was terrible. (dance)

3. _____ is one part of the competition. (sing)

TEACHER: Read the directions and questions in Part A and Part B to students. Guide students to complete each exercise, providing support as needed.

Name _____

> A **plural noun** names more than one person, place, thing, or idea. You can form the plural of many nouns by adding –s to the singular form.
>
> girl<u>s</u>   state<u>s</u>   chair<u>s</u>   thought<u>s</u>

Complete each sentence with the plural form of the noun in parentheses.

1. The (kitten) _____ play with yarn.

2. Mona's (book) _____ are on the shelf.

3. We grew (bean) _____ in our garden.

4. Take your (tray) _____ to the kitchen.

5. Did you find your (key) _____?

TEACHER: Read the directions and questions to students. Guide students to complete the exercise, providing support as needed.

Name _____

A **plural noun** names more than one person, place, thing, or idea. You can form the plural of many nouns by adding –s to the singular form.

girl<u>s</u>   chair<u>s</u>

A. Change the singular noun in parentheses to a plural noun.

1. The _____ like to play together. (cat)

2. My _____ are on the shelf. (book)

3. We grew _____ in our garden. (bean)

B. Rewrite each sentence to tell about two or more things. Change the underlined noun to a plural noun.

1. Take your <u>tray</u> to the kitchen.

_____

2. Did you find your <u>key</u>?

_____

3. After supper, we washed the <u>plate</u>.

_____

TEACHER: Read the directions and questions in Part A and Part B to students. Guide students to complete each exercise, providing support as needed.

Name _____

> A **plural noun** names more than one person, place, thing, or idea. You can form the plural of many nouns by adding –s to the singular form.

A. Circle the singular noun in each sentence. Write it on the line.

1. The kittens played with a toy. _____

2. Her books are on the table. _____

3. We grew beans in our garden. _____

4. Place the dishes in the sink. _____

5. Did you find your keys to the house? _____

B. Choose three of the singular nouns you circled above. Use their plural forms in three new sentences. Write the sentences on the lines.

1. _____

   _____

2. _____

   _____

3. _____

   _____

Name _____

> When a singular noun ends in *-s, -sh, -ch,* or *-x,* form the plural by adding *–es.*
>
> bus<u>es</u>   bush<u>es</u>   watch<u>es</u>   box<u>es</u>
>
> When a singular noun ends in a consonant + *y,* form the plural by changing the *y* to an *i,* then adding *–es.*
>
> city/cit<u>ies</u>   baby/bab<u>ies</u>
>
> Some words that end in *o* also form the plural with *–es.*
>
> tomato/tomato<u>es</u>

Write the plural form that correctly completes each sentence.

1. My little sister blew me _____.
    kises   kisses

2. The children got new _____.
    watches   watchs

3. The _____ are buzzing around my food.
    flys   flies

4. The _____ were in the parade.
    heros   heroes

5. We need camping _____.
    supplies   supplys

6. The _____ ran into the woods.
    foxs   foxes

TEACHER: Read the directions and questions to students. Guide students to complete the exercise, providing support as needed.

Name _____

When a singular noun ends in -s, -sh, -ch, or -x, form the plural by adding –es.

boxes

When a singular noun ends in a consonant + y, form the plural by changing the y to an i, then adding –es.

cities

Some words that end in o also form the plural with –es.

tomatoes

A. Write the correct plural form of each singular noun.

1. kiss _____

2. watch _____

3. fly _____

4. fox _____

B. Write the plural form of the noun in parentheses.

1. We need camping _____. (supply)

2. The _____ were in the parade. (hero)

3. Wash the _____. (dish)

TEACHER: Read the directions and questions in Part A and Part B to students. Guide students to complete each exercise, providing support as needed.

Name _____

> When a singular noun ends in *-s, -sh, -ch,* or *-x,* form the plural by adding *–es.*
>
> When a singular noun ends in a consonant + *y,* form the plural by changing the *y* to an *i,* then adding *–es.*
>
> Some words that end in *o* also form the plural with *–es.*

A. **Rewrite each sentence using the correct plural form of the noun in parentheses.**

1. My little sister blew me (kiss).

   _____

2. The children got new (watch).

   _____

3. The (fly) are buzzing around my food.

   _____

B. **Write the plural form of the noun in parentheses to complete each sentence.**

1. The _____ were in the parade. (hero)

2. We need camping _____. (supply)

3. Two red _____ live in our neighborhood. (fox)

TEACHER: Read the directions and questions in Part A and Part B to students. Guide students to complete each exercise, providing support as needed.

Name _____

> - To form the plural of some nouns ending in -f, -lf or -fe, change the f to v and add -es.
>
>   kni**ves**   wol**ves**
>
> - To form the plural of some nouns with oo in the middle, change the oo to ee.
>
>   f**ee**t   t**ee**th
>
> - To form the plural of some nouns, add en or ren to the end.
>
>   child**ren**   wom**en**

Write the correct plural noun to complete each sentence.

1. They have happy _____ .
   lifes   lives

2. The girl made three _____ .
   snowmen   snowmans

3. The husbands danced with their _____ .
   wife   wives

4. _____ fly south for winter.
   Geese   Gooses

5. Two of Sally's _____ fell out.
   toothes   teeth

TEACHER: Read the directions and questions to students. Guide students to complete the exercise, providing support as needed.

Name _____

> • To form the plural of some nouns ending in *-f, -lf* or *-fe*, change the *f* to *v* and add *-es*.
>
> kni**ves**   wol**ves**
>
> • To form the plural of some nouns with *oo* in the middle, change the *oo* to *ee*.
>
> f**ee**t   t**ee**th
>
> • To form the plural of some nouns, add *en* or *ren* to the end.
>
> child**ren**   wom**en**

A. Write *C* if the underlined plural noun is written correctly. Write *I* if the underlined plural noun is incorrect. Then write the correct form of the noun.

1. They have happy <u>lifes</u>. _____

2. The <u>children</u> like soccer. _____

3. The girl made three <u>snowmen</u>. _____

B. Correct each sentence by writing the plural form of the underlined noun.

1. The husbands danced with their <u>wife</u>. _____

2. <u>Goose</u> fly south for winter. _____

3. Dogs have four <u>foot</u>. _____

TEACHER: Read the directions and questions in Part A and Part B to students. Guide students to complete each exercise, providing support as needed.

Name _____

> - To form the plural of some nouns ending in *-f, -lf* or *-fe,* change the *f* to *v* and add *-es.*
> - To form the plural of some nouns with *oo* in the middle, change the *oo* to *ee.*
> - To form the plural of some nouns, add *en* or *ren* to the end.

A. Complete each sentence by writing the plural form of the noun in parentheses.

1. The (child) like soccer. _____

2. The husbands danced with their (wife). _____

3. (Goose) fly south for winter. _____

4. The (wolf) are howling. _____

5. Two of Sally's (tooth) fell out. _____

B. Choose three plural nouns from above and use them to write three new sentences. Write the sentences on the lines.

1. _____
   _____

2. _____
   _____

3. _____
   _____

TEACHER: Read the directions and questions in Part A and Part B to students. Guide students to complete each exercise, providing support as needed.

Name _____

> - To form the plural of some nouns, you need to memorize the spelling.
>
>   one person; two <u>people</u>   one mouse; two <u>mice</u>
>
> - To form the plural of some nouns, you use the same spelling as the singular form.
>
>   one deer; two <u>deer</u>   one sheep; two <u>sheep</u>
>
> - **Collective nouns** are for groups. They can be singular or plural.
>
>   The <u>band</u> played a concert. The <u>bands</u> competed with each other.

A. Choose the word that correctly completes each sentence. Write it on the line.

1. I see three _____ .

    mouses   mice

2. Roberto caught ten _____ .

    fish   fishes

3. There were five _____ at the party.

    persons   people

4. We saw several _____ in the field.

    deer   deers

B. Read each sentence. Write the collective noun on the line.

1. The bands played the last song together. _____

2. The class went on a trip to the museum. _____

3. The crowd cheered for the speaker. _____

TEACHER: Read the directions and questions in Part A and Part B to students. Guide students to complete each exercise, providing support as needed.

Name _____

- To form the plural of some nouns, you need to memorize the spelling.

  one person; two <u>people</u>

- To form the plural of some nouns, you use the same spelling as the singular form.

  one deer; two <u>deer</u>

- **Collective nouns** are for groups. They can be singular or plural.

  The <u>band</u> played a concert.

Complete each sentence by writing the correct plural form of the noun in bold.

1. I see a **mouse**.

   I see three _____

2. Roberto caught a **fish**.

   Roberto caught ten _____.

3. One **person** was at the party.

   Many _____ were at the party

4. A deer was in the field.

   Three _____ were in the field

5. The moose stared at us.

   Both _____ stared at us

6. The band played a song.

   All the _____ played a song together.

TEACHER: Read the directions and questions to students. Guide students to complete the exercise, providing support as needed.

Name _____

- To form the plural of some nouns, you need to memorize the spelling.
- To form the plural of some nouns, you use the same spelling as the singular form.
- **Collective nouns** are for groups. They can be singular or plural.

Read the passage. Circle each incorrect plural noun. Then rewrite the passage correctly on the lines below.

1. Two class from my school went on a trip to a farm. Many persons worked on the farm. There were also horses, cows, chickens, and sheeps. We got to pet many of the animals. My favorite animal was the cat that lived in the barn. Our guide said she helped keep all the mouses away. It was a fun day!

_____

_____

_____

_____

_____

TEACHER: Read the directions and questions to students. Guide students to complete the exercise, providing support as needed.

Name _____

> To show possession, add *'s* to the end of singular nouns, even nouns that end in –*s*.
>
> The pen belongs to Dave. It is Dave<u>'s</u> pen.
>
> The windows on the bus are dirty. The bus<u>'s</u> windows are dirty.

A. Select the correct answer for each question.

1. Which sentence has the correct possessive form of *Maria*?

   a. That is Maria pencil.

   b. That is Marias pencil.

   c. That is Maria's pencil.

   d. That is Marias' pencil.

2. Which sentence has the correct possessive form of *Mavis*?

   a. This is Mavis's crayon.

   b. This is Mavis crayon.

   c. This is Mavis' crayon.

   d. This is Mavi's crayon.

B. Circle the possessive noun that correctly completes each sentence.

1. I went to my (friends / friend's) house.

2. He wants to ride (Boris's / Boris') bike.

3. That is my (dogs / dog's) bone.

4. The book is in my (sisters / sister's) room.

TEACHER: Read the directions and questions in Part A and Part B to students. Guide students to complete each exercise, providing support as needed.

Grades 4-6   **67**

Name _____

To show possession, add *'s* to the end of singular nouns, even nouns that end in *–s*.

It is Dave's pen.

The bus's windows are dirty.

A. Add *'s* to each noun to show possession. Then write the word.

1. Maria + 's = _____

2. dog + 's = _____

3. house + 's = _____

4. Bess + 's = _____

B. Correct each sentence by writing the possessive form of the underlined noun.

1. I went to my <u>friend</u> house. _____

2. Look at the <u>duck</u> beautiful feathers. _____

3. This is <u>James</u> bike. _____

4. Where do you keep the <u>cat</u> food? _____

TEACHER: Read the directions and questions in Part A and Part B to students. Guide students to complete each exercise, providing support as needed.

Name _____

> To show possession, add 's to the end of singular nouns, even nouns that end in –s.

A. Complete each sentence by writing the possessive form of the noun in parentheses.

1. That is _____ pencil. (Maria)

2. This is _____ crayon. (Mavis)

3. This is that _____ car. (person)

4. That bone is my _____. (dog)

5. Look at the _____ beautiful feathers! (duck)

B. Write four new sentences using possessive nouns.

1. _____
   _____

2. _____
   _____

3. _____
   _____

4. _____
   _____

Copyright © McGraw-Hill Education

Name _____

> To show possession, add only an apostrophe (') to regular plural words that end in -s.
>
> Add 's to irregular plural words that do not end in -s.
>
> The <u>cats'</u> toys are new.   The <u>children's</u> teacher is sick today.

A. Select the correct answer for each question.

1. Which sentence uses the correct possessive form of the plural noun *children*?

    a. I want to see the childrens' art.

    b. I want to see the children's art.

    c. I want to see the children art.

    d. I want to see the childrens art.

2. Which sentence uses the correct possessive form of the plural noun *lions*?

    a. Do not get too close to the lion's cage!

    b. Do not get too close to the lions' cage!

    c. Do not get too close to the lions cage!

    d. Do not get too close to the lion cage!

B. Circle the plural possessive noun that completes each sentence correctly.

1. I went to my (cousin's / cousins') house.

2. The (children's / childrens') school is nearby.

3. My (brother's / brothers') room has a bunk bed.

4. The (men's / mens') team won the championship.

TEACHER: Read the directions and questions in Part A and Part B to students. Guide students to complete each exercise, providing support as needed.

Name _____

> - To show possession, add only an apostrophe (') to regular plural words that end in -*s*.
> - Add '*s* to irregular plural words that do not end in -*s*.
>
>   The <u>cats'</u> toys are new.   The <u>children's</u> teacher is sick today.

A. Add an ' or an 's to each plural noun to show possession. Then write the word.

1. Smiths _____

2. lions _____

3. women _____

4. kids _____

B. Correct each sentence by writing the possessive form of the underlined plural noun.

1. I went to my <u>cousins</u> house. _____

2. The <u>children</u> school is nearby. _____

3. My <u>brothers</u> room has a bunk bed. _____

4. The <u>men</u> team won the championship. _____

Name _____

- To show possession, add only an apostrophe (') to regular plural words that end in -s.
- Add 's to irregular plural words that do not end in -s.

A. Complete each sentence by writing the possessive form of the plural noun in parentheses.

1. Those are the _____ bicycles. (Smiths)

2. These are the _____ pens. (students)

3. I want to see the _____ art. (children)

4. She is the _____ choice for president. (people)

5. Do not get too close to the _____ cage! (lions)

B. Write three new sentences using plural possessive nouns.

1. _____

   _____

2. _____

   _____

3. _____

   _____

TEACHER: Read the directions and questions in Part A and Part B to students. Guide students to complete each exercise, providing support as needed.

Name _____

> A **noun phrase** functions as a noun. An entire noun phrase can be replaced by a pronoun.
>
> The bedroom windows are open.   They are open.

A. Circle the noun phrase under each sentence.

1. The boy's shoes are new.

    The boy's shoes   are new

2. The teacher's desk is big.

    The teacher's desk   is big

3. I like my little brother.

    I like   my little brother

4. This red ball is my favorite.

    This red ball   is my favorite

B. Fill in each blank with the correct pronoun for each noun phrase.

1. The boy's shoes are new. _____ are new.

2. The teacher's desk is big. _____ is big.

3. I like my little brother. I like _____ .

4. This red ball is my favorite. _____ is my favorite.

TEACHER: Read the directions and questions in Part A and Part B to students. Guide students to complete each exercise, providing support as needed.

Name _____

> A **noun phrase** functions as a noun. An entire noun phrase can be replaced by a pronoun.
>
> The bedroom windows are open.   They are open.

A. Underline the noun phrase in each sentence.

1. The boy's shoes are new.

2. The teacher's desk is big.

3. I like my little brother.

B. Rewrite each sentence using a pronoun to replace the noun phrase.

1. The boy's shoes are new.

   _____

2. The teacher's desk is big.

   _____

3. I like my little brother.

   _____

TEACHER: Read the directions and questions in Part A and Part B to students. Guide students to complete each exercise, providing support as needed.

Name _____

> A **noun phrase** functions as a noun. An entire noun phrase can be replaced by a pronoun.

A. Read each sentence. Write the noun phrase on the line.

1. The boy's shoes are new. _____

2. The teacher's desk is big. _____

3. I like my little brother. _____

4. This red ball is my favorite. _____

5. The small box was empty. _____

B. Choose three noun phrases that you wrote above. Use them in three new sentences. Write the sentences on the lines.

1. _____

    _____

2. _____

    _____

3. _____

    _____

Name _____

> A **noun phrase** functions as a noun. It can be expanded by adding adjectives that describe the noun. A noun phrase can always be replaced by a pronoun.
>
> The boy ran.   The tall boy ran.

A. Circle the noun phrase under each sentence.

1. The warm, tasty soup is hers.

    The warm, tasty soup   is hers

2. The larger, newer house is theirs.

    The larger, newer house   is theirs

3. He likes the smallest, fastest car.

    He likes   the smallest, fastest car

4. They want the louder and more playful puppy.

    They want   the louder and more playful puppy

B. Read each sentence. Circle the noun in each underlined noun phrase.

1. The warm, tasty soup is hers.

2. The larger, newer house is theirs.

3. He likes the smallest, fastest car.

4. They want the louder and more playful puppy.

TEACHER: Read the directions and questions in Part A and Part B to students. Guide students to complete each exercise, providing support as needed.

Name _____

> A **noun phrase** functions as a noun. It can be expanded by adding adjectives that describe the noun. A noun phrase can always be replaced by a pronoun.
>
> The boy ran.   The tall boy ran.

A. Underline the noun phrase in each sentence.

1. The warm, tasty soup is hers.

2. The larger, newer house is theirs.

3. He likes the smallest, fastest car.

B. Read each sentence. For each underlined noun phrase, write the noun and the words that describe the noun.

1. The warm, tasty soup is hers.

    Noun: _____   Describing Words: _____

2. The larger, newer house is theirs.

    Noun: _____   Describing Words: _____

3. He likes the smallest, fastest car.

    Noun: _____   Describing Words: _____

TEACHER: Read the directions and questions in Part A and Part B to students. Guide students to complete each exercise, providing support as needed.   Grades 4-6   77

Name _____

> A **noun phrase** functions as a noun. It can be expanded by adding adjectives that describe the noun. A noun phrase can always be replaced by a pronoun.

A. Read each sentence. Write the noun phrase on the line.

1.   The warm, tasty soup is hers. _____

2.   The larger, newer house is theirs. _____

3.   He likes the smallest, fastest car. _____

4.   They want the louder and more playful puppy. _____

5.   The shiny, blue marble is my favorite. _____

B. Choose three noun phrases that you wrote above. Use them in three new sentences. Write the sentences on the lines.

1.   _____

   _____

2.   _____

   _____

3.   _____

   _____

TEACHER: Read the directions and questions in Part A and Part B to students. Guide students to complete each exercise, providing support as needed.

Name _____

> - An **appositive** is a noun. It gives non-essential information about the noun next to it.
> - Appositives are set off by commas.
>
>   My sister, <u>Judy</u>, plays basketball.

A. Underline the appositive in each sentence.

1. My sister, Leticia, has long hair.

2. Our school, Lincoln Elementary, is on Willow Street.

3. My favorite story, *Huckleberry Finn*, was written by Mark Twain.

4. Our gym teacher, Mrs. Holmes, was born in Poland.

5. David's dog, Fluffy, is a poodle.

6. My parents' friend, Jacob, is coming to dinner.

TEACHER: Read the directions and questions in Part A and Part B to students. Guide students to complete each exercise, providing support as needed.

Name _____

> • An **appositive** is a noun. It gives non-essential information about the noun next to it.
>
> • Appositives are set off by commas.
>
> My sister, <u>Judy</u>, plays basketball.

A. Underline the appositive in each sentence.

1. Our school, Lincoln Elementary, is on Willow Street.

2. My favorite story, *Huckleberry Finn,* was written by Mark Twain.

3. Our gym teacher, Mrs. Holmes, was born in Poland.

B. Complete each sentence with the appositive that correctly combines the two sentences.

1. My sister has long hair. My sister is Leticia.

   My sister, _____, has long hair.

2. David's dog is Fluffy. David's dog is a poodle.

   David's dog, _____, is a poodle.

3. My parents' friend is Jacob. My parents' friend is coming to dinner.

   My parents' friend, _____, is coming to dinner.

TEACHER: Read the directions and questions in Part A and Part B to students. Guide students to complete each exercise, providing support as needed.

Name _____

- An **appositive** is a noun. It gives non-essential information about the noun next to it.
- Appositives are set off by commas.

Combine the two sentences with an appositive. The first sentence of each pair contains essential information. The second sentence does not.

1. My sister has long hair. My sister is Leticia.

   _____

   _____

2. David's dog is a poodle. David's dog is Fluffy.

   _____

   _____

3. My parents' friend is coming to dinner. My parents' friend is Jacob.

   _____

   _____

Name _____

> - An **appositive phrase** functions as a noun. It gives non-essential information about the noun next to it.
> - Appositive phrases are set off by commas.
>
>   **Marcus enjoys tennis, <u>which he started playing when he was five.</u>**

A. Underline the appositive phrase in each sentence.

1. Hillary Clinton, who was born in Illinois, was the U.S. Secretary of State for four years.

2. Mr. Hayes, who volunteers at a museum, is our art teacher.

3. The house was painted blue, my favorite color.

4. Math, my favorite subject, is easy for me.

5. The Lees, our neighbors for the last 10 years, are moving to Texas.

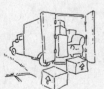

6. The building, which has 85 floors, was built in 1990.

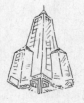

TEACHER: Read the directions and questions in Part A and Part B to students. Guide students to complete each exercise, providing support as needed.

Name _____

> • An **appositive phrase** functions as a noun. It gives non-essential information about the noun next to it.
>
> • Appositive phrases are set off by commas.
>
>   **Marcus enjoys tennis, <u>which he started playing when he was five.</u>**

A. Underline the appositive phrase in each sentence.

1. Math, my favorite subject, is easy for me.

2. The Lees, our neighbors for the last 10 years, are moving to Texas.

3. The building, which has 85 floors, was built in 1990.

B. Complete each sentence with the appositive phrase that correctly combines the two sentences.

1. Ronald Reagan was the U.S. president for eight years. He was born in Illinois.

   Ronald Reagan, _____, was the U.S. president for eight years.

2. Mr. Hayes is our art teacher. Mr. Hayes volunteers at a museum.

   Mr. Hayes, _____, is our art teacher.

3. The house was painted blue. Blue is my favorite color.

   The house was painted blue, _____.

TEACHER: Read the directions and questions in Part A and Part B to students. Guide students to complete each exercise, providing support as needed.

Name _____

> • An **appositive phrase** functions as a noun. It gives non-essential information about the noun next to it.
> • Appositive phrases are set off by commas.

Combine the two sentences with an appositive phrase.

1. Ronald Reagan was the U.S. president for eight years. He was born in Illinois.

   _____

   _____

2. Mr. Hayes is our art teacher. Mr. Hayes volunteers at a museum.

   _____

   _____

3. The house was painted blue. Blue is my favorite color.

   _____

   _____

TEACHER: Read the directions and questions to students. Guide students to complete the exercise, providing support as needed.

Name _____

> **Main verbs** are the key words in most sentences. They often show an action or a state.
>
> **She** <u>eats</u>.   **He** <u>reads</u>.   **They** <u>play</u>.

A.   **Write the correct main verb to complete each sentence.**

1.   I _____ lunch every day.
   carrots   eat

2.   Julio _____ basketball.
   plays   good

3.   Paula _____ in sixth grade.
   is   school

4.   Yuko _____ a puppy.
   wants   cute

5.   Peter _____ to the teacher.
   student   listens

B.   **Underline the main verb in each sentence.**

1.   Andrea reads books.

2.   Albert loves carrots.

3.   That house is beautiful.

Name _____

> **Main verbs** are the key words in most sentences. They often show an action or a state.
>
> **She <u>eats</u>.   He <u>reads</u>.   They <u>play</u>.**

Complete each sentence by adding a verb from the box. Then write the sentence correctly.

eat	is	listen	plays	wants

1. I _____ lunch every day.

_____

2. Julio _____ basketball.

_____

3. Paula _____ in sixth grade.

_____

4. Yuko _____ a puppy.

_____

5. We _____ to the teacher.

_____

TEACHER: Read the directions and questions to students. Guide students to complete the exercise, providing support as needed.

Name _____

> **Main verbs** are the key words in most sentences. They often show an action or a state.

A. **Underline the main verb in each sentence.**

1. My friend Andrea is 12 years old today.

2. Andrea reads books every day.

3. She loves fresh carrots from her garden.

4. At school, Andrea eats carrots every day for lunch.

5. She lives in the house next to mine.

6. Her house is big and beautiful.

TEACHER: Read the directions and questions in Part A and Part B to students. Guide students to complete each exercise, providing support as needed.

Grades 4-6   87

Name _____

> **Helping verbs** help the main verbs in sentences. Common helping verbs include:
>
> can   have   is   do

A. Choose the correct helping verb to complete each sentence.

1. Andrea _____ read.
    can   do

2. Nora _____ making fresh bread.
    has   is

3. Matt _____ planting flowers in his garden.
    can   is

4. Albert _____ eat carrots every day.
    can   do

5. We _____ been to this restaurant before.
    is   have

6. That house _____ five owners.
    had   were

TEACHER: Read the directions and questions in Part A and Part B to students. Guide students to complete each exercise, providing support as needed.

Name _____

> **Helping verbs** help the main verbs in sentences. Common helping verbs include:
>
> can   have   is   do

Complete each sentence by choosing a helping verb from the box. Then write the sentence.

> can   is   have   had   was

1. Nora _____ making fresh bread.

   _____

2. Matt _____ planting flowers when it started raining.

   _____

3. Albert loves carrots. He _____ eat them every day.

   _____

4. We _____ been to this restaurant before.

   _____

5. This house _____ five owners before we moved in.

   _____

TEACHER: Read the directions and questions to students. Guide students to complete the exercise, providing support as needed.

Grades 4-6   89

Name _____

> Helping verbs help the main verbs in sentences. Common helping verbs include the various forms of *can*, *have*, *is*, and *do*.

A. Underline the helping verb and main verb in each sentence.

1. I have eaten a sandwich for lunch every day this week.

2. Julio can play basketball.

3. Paula is going to school today.

4. Yuko can play with the puppy.

5. Do they listen to the teacher?

B. Write each helping verb from Part A on the lines below.

1. _____

2. _____

3. _____

4. _____

5. _____

Name _____

> **Verbs** can tell about actions. The tense of a verb lets you know when an action takes place.
>
> The dogs <u>bark</u>. (present)   The dogs <u>barked</u>. (past)
> The dogs <u>will bark</u>. (future)

A. **Underline the verb in each sentence. Then write** *past, present,* **or** *future* **to tell the time of the action.**

1. The pet shop will sell us a puppy. _____

2. The funny little puppies lick me. _____

3. Dad owned a puppy long ago. _____

4. I will love my new puppy forever. _____

B. **Circle the correct verb in parentheses to complete each sentence.**

1. We (picked, will pick) out our new puppy yesterday.

2. Now the puppy and I (snuggle, snuggled) together.

3. Tomorrow I (showed, will show) the puppy our park.

Name _____

> **Verbs** can tell about actions. The tense of a verb lets you know when an action takes place.
>
> The dogs <u>bark</u>. (present)   The dogs <u>barked</u>. (past)
> The dogs <u>will bark</u>. (future)

A. Underline the verb in each sentence. Then write *past, present,* or *future* to tell the time of the action.

1. Last winter, I asked my parents for a puppy.

    _____

2. We visited the best pet shop in town.

    _____

3. Now I hold one of the puppies.

    _____

4. Later, I will choose a name for my new pet.

    _____

B.   Write the past and future tense form of each verb.

		past	future
1.	growl	_____	_____
2.	guard	_____	_____
3.	lick	_____	_____
4.	follow	_____	_____

TEACHER: Read the directions and questions in Part A and Part B to students. Guide students to complete each exercise, providing support as needed.

Name _____

> **Verbs** can tell about actions. The tense of a verb lets you know when an action takes place.

A. Read each sentence. On the line, write the underlined verb in the tense given in parentheses.

1. My parents <u>promise</u> me a new puppy for my birthday. (past) _____

2. Tomorrow, we <u>visit</u> a dog breeder in our town. (future) _____

3. I already <u>ask</u> the breeder about different kinds of dogs. (past) _____

4. Dave <u>like</u> small breeds, such as terriers. (present) _____

5. The breeder <u>find</u> the right dog for us. (future) _____

B. Choose one past-tense verb and one future-tense verb from the sentences above. Use each verb in a new sentence. Write your sentences on the lines.

1. _____

   _____

   _____

2. _____

   _____

   _____

TEACHER: Read the directions and questions in Part A and Part B to students. Guide students to complete each exercise, providing support as needed.

Name _____

> Most **verbs** that tell about the past end in *-ed*. Most verbs that tell about the future use the helping verb *will*.
>
> **Past:** we worked   **Present:** we work   **Future:** we will work

Circle the verb that completes each sentence with the tense shown in parentheses. Then write the verb.

1. Two of us _____ the paint. (present).

    mix   mixed

2. Anya _____ the color. (past).

    picked   will pick

3. That color _____ nice. (future).

    looked   will look

4. Anya _____ a brush. (future)

    used   will use

5. I _____ my room last year. (past)

    paint   painted

TEACHER: Read the directions and questions to students. Guide students to complete the exercise, providing support as needed.

Name _____

> Most **verbs** that tell about the past end in *-ed*. Most verbs that tell about the future use the helping verb *will*.
>
> **Past:** worked   **Present:** work   **Future:** will work

A.   Write the past and future tense of each verb.

	past	future

1. paint   _____   _____

2. mix   _____   _____

3. select   _____   _____

4. finish   _____   _____

B.   Write the given form of the word in parentheses to complete each sentence.

1. This color (cover) _____ the old paint. (future tense)

2. The old paint (fade) _____ in several places. (past tense)

3. The new color (match) _____ the curtains. (future tense)

Name _____

Most **verbs** that tell about the past end in *-ed*. Most verbs that tell about the future use the helping verb *will*.

Read the passage. Circle each mistake in verb tense. Then rewrite the passage correctly on the lines below.

1. Yesterday, Anya pick out a new color for her room. Then she cover the furniture and the floor. Now Anya and her mom mix the paint. By next week, the walls look shiny and new. At last, they match her curtains and bedspread.

_____

_____

_____

_____

_____

TEACHER: Read the directions and questions to students. Guide students to complete the exercise, providing support as needed.

Name _____

> The **direct object** of a verb is a noun or pronoun that receives the action of the verb.
>
> I sing. What do I sing? I sing a <u>song</u>.
>
> We entertain. Whom do we entertain? We entertain the <u>people</u>.

Circle the direct object in each sentence.

1. I read the notes.

2. Mrs. Duncan leads us.

3. Joelle sings a solo.

4. Our voices delight everyone.

5. People clap their hands loudly.

6. Dad records the concert for us.

TEACHER: Read the directions and questions to students. Guide students to complete the exercise, providing support as needed.

Grades 4-6   97

Name _____

The **direct object** of a verb is a noun or pronoun that receives the action of the verb.

I sing. What do I sing? I sing a <u>song</u>.

A. **Underline the sentences that have direct objects.**
Circle the direct objects.

1. **a.** Mrs. Duncan leads our chorus.

   b. She teaches music at our school.

   c. Her daughter is in my class.

2. **a.** Everyone loves our concert.

   b. They clap loudly and long.

   c. A few people throw flowers.

B. **Decide whether the direct object answers the question *Whom?* or *What?***
Circle the answer. Then write the direct object on the line.

1. Mr. Hang will record the performance.   Whom?   What?

   _____

2. Mrs. Duncan invited a newspaper reporter.   Whom?   What?

   _____

3. The reporter is taking notes.   Whom?   What?

   _____

TEACHER: Read the directions and questions in Part A and Part B to students. Guide students to complete each exercise, providing support as needed.

Name _____

> The **direct object** of a verb is a noun or pronoun that receives the
> action of the verb.
>
> I sing. What do I sing? I sing a <u>song</u>.

A. Read each sentence. Circle the direct objects.

1. I read the notes in the music book.

2. Mrs. Duncan leads the children's chorus.

3. The audience members found their seats.

4. The conductor raised her arms high.

5. We opened our mouths and sang.

6. A few people throw flowers at the end of the show.

**B. Add a direct object to each sentence. The direct object should answer the
question in parentheses.**

1. Everyone enjoyed the _____. (What?)

2. Our conductor introduced _____. (Whom?)

3. A high school student played the _____. (What?)

4. A reporter wrote a(n) _____ about us. (What?)

5. The choir thanked the _____. (Whom?)

**TEACHER: Read the directions and questions in Part A and Part B to students. Guide
students to complete each exercise, providing support as needed.**

Name _____

> Direct objects tell *what* or *whom* about the action verb. **Indirect objects** tell *to whom* or *for whom*.
>
> I made <u>Joe</u> a valentine. (for whom)   I handed <u>him</u> the card. (to whom)

Circle the indirect object in each sentence.

1. Mom bought me some art supplies.

2. I asked her for some help.

3. She made Dad a paper heart.

4. I showed them my finished cards.

5. We mailed Grandma one pretty card.

6. I gave everyone a valentine.

TEACHER: Read the directions and questions to students. Guide students to complete the exercise, providing support as needed.

Name _____

> Direct objects tell *what* or *whom* about the action verb. **Indirect objects** tell *to whom* or *for whom*.
>
> I made <u>Joe</u> a valentine. (for whom)   I handed <u>him</u> the card. (to whom)

A. Underline the sentences that have indirect objects. Circle the indirect objects.

1. **a.** I mailed Grandma a valentine.

    b. She loves Valentine's Day.

    c. I made her a pretty card.

2. **a.** Cutting paper hearts was hard.

    b. I asked Mom for some help.

    c. She showed me the easiest way.

B. Decide whether the indirect object tells *to whom* or *for whom*. Circle the answer. Then write the direct object on the line.

1. Mom made Dad a paper heart.   to whom   for whom

    _____

2. I gave my classmates valentines.   to whom   for whom

    _____

3. Many people sent me cards.   to whom   for whom

    _____

Name _____

> Direct objects tell *what* or *whom* about the action verb. **Indirect objects** tell *to whom* or *for whom*.
>
> I made <u>Joe</u> a valentine. (for whom)   I handed <u>him</u> the card. (to whom)

A. Read each sentence. Circle the indirect objects.

1. Mom bought me paper, scissors, and glue.

2. I asked her for help in cutting out hearts.

3. She designed Dad a lovely paper heart.

4. I made my classmates beautiful valentines.

5. Some of the parents baked us Valentine's Day snacks.

B. Add an indirect object to each sentence. The indirect object should answer the question in parentheses.

1. Ella drew _____ a big red heart. (For whom?)

2. Our teacher told _____ a holiday story. (To whom?)

3. We brought _____ cookies and juice. (For whom?)

4. Franco handed _____ a heart-shaped cookie. (To whom?)

TEACHER: Read the directions and questions in Part A and Part B to students. Guide students to complete each exercise, providing support as needed.

Name _____

> The present tense tells about an action that is happening now. The **present progressive form** tells about an action that is continuing. It uses a helping verb *am*, *is* or *are* and the *–ing* form of the verb.
>
> The baby is crawling across the floor. (present progressive form)

Write *P* if the underlined verb is in the present-tense. Write *PP* if the verb is in the present progressive form.

1. The baby is riding in a stroller. _____

2. We push the stroller along. _____

3. People are crossing the street. _____

4. I am looking both ways. _____

5. The little baby laughs. _____

TEACHER: Read the directions and questions to students. Guide students to complete the exercise, providing support as needed.

Grades 4-6   **103**

Name _____

> The present tense tells about an action that is happening now. Add –s to a regular verb to tell about one person's action.
>
> | The babies <u>crawl</u>. | The baby <u>crawls</u>. |
>
> The **present progressive** form tells about an action that is continuing. It uses a helping verb, *am, is* or *are* and the *–ing* form of the verb.
>
> | The babies <u>are crawling</u>. | The baby <u>is crawling</u>. |

Change the verb in bold to match the new subject. Write the new verb.

1. The strollers **roll** along.   The stroller _____ along.

2. The babies **are laughing**.   The baby _____.

3. People **are crossing** the street.   I _____ the street.

4. Babies **ride** in strollers.   The baby _____ in a stroller.

5. The sign **is blinking**.   The signs _____.

TEACHER: Read the directions and questions to students. Guide students to complete the exercise, providing support as needed.

Name _____

> The present tense tells about an action that is happening now. Add *–s* to a regular verb to tell about one person's action.
>
> The **present progressive** form tells about an action that is continuing. It uses a helping verb, *am, is* or *are* and the *–ing* form of the verb.

Read the passage. Circle each mistake in verb use. Then rewrite the passage correctly on the lines below.

1. I is taking the baby for a walk. The baby ride in his stroller. The stroller roll along the sidewalk. At the crosswalk, the sign are blinking. People is crossing carefully.

_____

_____

_____

_____

_____

Name _____

> Present-tense verbs can tell about an action that is happening now. They may also tell about an action that happens a lot, an action that happens all the time, and an action that has no specific time.

A. Read each sentence. Circle the letter of the sentence that has a timeless present-tense verb.

1. a. Raindrops filled the creek.

    b. The river sometimes overflows.

    c. This storm will end soon.

2. a. All clouds hold water.

    b. Dark clouds gathered overhead.

    c. The sun will shine later today.

B. Read each sentence. Write the present-tense verb that best completes each sentence on the line.

1. Rain usually (fall, falls) for an hour or two. _____

2. Sometimes Luke (play, plays) in the puddles. _____

3. All living things (need, needs) rain. _____

4. Flowers (grow, grows) well in our town. _____

TEACHER: Read the directions and questions in Part A and Part B to students. Guide students to complete each exercise, providing support as needed.

Name _____

Present-tense verbs can tell about an action that is happening now. They may also tell about an action that happens a lot, an action that happens all the time, and an action that has no specific time.

A. Read each sentence. Circle the letters the sentences that have a timeless present-tense verb.

1. **a.** Usually, rain seems harmless.

    b. Sometimes rivers overflow.

    c. Our river flooded last year.

2. **a.** All clouds hold water.

    b. I watched a big, black cloud.

    c. Nimbus clouds produce rain.

B. Write the correct present-tense form of the verb in parentheses to complete each sentence.

1. The rain usually (fall) _____ for no more than an hour.

2. Luke often (play) _____ in the puddles.

3. All living things (need) _____ water.

Name _____

> Present-tense verbs can tell about an action that is happening now. They may also tell about an action that happens a lot, an action that happens all the time, and an action that has no specific time.

A. Underline the timeless present-tense verb in each sentence. Write it on the line.

1. Thunderstorms usually involve lightning. _____

2. Flooding sometimes occurs in the valleys. _____

3. The river overflows once or twice a year. _____

4. People always prepare for the flood season. _____

5. Flood waters leave good soil behind. _____

B. Use a timeless present-tense verb to complete each sentence.

1. On rainy days, we often _____

_____.

2. Ordinarily, the rain _____

_____.

TEACHER: Read the directions and questions in Part A and Part B to students. Guide students to complete each exercise, providing support as needed.

Name _____

> Most verbs add *–ed* to tell about the past.
>
> Use the past progressive form when action happens over a long period of time. The past progressive uses a form of the verb *be* and the *–ing* form of the verb.

A. **Circle the past-tense verb to complete each sentence. Then write the verb.**

1. We _____ a poster.
   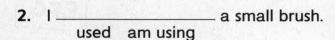
   paint   painted

2. I _____ a small brush.
   used   am using

3. I _____ the brush in paint.
   dip   dipped

4. Then I _____ some letters.
   traced   was tracing

5. My teacher _____ my work.
   liked   likes

B. **Underline the verb. Then complete the second sentence using the past progressive form of the same verb.**

1. Art class ended.   Art class was _____.

2. We cleaned up.   We were _____ up.

3. Ms. Quinn smiled.   Ms. Quinn was _____.

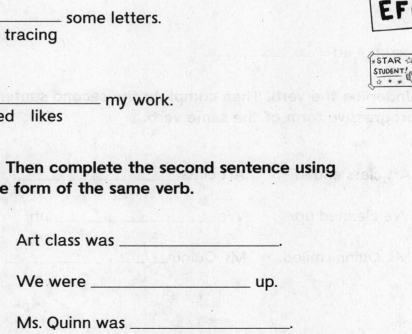

Name _____

> Most verbs add –ed to tell about the past.
>
> Use the past progressive form when an action happens over a long period of time. This form uses a helping verb and the –ing form of the verb.

A. Add –ed to tell about the past. Then write the verb. If a verb ends with a vowel + consonant, double the consonant before adding -ed

1. paint + ed = _____

2. trace + ed = _____

3. dip + ed = _____

4. scrub + ed = _____

B. Underline the verb. Then complete the second sentence using the past progressive form of the same verb.

1. Art class ended.   Art class _____.

2. We cleaned up.   We _____ up.

3. Ms. Quinn smiled.   Ms. Quinn _____.

TEACHER: Read the directions and questions in Part A and Part B to students. Guide students to complete each exercise, providing support as needed.

Name _____

> Most verbs add *-ed* to tell about the past.
>
> Use the past progressive when an action happens over a long period of time. The past progressive uses a form of the verb *be* and the *-ing* form of the verb.

Rewrite the sentences below, correcting any mistakes in spelling or usage.

1.   I were painting a poster.

   _____

   _____

2.   My classmates was finishing up their posters.

   _____

   _____

3.   Our teacher is helping all of us yesterday.

   _____

   _____

Name _____

> Most verbs use *will* to tell about the future. When action will happen over a period of time, use *will*, the verb *be,* and the *–ing* form of the verb.
>
> Joe <u>will carry</u> the flag. (future)
>
> Joe <u>will be carrying</u> the flag. (future progressive)

A. Write *F* if the sentence has a verb in the future tense. Write *FP* if the sentence has a verb in the future progressive form.

1. The parade will pass our school. _____

2. We will be standing on the sidewalk. _____

3. Joe will hold the flag high. _____

4. I will be waving wildly at him. _____

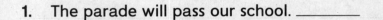

B. Underline the verb in the future progressive in each sentence.

1. My cousin will be twirling her baton.

2. The high school band will be marching.

3. The mayor will be leading the parade.

4. He will be wearing a big cowboy hat.

TEACHER: Read the directions and questions in Part A and Part B to students. Guide students to complete each exercise, providing support as needed.

Name _____

> Most verbs use *will* to tell about the future. When action will happen over a period of time, use *will*, the verb *be*, and the *–ing* form of the verb.
>
> Joe <u>will carry</u> the flag. (future)
> Joe <u>will be carrying</u> the flag. (future progressive)

Underline the verb in the future progressive in each sentence.

1. The mayor will be marching at the front of the parade.

2. High school students will be playing tubas and flutes.

3. The people on the sidewalk will be cheering happily.

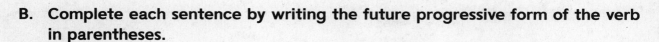

4. Kris will be taking pictures with her new camera.

B. Complete each sentence by writing the future progressive form of the verb in parentheses.

1. Kate and Chen (hold) _____ a banner.

2. The band (wear) _____ their uniforms.

3. Police officers (direct) _____ traffic.

4. The whole town (watch) _____ the parade.

TEACHER: Read the directions and questions in Part A and Part B to students. Guide students to complete each exercise, providing support as needed.

Name _____

> Most verbs use *will* to tell about the future. When action will happen over a period of time, use the **future progressive**. To form the future progressive form, use *will*, the verb *be*, and the *-ing* form of the verb.

Read the passage. Rewrite the passage on the lines below. Change verbs in the future tense to verbs in the future progressive form.

1. The whole town will watch the parade. Officer Trombley will direct traffic. The mayor will lead the marchers. Townspeople will line the sidewalks. Everyone will cheer as loudly as possible.

    _____

    _____

    _____

    _____

    _____

TEACHER: Read the directions and questions to students. Guide students to complete the exercise, providing support as needed.

Name _____

> Verb tenses help people to understand the time of an action. Do not switch back and forth between tenses.
>
> **INCORRECT:** When our team <u>scored</u>, we <u>cheer</u>.
>
> **CORRECT:** When our team <u>scores</u>, we <u>cheer</u>.
> When our team <u>scored</u>, we <u>cheered</u>.

Circle the verb that completes each sentence correctly. Then write the word.

1. I rolled and _____ the ball.
   kick   kicked

2. Pete reaches out and _____ it.
   stops   stopped

3. As I run, I _____ my team.
   watch   watched

4. The ball wobbled and _____ up.
   sails   sailed

5. I tag Mike, and he _____ in.
   rushes   rushed

6. When we win, we _____ up.
   jump   jumped

TEACHER: Read the directions and questions to students. Guide students to complete the exercise, providing support as needed.

Name _____

Verb tenses help people to understand the time of an action. Do not switch back and forth between tenses.

INCORRECT: When our team <u>scored</u>, we <u>cheer</u>.

CORRECT: When our team <u>scores</u>, we <u>cheer</u>.
When our team <u>scored</u>, we <u>cheered</u>.

Choose a verb from the box to complete each sentence. Then write the sentence on the line using the correct tense of the verb you chose.

jump   rush   sail   stop   yell

1. I kicked the ball, and it _____ slowly into the air.

_____

2. Pete reached out and _____ the ball with his hand.

_____

3. I tag Mike, and he _____ out onto the field.

_____

4. The coach _____ and encourages us from the sidelines.

_____

5. When we win, we all _____ for joy.

_____

TEACHER: Read the directions and questions to students. Guide students to complete the exercise, providing support as needed.

Name _____

> Verb tenses help people to understand the time of an action. Do not switch back and forth between tenses.

Find the error in the use of verb tenses. Choose one way to correct the sentence. Rewrite the sentence correctly on the lines.

1. I kick the ball, and it sailed into the air.

   _____

   _____

2. Pete reaches out and stopped the ball.

   _____

   _____

3. The coach encourages us and yelled from the sidelines.

   _____

   _____

TEACHER: Read the directions and questions to students. Guide students to complete the exercise, providing support as needed.

Grades 4-6   **117**

Name _____

In a paragraph or essay, use verbs that are in the same tense. If the writing is set in the past, use verbs in the past tense. If the writing tells about the future, use verbs in the future tense.

A. Choose the correct form of each verb to make the story tell about the future. Circle your answer.

1. Next Tuesday, Maha _____ a bus to the city.

   a. takes   **b.** will take   **c.** took

2. She _____ her grandmother.

   a. visited   **b.** visits   **c.** will visit

3. The two of them _____ the day together.

   a. spend   **b.** spent   **c.** will spend

B. Circle the correct verb to make the story tell about the past.

1. The train (stops, stopped) near Broadway.

2. Maha and her grandmother (enter, entered) the theater.

3. The show (started, starts) at three o'clock.

4. The people (settled, settle) in their seats.

TEACHER: Read the directions and questions in Part A and Part B to students. Guide students to complete each exercise, providing support as needed.

Name _____

> In a paragraph or essay, use verbs that are in the same tense. If the writing is set in the past, use verbs in the past tense. If the writing tells about the future, use verbs in the future tense.

Circle the verb in each sentence. Then write the verb you would use to change the story to tell about something that happened in the past.

1. Maha travels to the city by bus. _____

2. She visits her grandmother's house. _____

3. Their train stops near Broadway. _____

4. They enter the theater. _____

5. The lights dim at three o'clock. _____

6. The curtain opens on a lovely scene. _____

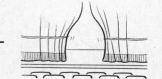

TEACHER: Read the directions and questions to students. Guide students to complete the exercise, providing support as needed.

Name _____

In a paragraph or essay, use verbs that are in the same tense. If the writing is set in the past, use verbs in the past tense. If the writing tells about the future, use verbs in the future tense.

Read the passage. Decide whether to write the verbs in the past or the future. Then rewrite the passage on the lines below.

1. Maha travels to the city by bus. She visited her grandmother's house. They plan a trip to Broadway. They hand their tickets to an usher. Later, they dined at Maha's favorite restaurant.

_____

_____

_____

_____

_____

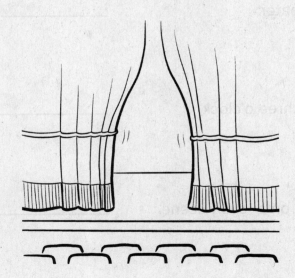

TEACHER: Read the directions and questions to students. Guide students to complete the exercise, providing support as needed.

Name _____

> You can form the **present perfect** tense by using *has* or *have* and the past participle of the main verb.
>
> I <u>have read</u> that book.

A. Read the first sentence with the underlined verb in the past tense. Then fill in the blank to rewrite the sentence with the verb in the present perfect.

1. I <u>watched</u> the game.

   I _____ the game.

2. She <u>started</u> making a sweater.

   She _____ making a sweater.

3. He <u>lost</u> his watch.

   He _____ his watch.

4. Jesse <u>ate</u> a sandwich.

   Jesse _____ a sandwich.

B. Circle the correct word in parentheses to complete each sentence.

1. I (has, have) enjoyed fishing.

2. Max (has, have) climbed a mountain.

3. We (has, have) sung in the choir.

Name _____

> You can form the **present perfect** tense by using *has* or *have* and the past participle of the main verb.

A. Complete the sentence using the present perfect tense of the verb in parentheses.

1. I _____ the game. (watch)

2. She _____ making a sweater. (start)

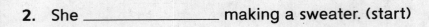

3. He _____ his watch. (lose)

4. Jesse _____ a sandwich. (eat)

B. Complete the sentences by writing the present perfect tense of each verb in parentheses.

1. I _____ fishing. (enjoy)

2. Max _____ a mountain. (climb)

3. We _____ in the choir. (sing)

TEACHER: Read the directions and questions in Part A and Part B to students. Guide students to complete each exercise, providing support as needed.

Name _____

> You can form the **present perfect** tense by using *has* or *have* and the past participle of the main verb.

A. Rewrite each sentence using the present perfect tense.

1. I watched the game.

   _____

2. She started making a sweater.

   _____

3. He lost his watch.

   _____

B. Write the present perfect tense of the verb in parentheses to complete each sentence.

1. Jesse _____ a sandwich. (eat)

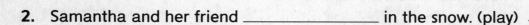

2. Samantha and her friend _____ in the snow. (play)

3. We _____ in the choir. (sing)

TEACHER: Read the directions and questions in Part A and Part B to students. Guide students to complete each exercise, providing support as needed.

Name _____

> You can form the **past perfect** tense by using *had* and the past
> participle of the main verb. You can form the **future perfect** tense by
> using *will have* and the past participle of the main verb.
>
> <u>had</u> traveled (past perfect)   <u>will have</u> traveled (future perfect)

**A. Choose the verb in the past perfect tense to complete each sentence.
Circle the answer.**

1. Mara _____ a letter to her friend.

   a. writes   **b.** wrote   **c.** had written   **d.** has written

2. She _____ a present.

   a. wrapped   **b.** had wrapped   **c.** has wrapped   **d.** have wrapped

3. Kelsey _____ dinner for his parents.

   a. cooked   **b.** have cooked   **c.** has cooked   **d.** had cooked

**B. Choose the verb in the future perfect tense to complete each sentence.
Circle the answer.**

1. George (will place, will have placed) the book
   on the shelf.

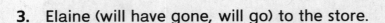

2. The dog (will have run, will run) onto the road.

3. Elaine (will have gone, will go) to the store.

4. Lita (will have carried, will carry) the
   groceries inside.

**TEACHER: Read the directions and questions to students. Guide students to complete
each exercise, providing support as needed.**

Name _____

> You can form the **past perfect** tense by using *had* and the past participle of the main verb. You can form the **future perfect** tense by using *will have* and the past participle of the main verb.
>
> <u>had</u> traveled   <u>will have</u> traveled

A. Write the past perfect tense of the given verb on the line.

1. carry _____

2. write _____

3. wrap _____

4. cook _____

B. Read each sentence. Write the future perfect tense of the verb in parentheses.

1. George (place) the book on the shelf. _____

2. The dog (run) onto the road. _____

3. Elaine (shop) at the store. _____

TEACHER: Read the directions and questions in Part A and Part B to students. Guide students to complete each exercise, providing support as needed.

Name _____

> You can form the **past perfect** tense by using *had* and the past participle of the main verb. You can form the **future perfect** tense by using *will have* and the past participle of the main verb.

A. Read each sentence and underline the verb. Then rewrite the sentence, using the verb in the past perfect tense.

1. Mara writes a letter to her friend.

   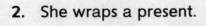

   _____

2. She wraps a present.

   _____

3. Kelsey cooks dinner for his father.

   _____

B. Complete each sentence using the future perfect tense of the verb in parentheses.

1. George _____ the book on the shelf. (place)

2. The dog _____ onto the road. (run)

3. Elaine _____ to the store. (go)

TEACHER: Read the directions and questions in Part A and Part B to students. Guide students to complete each exercise, providing support as needed.

Name _____

> Use the **helping verbs** *is, am, are, was, were,* and *will* to form the past
> progressive, present progressive, and simple future.
>
>   I drive. (present)   I drove. (past)   I <u>will</u> drive. (future)
>
> I <u>was </u>driving. (past progressive)   I <u>am</u> driving. (present progressive)

A. Read each sentence. Write *future, past progressive,* or *present progressive*
   on the line.

1. The brown horse was galloping. _____

2. He is walking now. _____

3. I am waiting for him to rest. _____

4. Later, I will ride him. _____

B. Read each sentence. Circle the helping verb.

1. Jacob was riding his bike.

2. Now he is playing with his dog.

3. He will throw the ball for the dog.

4. Later, he will put his bike away.

**TEACHER: Read the directions and questions in Part A and Part B to students. Guide
students to complete each exercise, providing support as needed.**

Name _____

> Use the **helping verbs** *is, am, are, was, were,* and *will* to form the past progressive, present progressive, and simple future.
>
> I <u>was</u> driving. (past progressive)   I <u>am</u> driving. (present progressive)
>
> I <u>will</u> drive. (future)

A. Circle the correct helping verb. Write *future, past progressive,* or *present progressive* on the line.

1. The brown horse (are/was)

   galloping. _____

2. He (is/are) walking now. _____

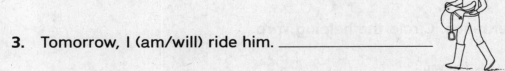

3. Tomorrow, I (am/will) ride him. _____

B. Circle the helping verb in each sentence.

1. Jacob was riding his bike.

2. Now he is playing with his dog.

3. He will throw the ball for the dog.

TEACHER: Read the directions and questions in Part A and Part B to students. Guide students to complete each exercise, providing support as needed.

Name _____

> Use the **helping verbs** *is, am, are, was, were,* and *will* to form the present progressive, past progressive and simple future.

A. **Circle the correct helping verb. Write *future, past progressive,* or *present progressive* on the line.**

1. The brown horse (are/was) galloping. _____

2. He (is/are) walking now. _____

3. I (am/will) ride him later. _____

B. **Write a helping verb to form the tense in parentheses.**

1. Jacob _____ riding his bike. (past progressive)

2. Now he _____ playing with his dog. (present progressive)

3. Later, he _____ throw the ball for the dog. (future)

C. **Rewrite each sentence using the past progressive form.**

1. I am cooking dinner.

_____

2. They are playing hockey.

_____

Name _____

> The **helping verb** *can* is used to express that you are able to do an action. The **helping verb** *may* is used to express that an action is possible.
>
> I <u>can</u> throw this ball. = I <u>have the ability</u> to throw the ball.
>
> I <u>may</u> throw this ball. = <u>It is possible</u> that I will throw the ball.

Write *can* or *may* to complete each sentence.

1. You _____ enjoy this music.

2. She _____ dance well because she practices each day.

3. Josie _____ want to get pizza.

4. The game _____ end early because it is raining.

5. We _____ go into the museum because we paid the fee.

TEACHER: Read the directions and questions to students. Guide students to complete the exercise, providing support as needed.

Name _____

> The **helping verb** *can* is used to express that you are able to do an action. The **helping verb** *may* is used to express that an action is possible.
>
> can = able to   may = it is possible that

A. Write *can* or *may* to complete each sentence.

1. You _____ enjoy this music.

2. She _____ dance well because she practices each day.

3. Josie _____ want to get pizza.

B. Rewrite each sentence using *can* or *may*. You may need to add, delete, or rearrange words.

1. It is possible that the game will end early because it is raining.

_____

2. We are able to go into the museum because we paid the fee.

_____

3. She has the ability to run fast.

_____

TEACHER: Read the directions and questions in Part A and Part B to students. Guide students to complete each exercise, providing support as needed.

Name _____

> The **helping verb** *can* is used to express that you are able to do an action.
> The **helping verb** *may* is used to express that an action is possible.

Rewrite each sentence using *can* or *may*.

1. It is possible that the game will end early because it is raining.

    _____

2. We are able to go into the museum because we paid the fee.

    _____

3. My mother has the ability to run very fast.

    _____

Write *can* or *may* to complete each sentence.

1. I think that you _____ enjoy this music.

2. The woman _____ dance well because she
    practices for several hours each day.

3. Josie _____ not want to get pizza, because
    she just had dinner.

TEACHER: Read the directions and questions in Part A and Part B to students. Guide students to complete each exercise, providing support as needed.

Name _____

> Use *ought* to say that something is correct or right to do.
>
> Use *will* to say that something is certain to happen.
>
> Use *shall* to politely make a suggestion.

Write *ought, will,* or *shall* to complete each sentence.

1. You _____ to do your homework before dinner.

2. _____ I make breakfast?

3. Stephan _____ to mow the grass before the rain starts.

4. The sun _____ come out today.

5. They _____ catch the next bus.

TEACHER: Read the directions and questions to students. Guide students to complete the exercise, providing support as needed.

Name _____

Use *ought* to say that something is correct or right to do. Use *will* to say that something is certain to happen. Use *shall* to politely make a suggestion.

A. Choose *ought, will,* or *shall* to complete each sentence.

1. You (ought, will, shall) to do your homework before dinner.

2. (Ought, Will, Shall) I make breakfast?

3. Stephan (ought, will, shall) to mow the grass before the rain starts.

B. Read each sentence. Rewrite the sentence using *ought* or *will*.

1. The sun is sure to come out today.

_____

2. Ben should be sure to eat his vegetables.

_____

3. They are certain to catch the next bus.

_____

TEACHER: Read the directions and questions in Part A and Part B to students. Guide students to complete each exercise, providing support as needed.

Name _____

Use **ought** to say that something is correct or right to do. Use **will** to say that something is certain to happen. Use **shall** to politely make a suggestion.

A. Rewrite each sentence using *ought*, *will*, or *shall*.

1. Would it be fun if we went swimming?

   _____

2. Ben should be sure to eat his vegetables.

   _____

3. They are certain to catch the next bus.

   _____

B. Write *ought*, *will*, or *shall* to complete each sentence.

1. You _____ to do your homework before dinner.

2. _____ I make you some fried eggs for breakfast?

3. Stephan _____ to mow the grass before the rain starts.

Name _____

> Use *prefer to* or *would rather* to say that you like one thing more than another.
>
> I <u>prefer to</u> swim.   I <u>would rather</u> swim than walk.

A. Write the word or words that complete each sentence.

1. She _____ speak than write.
   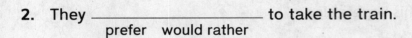
   prefers   would rather

2. They _____ to take the train.
   prefer   would rather

3. Nell _____ to sew her own clothes.
   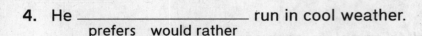
   prefers   would rather

4. He _____ run in cool weather.
   prefers   would rather

5. I _____ walk than run.

   prefer   would rather

B. Write *prefer* or *rather* to complete each sentence.

1. She would _____ dance.

2. They _____ to eat later.

3. Martha would _____ practice piano than go outside.

TEACHER: Read the directions and questions in Part A and Part B to students. Guide students to complete each exercise, providing support as needed.

Name _____

> Use **prefer to** or **would rather** to say that you like one thing more than another.
>
> I prefer to swim.   I would rather swim than walk

A. Circle the word or words that complete each sentence.

1. She (prefers/would rather) speak than write.

2. They (prefer/would rather) to take the train.

3. Nell (prefers/would rather) to sew her own clothes.

4. The runner (prefers/would rather) train in cool weather.

B. Write *prefer, prefers,* or *rather* to complete each answer.

1. Would she like to dance or sing?

    She _____ to dance.

2. Do you want to cook or go out to eat?

    I would _____ cook.

3. Do you like to walk or run?

    I would _____ walk.

TEACHER: Read the directions and questions in Part A and Part B to students. Guide students to complete each exercise, providing support as needed.   Grades 4-6   **137**

Name _____

> Use *prefer to* or *would rather* to say that you like one thing more than another.

A. Answer each question using *prefer to* or *would rather*.

1. Would she like to dance or sing in the show?

   _____

2. Do you want to cook or go out to eat?

   _____

3. Would you rather go to the movies or go bowling?

   _____

B. Write *prefer, prefers,* or *would rather* to complete each sentence.

1. She _____ speak than write.

2. They _____ to take the train.

3. Nell _____ to sew her own clothes.

TEACHER: Read the directions and questions in Part A and Part B to students. Guide students to complete each exercise, providing support as needed.

Name _____

A **linking verb** is not an action verb. Linking verbs are used to tell the condition or state of something.

Read each sentence. Circle the linking verb.

1.   That puzzle seems difficult.

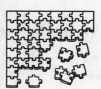

2.   The horse appeared tired after the long ride.

3.   You are my best friend.

4.   I was worried about driving on icy roads.

5.   That building is very tall.

6.   Reva looks excited about her new bike.

TEACHER: Read the directions and questions to students. Guide students to complete the exercise, providing support as needed.

Name _____

> A **linking verb** is not an action verb. Linking verbs are used to tell the condition or state of something.

A. Read each sentence. Circle the linking verb.

1. That puzzle seems difficult.

2. The horse appeared tired after the long ride.

3. You are my best friend.

B. Write a linking verb to complete each sentence.

1. I _____ worried about driving on icy roads.

2. That building _____ very tall.

3. Reva _____ excited about her new bike.

TEACHER: Read the directions and questions in Part A and Part B to students. Guide students to complete each exercise, providing support as needed.

Name _____

> A **linking verb** is not an action verb. Linking verbs are used to tell the condition or state of something.

A. Read each sentence. Write the linking verb on the line.

1. That puzzle seems very difficult. _____

2. The brown horse appeared tired after the long ride. _____

3. Those boys are my older brothers. _____

4. I was worried about driving on icy roads. _____

5. That building is made of metal and glass. _____

6. The clean car looked brand new. _____

7. After the game, the entire team was tired. _____

B. Choose two of the linking verbs you wrote above. Use them in two new sentences. Write the sentences on the lines below.

1. _____

_____

_____

2. _____

_____

_____

Name _____

> **Linking verbs** are used to tell the condition or state of something.

A. Circle the linking verb that correctly completes each sentence.

1. This salad _____ fresh.

   becomes   tastes

2. Our dog _____ excited at dinnertime.

   smells   becomes

3. This pineapple _____ rotten.

   smells   grows

4. I _____ tired after staying up late.

   smells   feel

5. The lights _____ dim as the concert began.

   grew   taste

B. Read each sentence. Underline the linking verb.

1. This sauce tastes great.

2. That candle smells nice.

3. I feel warm in my new coat.

TEACHER: Read the directions and questions in Part A and Part B to students. Guide students to complete each exercise, providing support as needed.

Name _____

> **Linking verbs** are used to tell the condition or state of something.

A. Circle the linking verb that correctly completes each sentence.

1. Our dog (smells / becomes) excited at dinnertime.

2. This pineapple (smells / grows) rotten.

3. I (smell / feel) tired after staying up late.

4. The lights (grew/felt) dim as the concert began.

**B. Write *L* if the underlined word is used as a linking verb.
Write *A* if the underlined word is used as an action verb.**

1. I will <u>taste</u> the sauce to see if it needs salt.

_____

2. That candle <u>smells</u> nice. _____

3. Do you <u>grow</u> your own vegetables?

_____

Name _____

> **Linking verbs** are used to tell the condition or state of something.

A. Write a linking verb to complete each sentence. Choose from *become(s),* *feel(s),* or *smell(s).*

1. Our dog _____ excited at dinnertime.

2. This pineapple _____ rotten.

3. I _____ tired when I stay up late.

B. Write *L* if the underlined word is used as a linking verb. Write *A* if it is used as an action verb.

1. I will <u>taste</u> the sauce to see if it needs salt. _____

2. That candle <u>smells</u> nice. _____

3. Do you <u>grow</u> your own vegetables? _____

C. Underline the linking verb in each sentence. Then write your own sentence using that linking verb.

1. The chocolate becomes warm in the sun.

   _____

2. Why does she feel disappointed?

   _____

3. The theater grew dark as the concert began.

   _____

TEACHER: Read the directions and questions in Part A, Part B, and Part C to students. Guide students to complete each exercise, providing support as needed.

Name _____

> A **predicate noun** is a noun that follows a linking verb and renames the subject.

A. Circle the letter next to the predicate noun for each sentence.

1. That man is a teacher.
   - **a.** that
   - **b.** man
   - **c.** a
   - **d.** teacher

2. Waffles are my favorite breakfast.
   - **a.** waffles
   - **b.** favorite
   - **c.** breakfast
   - **d.** are

3. Zane is Cassidy's younger brother.
   - **a.** Cassidy
   - **b.** brother
   - **c.** Zane
   - **d.** younger

B. Read each sentence. Circle the predicate noun.

1. Samantha is a basketball player.

2. River is a musician.

3. Mozart was a famous composer.

4. Albany is a state capital.

TEACHER: Read the directions and questions in Part A and Part B to students. Guide students to complete each exercise, providing support as needed.

Name _____

A **predicate noun** is a noun that follows a linking verb and renames the subject.

A. Read each sentence. Circle the predicate noun.

1. Samantha is a basketball player.

2. River is a musician.

3. Mozart was a famous composer.

4. Albany is a state capital.

5. The man in the hat is my piano teacher.

B. Circle the letter next to the predicate noun for each sentence.

1. Waffles are my favorite breakfast food.
   a. food
   b. favorite
   c. waffle

2. The boy in the striped shirt is Cassidy's younger brother.
   a. Cassidy
   b. brother
   c. boy

TEACHER: Read the directions and questions in Part A and Part B to students. Guide students to complete each exercise, providing support as needed.

Name _____

> A **predicate noun** is a noun that follows a linking verb and renames the subject.

Two Points!

Samantha is a basketball player.

She scored two points in the last game.

She was happy. The team was happy, too.

They won the game.

Anna is their coach. She took the players out for ice cream.

Samantha ordered chocolate ice cream.

Chocolate is her favorite flavor.

Many other players had chocolate, but some had vanilla.

People had fun. It was a celebration!

1. **Circle the predicate nouns in the sentences above.**

2. **Write a sentence with a predicate noun.**

_____

TEACHER: Read the directions and questions to students. Guide students to complete the exercise, providing support as needed.

Name_____

> A **predicate adjective** follows a linking verb and tells more about the subject.

A. Circle the letter next to the predicate adjective for each sentence.

1. The new puppy is black.

   a. is   **b.** new   **c.** black   **d.** puppy

2. The red cabbage was crunchy.

   a. was   **b.** red   **c.** cabbage   **d.** crunchy

3. The twin baby lambs were cute.

   a. twin   **b.** cute   **c.** baby   **d.** lambs

B. Read each sentence. Circle the predicate adjective.

1. Trees in the Redwood Forest are tall.

2. The curry soup was spicy.

3. The actor's hair is curly.

4. The ice skaters are graceful.

TEACHER: Read the directions and questions in Part A and Part B to students. Guide students to complete each exercise, providing support as needed.

Name _____

> A **predicate adjective** follows a linking verb and tells more about the subject.

A. Read each sentence. Circle the predicate adjective.

1. Trees in the Redwood Forest are tall.

2. Mom's curry soup was spicy.

3. The tall actor's hair is curly.

4. The figure skaters are graceful.

5. That skier is brave.

B. Circle the letter next to the predicate adjective for each sentence.

1. The new puppy is black.
   a. is
   b. new
   c. black
   d. puppy

2. The twin lambs were cute.
   a. twin
   b. cute
   c. were
   d. lambs

TEACHER: Read the directions and questions in Part A and Part B to students. Guide students to complete each exercise, providing support as needed.

Grades 4-6   149

Name _____

> A **predicate adjective** follows a linking verb and tells more about the subject.

A. Read each sentence. Circle the predicate adjective.

1. Trees in the Redwood Forest are tall.

2. Mom's curry soup was spicy.

3. The tall actor's hair is curly.

B. Write a predicate adjective to complete each sentence.

1. The figure skaters are _____.

2. That skier is _____.

3. The campfire was _____.

C. Circle the predicate adjective in each sentence. Then write a new sentence using the circled word as a predicate adjective.

1. The new puppy is small.

   _____

   _____

2. The twin lambs were cute.

   _____

   _____

TEACHER: Read the directions and questions in Part A, Part B, and Part C to students. Guide students to complete each exercise, providing support as needed.

Name _____

> **Linking verbs** do not express action. They link the subject with additional information about the subject. Forms of the verb *be* are linking verbs.
>
> **Present:** am, is, are **Past:** was, were

A. Underline the linking verb in each sentence and write *past* or *present* on the line.

1. I am sleepy today. _____

2. I was happy yesterday. _____

3. You were in fourth grade last year. _____

4. My mother is working today. _____

B. Choose the correct verb in parentheses to complete each sentence.

1. Cho (is, am) South Korean.

2. I (am, was) in fifth grade last year.

3. They (are, were) running now.

4. They (are, were) walking yesterday.

TEACHER: Read the directions and questions in Part A and Part B to students. Guide students to complete each exercise, providing support as needed.

Grades 4-6   151

Name _____

> **Linking verbs** do not express action. They link the subject with additional information about the subject. Forms of the verb *be* are linking verbs.
>
> **Present:** am, is, are   **Past:** was, were

A. Circle the letter next to the correct verb for each sentence.

1. Cho _____ South Korean.

    a. is

    b. are

    c. am

2. I _____ in fifth grade last year.

    a. am

    b. were

    c. was

B. Fill in the blank with the correct form of the verb *be* and then write *past* or *present* on the line.

1. I _____ sleepy today.

    _____

2. I _____ happy yesterday.

    _____

3. You _____ in fourth grade last year.

    _____

TEACHER: Read the directions and questions in Part A and Part B to students. Guide students to complete each exercise, providing support as needed.

Name _____

> **Linking verbs** do not express action. They link the subject with additional information about the subject. Forms of the verb *be* are linking verbs.

A. **Rewrite each sentence. Change the verb from present to past or from past to present.**

1. I am sleepy today.

    _____ yesterday.

2. I was happy yesterday.

    _____ today.

3. You were in fourth grade last year.

    _____ this year.

B. **Write the correct form of *be* to complete each sentence.**

1. My friend Cho _____ South Korean.

2. I _____ in fifth grade last year.

3. They _____ running now.

Name _____

> When the verb *look* follows a singular noun or the words *he, she,* or *it,* add the ending *-s.* **(looks)**
>
> When the verb *look* follows a plural noun or the words *you, we,* or *they,* do not add *-s.* **(look)**
>
> For things that happened in the past, add *-ed* to the end of *look.* **(looked)**

Circle the word that correctly completes each sentence. Then write the word.

1. I _____ sleepy now.

   look   looks

2. Jaylen _____ happy now.

   looks   looked

3. Roshni _____ at her calendar every day.

   looked   looks

4. Those two boys _____ like brothers.

   look   looks

5. Our teacher _____ for her lost keys yesterday.

   looks   looked

TEACHER: Read the directions and questions to students. Guide students to complete the exercise, providing support as needed.

Name _____

> When the verb *look* follows a singular noun or the words *he, she,* or *it,* add the ending –*s.* **(looks)**
>
> When the verb *look* follows a plural noun or the words *you, we,* or *they,* do not add –*s.* **(look)**
>
> For things that happened in the past, add –*ed* to the end of *look.* **(looked)**

Write *look, looks,* or *looked* to complete each sentence.

1. I _____ sleepy now.

2. Yusef _____ happy now.

3. Roshni _____ at her calendar every day.

4. Those two boys _____ like brothers.

5. Our teacher _____ for her lost keys yesterday.

TEACHER: Read the directions and questions to students. Guide students to complete the exercise, providing support as needed.

Name _____

> When the verb *look* follows a singular noun or the words *he, she,* or *it,* add the ending *–s.* **(looks)**
>
> When the verb *look* follows a plural noun or the words *you, we,* or *they,* do not add *–s.* **(look)**
>
> For things that happened in the past, add *–ed* to the end of *look.* **(looked)**

Rewrite each sentence using the new subject in parentheses.

1. I look sleepy now. (She)

   _____

   _____

2. Those boys look like baseball players. (That boy)

   _____

   _____

3. Yusef looks happier now. (Yusef and Rodney)

   _____

   _____

TEACHER: Read the directions and questions to students. Guide students to complete the exercise, providing support as needed.

Name _____

> A verb is a word that tells about an action or a state of being. **Present-tense verbs** tell about actions that are happening now or the current state of something. Regular present-tense verbs add –s when they are used with *he, she,* or *it.*

A. **Choose the correct form of the verb for the given subject. Write the verb on the line.**

1. I   cook / cooks   _____

2. she   like / likes   _____

3. we   wash / washes   _____

4. it   move / moves   _____

B. **Circle the correct form of the verb to complete each sentence.**

1. I (fill / fills) my glass with water.

2. Daniel (win / wins) the race.

3. Carol (type / types) her report.

4. They (enjoy / enjoys) doing puzzles.

Name _____

A verb is a word that tells about an action or a state of being. **Present-tense verbs** tell about actions that are happening now or the current state of something. Regular present-tense verbs add *–s* when they are used with *he, she,* or *it.*

Change each verb in bold to match the subject in the second sentence. Write the new verb on the line.

1. I **fill** the glass with water. She _____ the glass with water.

2. Daniel **wins** the race. I _____ the race.

3. Carol **types** her report. We _____ our report.

4. They **enjoy** puzzles. Enrique _____ puzzles.

5. You **sit** on the couch. The dog _____ on the couch.

6. I **write** a story. Dave _____ a story.

7. We **eat** soup for lunch. She _____ soup for lunch.

TEACHER: Read the directions and questions to students. Guide students to complete the exercise, providing support as needed.

Name _____

> **Present-tense verbs** tell about actions that are happening now or the current state of something. Regular present-tense verbs add *-s* when they are used with *he, she,* or *it.*

Rewrite each sentence with the new subject in parentheses.

1. I fill all the glasses on the table with water. (She)

   _____

   _____

2. Daniel wins the race. (I)

   _____

   _____

3. Carol types a report about the book she read. (We)

   _____

   _____

TEACHER: Read the directions and questions to students. Guide students to complete the exercise, providing support as needed.

Grades 4-6   159

Name _____

> The **past tense** tells about action that has already happened.
>
> For regular verbs ending in –e add –d: mov<u>e</u>   move<u>d</u>
>
> For regular verbs ending in a letter other than –e add -ed: wai<u>t</u>   wait<u>ed</u>
>
> For regular verbs ending in a consonant + -y change the y to i
> and add –ed: tr<u>y</u>   tr<u>ied</u>.

A. Circle the correct past-tense form of each verb. Write it on the line.

1. move   moves / moved   _____

2. cry   cryed / cried   _____

3. pack   packed / packs   _____

4. travel   traveled / traveld   _____

B. Add –d, –ed or change –y to –ied and write the past-tense verbs.

1. carry (change y to ied) _____

2. shove (add –d) _____

3. walk (add –ed) _____

4. play (add –ed) _____

**TEACHER: Read the directions and questions in Part A and Part B to students. Guide
students to complete each exercise, providing support as needed.**

Name _____

The **past tense** tells about action that has already happened.

For regular verbs ending in –e add –d: mov<u>e</u>   move<u>d</u>

For regular verbs ending in a letter other than –e add -ed: wai<u>t</u>   wait<u>ed</u>

For regular verbs ending in a consonant + -y change the y to i and add –ed: tr<u>y</u>   tr<u>ied</u>.

Complete each sentence with the past tense of the verb in bold.

1. I **carry** groceries inside.   I _____ groceries inside.

2. He **shoves** the heavy box.   He _____ the heavy box.

3. We **walk** to the park.   We _____ to the park.

4. They **play** soccer.   They _____ soccer.

5. Johnny **cheers** for us.   Johnny _____ for us.

TEACHER: Read the directions and questions to students. Guide students to complete the exercise, providing support as needed.

Name _____

The **past tense** tells about action that has already happened.

For regular verbs ending in –*e* add –*d*: move   move<u>d</u>

For regular verbs ending in a letter other than –*e* add -*ed*: wai<u>t</u>   wai<u>ted</u>

For regular verbs ending in a consonant + -*y* change the *y* to *i* and add –*ed*: tr<u>y</u>   tr<u>ied</u>.

Rewrite each sentence in the past tense.

1. I carry groceries from the car to the house.

    _____

    _____

2. After dinner, we all walk to the park.

    _____

    _____

3. They move into the new house.

    _____

    _____

TEACHER: Read the directions and questions to students. Guide students to complete the exercise, providing support as needed.

Name _____

> **Irregular verbs,** like *have* and *be,* do not follow normal patterns.
>
> **Have** becomes *has* when it is used with *he, she,* or *it.*
>
> **Be** has three different forms in the present tense:
>
> I <u>am</u>; you/we/they <u>are</u>; he/she/it *is*

A. Circle the correct verb to complete each sentence. Then write the word on the line.

1. The library _____ the book I want.
                   has   have

2. I _____ doing my homework.
        is   am

3. I _____ tickets to the game.
       has   have

4. My bedroom _____ messy.
           is   are

5. We _____ partners today.
         am   are

6. The cat _____ afraid of loud noises.
         is   are

TEACHER: Read the directions and questions to students. Guide students to complete the exercise, providing support as needed.

Name _____

> **Irregular verbs,** like *have* and *be,* do not follow normal patterns.
>
> *Have* becomes *has* when it is used with *he, she,* or *it.*
>
> *Be* has three different forms in the present tense:
>
> I a<u>m</u>; you/we/they <u>are</u>; he/she/it *is*

Complete each sentence by adding a verb from the box. Then write the sentence correctly.

> am   are   has   have   is

1. The library _____ the book I want.

   _____

2. I _____ doing my homework.

   _____

3. I _____ tickets to the game today.

   _____

4. My bedroom _____ messy.

   _____

5. We _____ partners for this assignment.

   _____

TEACHER: Read the directions and questions to students. Guide students to complete the exercise, providing support as needed.

Name _____

> **Irregular verbs,** like *have* and *be*, do not follow normal patterns.
>
> **Have** becomes *has* when it is used with *he, she,* or *it.*
>
> **Be** has three different forms in the present tense:
>
> I <u>am</u>; you/we/they <u>are</u>; he/she/it *is*

Write the correct present-tense form of the verb in parentheses.

1. The library (have) the book I want. _____

2. I (be) doing my homework. _____

3. I (have) tickets to the game. _____

4. My bedroom (be) messy. _____

5. We (be) partners for this assignment. _____

6. The cat (be) afraid of loud noises. _____

**TEACHER: Read the directions and questions to students. Guide students to complete
the exercise, providing support as needed.**

Name _____

> **Irregular verbs,** like *have* and *be,* do not follow normal patterns in the past tense.
>
> ***Have*** changes to <u>*had*</u> in the past tense.
>
> ***Be*** changes to <u>*was*</u> when it is used with *I, he, she,* or *it* and to <u>*were*</u> with *you, we,* or *they*.

A. Circle the correct past-tense verb to complete each sentence.

1. I _____ some milk with dinner.
       have   had

2. We _____ at the pool yesterday.
       was   were

3. Julia _____ a member of the choir.
       was   were

4. Alec _____ his keys yesterday.
       have   had

5. A firefighter _____ the class speaker yesterday.
       was   were

6. The plants _____ three inches tall last week.
       was   were

Copyright © McGraw-Hill Education

TEACHER: Read the directions and questions to students. Guide students to complete the exercise, providing support as needed.

Name _____

Irregular verbs, like *have* and *be,* do not follow normal patterns in the past tense.

Have changes to *had* in the past tense.

Be changes to *was* when it is used with *I, he, she,* or *it* and to *were* with *you, we,* or *they.*

Complete each sentence with the past tense of the verb in bold.

1. I **have** milk with dinner.   I _____ milk with dinner.

2. We **are** at the pool.   We _____ at the pool.

3. Julia **is** in the choir.   Julia _____ in the choir.

4. Alec **has** his keys.   Alec _____ his keys.

5. The firefighter **is** brave.   The firefighter _____ brave.

6. The plants **are** tall.   The plants _____ tall.

TEACHER: Read the directions and questions to students. Guide students to complete the exercise, providing support as needed.

Name _____

> **Irregular verbs,** like *have* and *be,* do not follow normal patterns in the past tense.
>
> **Have** changes to <u>had</u> in the past tense.
>
> **Be** changes to <u>was</u> when it is used with *I, he, she,* or *it* and to <u>were</u> with *you, we,* or *they.*

Write the past-tense form of the verb in parentheses to complete each sentence.

1. I (have) some milk with dinner. _____

2. We (be) at the pool yesterday. _____

3. Julia (be) a member of the choir. _____

4. Alec (have) his keys yesterday. _____

5. A firefighter (be) the class speaker yesterday. _____

6. The plants (be) three inches tall last week. _____

TEACHER: Read the directions and questions to students. Guide students to complete the exercise, providing support as needed.

Name _____

> Some **irregular past-tense verbs,** such as *did (do),* follow no spelling pattern. They need to be memorized.
>
> Other irregular verbs, such as *let (let),* are the same in the past and present tense. These need to be memorized too.

A. Draw a line to match the present and past tense of each verb.

1. become   a. hurt

2. hurt   b. became

3. eat   c. hit

4. hit   d. ate

B. Read each verb. Circle the correct past-tense form for each verb.

1. go   goed   went

2. cut   cuted   cut

3. get   got   get

4. cost   costed   cost

Name _____

Some **irregular past-tense verbs,** such as *did (do),* follow no spelling pattern. They need to be memorized.

Other irregular verbs, such as *let (let),* are the same in the past and present tense. These need to be memorized too.

A.   Write the correct past-tense form of each verb

1.   become _____

2.   cut _____

3.   get _____

4.   cost _____

B.   Write the correct past-tense form of the verb in parentheses.

1.   I (go) to my aunt's house yesterday. _____

2.   We (eat) our lunches outside because it was no nice. _____

3.   Jared (hit) a homerun to win the game. _____

TEACHER: Read the directions and questions in Part A and Part B to students. Guide students to complete each exercise, providing support as needed.

Name _____

> Some **irregular past-tense verbs,** such as *did (do),* follow no spelling pattern. They need to be memorized.
>
> Other irregular verbs, such as *let (let),* are the same in the past and present tense. These need to be memorized too.

Rewrite each sentence in the past tense.

1. I go to my aunt's house after school.

   _____

   _____

2. We eat our lunches outside on the grassy field.

   _____

   _____

3. I hit a homerun to win the game for our team.

   _____

   _____

4. The caterpillar becomes a butterfly.

   _____

   _____

TEACHER: Read the directions and questions to students. Guide students to complete the exercise, providing support as needed.

Grades 4-6   171

Name _____

Some **irregular past-tense verbs,** such as *did (do)*, follow no spelling pattern. They need to be memorized.

Other irregular verbs, such as *let (let)*, are the same in the past and present tense. These need to be memorized too.

A.   Draw a line to match the present and past tense of each verb.

1.   put   **a.**   left

2.   leave   **b.**   put

3.   say   **c.**   set

4.   set   **d.**   said

B.   Read each verb. Circle the correct past-tense form for each verb.

1.   see   seed   saw

2.   shut   shuted   shut

3.   take   take   took

4.   spread   spread   spreaded

TEACHER: Read the directions and questions in Part A and Part B to students. Guide students to complete each exercise, providing support as needed.

Name _____

> Some **irregular past-tense verbs,** such as *did (do),* follow no spelling pattern. They need to be memorized.
>
> Other irregular verbs, such as *let (let),* are the same in the past and present tense. These need to be memorized too.

A. Write the correct past-tense form of each verb.

1. put _____

2. shut _____

3. say _____

4. take _____

B. Write the correct past-tense form of each verb in parentheses.

1. I (leave) my house at 7:00. _____

2. Michelle (spread) peanut butter on her sandwich. _____

3. Carlos (see) the movie last Friday. _____

TEACHER: Read the directions and questions in Part A and Part B to students. Guide students to complete each exercise, providing support as needed.

Name _____

Some **irregular past-tense verbs,** such as *did (do),* follow no spelling pattern. They need to be memorized.

Other irregular verbs, such as *let (let),* are the same in the past and present tense. These need to be memorized too.

Rewrite each sentence in the past tense.

1. Michelle spreads peanut butter on her sandwich.

   _____

   _____

2. Then she takes the jelly off of the shelf.

   _____

   _____

3. "This sandwich looks delicious," she says.

   _____

   _____

TEACHER: Read the directions and questions to students. Guide students to complete the exercise, providing support as needed.

Name _____

> The **passive voice** always includes some form of *be* and a past participle.
>
> Passive sentences do not always include the person or thing doing the action (the agent). When the agent is included, it is placed after the verb.

A. Underline the form of the verb *be* and circle the main verb in each sentence.

1. That sandwich was made by Leo.

2. That story was written by Marci.

3. Many computers are made in China.

4. That soccer field is used every day.

B. Write the correct form of *be* and the past participle of the verb in parentheses to create a passive-voice sentence.

1. That pie (be + make) _____ by the chef.

2. That bridge (be + build) _____ 10 years ago.

3. English (be + speak) _____ in this class.

Hello, my name is Li!

4. The award (be + give) _____ to the winner.

TEACHER: Read the directions and questions in Part A and Part B to students. Guide students to complete each exercise, providing support as needed.

Grades 4-6   175

Name _____

> The **passive voice** always includes some form of *be* and a past participle.
>
> Passive sentences do not always include the person or thing doing the action (the agent). When the agent is included, it is placed after the verb.

A. Underline the form of the verb *be* and circle the main verb in each sentence.

1. That sandwich is being made by Leo.

2. That story was written by Marci.

3. Many computers are made in China.

B. Change each active sentence to a passive sentence.

1. The chef made that pie.

   _____

2. Workers are building that bridge.

   _____

3. The students speak English.

   _____

TEACHER: Read the directions and questions in Part A and Part B to students. Guide students to complete each exercise, providing support as needed.

Name _____

> The **passive voice** always includes some form of *be* and a past participle.
>
> Passive sentences do not always include the person or thing doing the action (the agent). When the agent is included, it is placed after the verb.

Rewrite each sentence in the active voice.

1. That sandwich is being made by Leo.

   _____

   _____

2. That bridge is being built by workers.

   _____

   _____

3. English will be spoken by the students today.

   _____

   _____

Hello, my name is Li!

TEACHER: Read the directions and questions to students. Guide students to complete the exercise, providing support as needed.

Name _____

> **Future conditionals** contain present tense and future-tense verbs. The order of these sentences can be flipped. The word *then* can be used when the *if*-clause is first.

A. Underline the present-tense verb and circle the future-tense verbs in each sentence.

1. If you are careful, I will share my toy with you.

2. If Yolanda makes dinner, I am going to make dessert.

3. I will clean the bathroom if you clean the bedroom.

4. I am going to do well if I study.

B. Circle the correct word in parentheses to make a conditional sentence.

1. Our class will have a picnic if the weather (is, was) nice.

2. If you (send, sending) the letter now, then she is going to get it by Wednesday.

3. My father (shopped, is going shopping) tonight if he is not busy.

4. Sofia will return your ring if she (finds, found) it.

TEACHER: Read the directions and questions in Part A and Part B to students. Guide students to complete each exercise, providing support as needed.

Name _____

> **Future conditionals** contain present tense and future-tense verbs. The order of these sentences can be flipped. The word *then* can be used when the *if*-clause is first.

A. Write the correct form of the verb in parentheses to make a conditional sentence.

1. Our class will have a picnic if the weather _____ nice. (be)

2. If you _____ the letter now, then she is going to get it by Wednesday. (send)

3. My father _____ tonight if he is not busy. (shop)

4. Sofia will return your ring if she _____ it. (find)

B. Draw a line from each clause on the left to each clause on the right to create conditional sentences.

1. If you are careful,   if I have the money.

2. I am going to buy a new car   you are going to do well.

3. I will clean the bathroom   if you clean the bedroom.

4. If you study,   I will share my toy with you.

TEACHER: Read the directions and questions in Part A and Part B to students. Guide students to complete each exercise, providing support as needed.

Grades 4-6   179

Name _____

> **Future conditionals** contain present tense and future-tense verbs. The order of these sentences can be flipped. The word *then* can be used when the *if*-clause is first.

A. Draw a line from each clause on the left to each clause on the right to create conditional sentences.

1. If you are careful,   if I have the money.

2. I am going to buy a new car   you are going to do well.

3. I will clean the bathroom   if you clean the bedroom.

4. If you study,   I will share my toy with you.

B. Circle the letter of the sentence that is a logical conditional.

1. **a.** Our class will have a picnic if the weather is nice.

   b. Our class will have a picnic if the weather was nice.

   c. Our class has a picnic if the weather is going to be nice.

   d. Our class has had a picnic when the weather is nice.

2. **a.** If you send the letter now, then she is going to get it by Wednesday.

   b. If you sending the letter now, then she is going to get it by Wednesday.

   c. If you had sent the letter now, then she will get it by Wednesday.

   d. If you send the letter now, the she was getting it by Wednesday.

Copyright © McGraw-Hill Education

TEACHER: Read the directions and questions in Part A and Part B to students. Guide students to complete each exercise, providing support as needed.

Name _____

> The **progressive perfect tense** tells about action started in the past that continues in the present or future. It usually includes a verb ending in *-ing*.
>
> The **future perfect tense** tells about action that takes place before another action in the future.
>
> The **conditional perfect tense** tells about action that might have happened in the past.

Underline each verb. Write *PP* if the verb is progressive perfect, *FP* if it is future perfect, or *CP* if it is conditional perfect.

1. If the author were living today, he

   would have described things differently. _____

2. He would have used different words

   if he were writing now. _____

3. By Friday, I will have completed ten

   chapters. _____

4. I have been discussing the book with

   my teacher. _____

5. Before the due date, I will have drafted

   my book report. _____

Name _____

> The **progressive perfect tense** tells about action started in the past that continues in the present or future. It usually includes a verb ending in *-ing*.
>
> The **future perfect tense** tells about action that takes place before another action in the future.
>
> The **conditional perfect tense** tells about action that might have happened in the past.

A. Underline the verbs described above. Write *progressive perfect, future perfect,* or *conditional perfect* to describe each.

1. I have been working on my book report all day.

   _____

2. Before the due date, I will have drafted my book report.

   _____

3. If I had known how long the book was, I would have asked for more time.

   _____

B. Write the progressive, future, and conditional perfect form of each verb.

	progressive perfect	future perfect	conditional perfect
1. end	_____	_____	_____
2. skim	_____	_____	_____
3. study	_____	_____	_____

TEACHER: Read the directions and questions in Part A and Part B to students. Guide students to complete each exercise, providing support as needed.

Name _____

> The **progressive perfect tense** tells about action started in the past that continues in the present or future. It usually includes a verb ending in *-ing*.
>
> The **future perfect tense** tells about action that takes place before another action in the future.
>
> The **conditional perfect tense** tells about action that might have happened in the past.

A. Underline the verbs described above. Write *PP* if the verb is progressive perfect, *FP* if it is future perfect, and *CP* if it is conditional perfect.

1. If the author were living today, he would have described things differently.

   _____

2. I have been working on my book report all day. _____

3. By Friday, I will have completed ten chapters. _____

4. If I had known how long the book was, I would have asked for more time.

   _____

B. Choose two verbs from the sentences in Part A. Use each verb in a new sentence. Write your sentences on the lines.

1. _____

   _____

2. _____

   _____

Name _____

> Use the **progressive perfect** form to tell about something that started in the past but is still happening or will still be happening in the future.
>
> Use the **future perfect** form to tell about something that will happen before something else happens in the future.
>
> Use **the conditional perfect** form to tell about something that might have happened.

Circle the verb that completes each sentence correctly. Then write the verb.

1. If I had remembered the tune,

    I _____ much better.

    will have sounded   would have sounded

    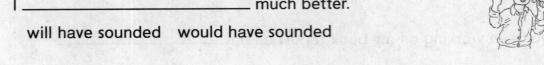

2. I _____ this song for a week now.

    have been practicing   would have practiced

3. If you had reminded me, I _____ my
    voice teacher.

    will have called   would have called

4. Before we meet next week, I _____ this
    difficult lesson.   will have mastered   would have mastered

TEACHER: Read the directions and questions to students. Guide students to complete the exercise, providing support as needed.

Name _____

> Use the **progressive perfect** form to tell about something that started in the past but is still happening or will still be happening in the future.
>
> Use the **future perfect** form to tell about something that will happen before something else happens in the future.
>
> Use **the conditional perfect** form to tell about something that might have happened.

A. Write the progressive perfect, future perfect, or conditional perfect form of each verb as indicated in parentheses.

1. learn (conditional perfect)   _____

2. practice (future perfect)   _____

3. call (progressive perfect)   _____

4. train (conditional perfect)   _____

B. Complete each sentence by writing the correct form of the verb in parentheses.

1. If I had remembered the tune, I (sound) _____ better.

2. I (practice) _____ this song for a week now.

3. If you had reminded me, I (ask) _____ my voice teacher.

Name _____

> Use the **progressive perfect** form to tell about something that started in the past but is still happening or will still be happening in the future.
>
> Use the **future perfect** form to tell about something that will happen before something else happens in the future.
>
> Use **the conditional perfect** form to tell about something that might have happened.

Read the passage. Circle each mistake in verb tense. Then rewrite the passage correctly on the lines below.

1.   I have not been practiced this music. If I had practiced more, I will have sounded better today. My teacher will have praised me more if I had performed better. However, by my next lesson, I have mastered the entire piece.

_____

_____

_____

_____

_____

TEACHER: Read the directions and questions to students. Guide students to complete the exercise, providing support as needed.

Name _____

> Some verbs are used with a connected word. The words form a **phrasal verb**.
>
> Juan <u>turned on</u> the computer. He <u>filled out</u> the form.

Underline the phrasal verb in each sentence.

1. Juan keeps on playing the same game.

2. In the game, you knock over pins.

3. You must look out for monsters.

4. The monsters knock down everyone.

5. We check in and play with Juan.

6. Come on and try this great game!

TEACHER: Read the directions and questions to students. Guide students to complete the exercise, providing support as needed.

Name _____

> Some verbs are used with a connected word. The words form a **phrasal verb**.
>
> Juan <u>turned on</u> the computer.

A. Circle the letters of the sentences that have phrasal verbs. Underline the phrasal verbs.

1. **a.** Juan keeps on playing the same game.

    b. Everyone in school loves the game.

    c. You must look out for monsters.

2. **a.** In the game, Juan knocks over pins.

    b. The monsters try to knock down Juan.

    c. Some of the monsters look scary.

B. Underline each phrasal verb. Then write its meaning on the line.

1. We must check in with the game manager before we play with Juan.

    _____

2. Come on and give me your password.

    _____

3. Look out for that huge monster in the corner!

    _____

TEACHER: Read the directions and questions in Part A and Part B to students. Guide students to complete each exercise, providing support as needed.

Name _____

> Some verbs are used with a connected word. The words form a **phrasal verb**.

Our Favorite Game

Juan and I are playing our favorite game.

"Look out for the monster!" I warn him.

Too late! The monster knocks down Juan's castle.

"Come on, try that again," Juan tells the monster.

He keeps on trying to escape.

"Can you turn on your shield?" I ask.

"Let me check out the tool belt," he answers.

I knock over a big monster.

At the end of the game, we fill in our score.

1. **Underline each phrasal verb.**

2. **Write the meaning of the phrasal verbs listed below.**

   Look out means _____

   Knocks down means _____

TEACHER: Read the directions and questions to students. Guide students to complete the exercise, providing support as needed.

Name _____

> Some verbs are used with a connected word. The words form a **phrasal verb**.
>
> I <u>wake up</u> at 7:00.   I <u>clean up</u> my room.

Underline the phrasal verb in each sentence.

1. I grew up in this house.

2. Now, Mom shows around a buyer.

3. I hurry up with my cleaning.

4. My brother throws away some old papers.

5. Let's slow down before we sell our house.

6. We speak up about it to Mom.

TEACHER: Read the directions and questions to students. Guide students to complete the exercise, providing support as needed.

Name _____

> Some verbs are used with a connected word. The words form a **phrasal verb**.
>
> I <u>wake up</u> at 7:00.

A. Circle the letters of the sentences that have phrasal verbs. Underline the phrasal verbs.

1. **a.** My brother and I grew up here.

    b. Now our house is for sale.

    c. Mom shows around a buyer.

2. **a.** We do not want to leave our home.

    b. My brother and I speak up about our fears.

    c. Let's slow down and sell the house later!

B. Underline each phrasal verb. Then write its meaning on the line.

1. Mom throws out many of our old toys.

    _____

2. Then she cleans up the entire back yard.

    _____

3. We hurry up with our chores.

    _____

TEACHER: Read the directions and questions in Part A and Part B to students. Guide students to complete each exercise, providing support as needed.

Name _____

Some verbs are used with a connected word. The words form a **phrasal verb**.

House for Sale

We are selling the house where I grew up.

Mom shows around a buyer and her family.

They hurry up through the upstairs rooms.

Then they slow down in the beautiful garden.

"What kind of trees are these?" they ask.

I speak up politely.

"Those are fig trees," I tell them.

"In summer, I clean up a lot of fruit from the ground."

1. Underline each phrasal verb.

2. Write the meaning of the phrasal verbs listed below.

   Slow down means _____

   Speak up means _____

TEACHER: Read the directions and questions to students. Guide students to complete the exercise, providing support as needed.

Name _____

> Some **phrasal verbs** have more than one meaning. Listen to or read the sentence to know which meaning is being used.
>
> Bao <u>works out</u> at the gym. (Bao exercises.)
>
> Bao <u>works out</u> a problem. (Bao solves it.)

Read the underlined phrasal verb. Circle the meaning of the verb as it is used in the sentence.

1. The two friends <u>made up</u> after their fight.

   put on makeup   made peace

2. We can <u>pick up</u> Charlie after school.

   give a ride to   raise up

3. The workers <u>blew up</u> the balloons.

   exploded   made bigger

4. The truck beeps as it <u>backs up</u>.

   supports   goes backward

5. The store's owner is <u>passing out</u> candy.

   fainting   handing out

TEACHER: Read the directions and questions to students. Guide students to complete the exercise, providing support as needed.

Name _____

> Some **phrasal verbs** have more than one meaning. Listen to or read the sentence to know which meaning is being used.
>
> Bao <u>works out</u> at the gym. (Bao exercises.)
>
> Bao <u>works out</u> a problem. (Bao solves it.)

Underline each phrasal verb. Then tell what it means. Use the picture to help you. Write the meaning on the line.

1. The two friends made up. _____

2. The car picked up Charlie. _____

3. Workers blew up the balloons. _____

4. The truck beeps and backs up. _____

5. Mr. Chan passed out candy. _____

TEACHER: Read the directions and questions to students. Guide students to complete the exercise, providing support as needed.

Name _____

> Some **phrasal verbs** have more than one meaning. Listen to or read the sentence to know which meaning is being used.

Read the phrasal verb and its meaning. Then write a sentence that uses that meaning of the phrasal verb.

1. pick up (lift)

    _____

    _____

2. pick up (give someone a ride)

    _____

    _____

3. work out (solve)

    _____

    _____

4. work out (exercise)

    _____

    _____

TEACHER: Read the directions and questions to students. Guide students to complete the exercise, providing support as needed.

Grades 4-6   **195**

Name _____

> Some **phrasal verbs** can be used as commands.
>
> I <u>sit down</u> on the sofa.   <u>Sit down!</u>

A. Read each question. Circle the letter of the correct answer.

1. Which sentence uses a phrasal verb as a command?

   a. The trucks go away.

   b. Go away!

   c. Let's go away in a truck.

   d. The drivers go away when their trip is done.

2. Which sentence uses a phrasal verb as a command?

   a. The drivers get in.

   b. They get in their trucks.

   c. Get in!

   d. The trucks get in line to be weighed.

B. Underline each phrasal verb. Then write it as a command.

1. The trucks quiet down at last. _____

2. They finish up their deliveries. _____

3. Drivers get out of their seats. _____

4. We watch out for the trucks. _____

TEACHER: Read the directions and questions in Part A and Part B to students. Guide students to complete each exercise, providing support as needed.

Name _____

> Some **phrasal verbs** can be used as commands.
>
> <u>Sit down!</u>

A. Underline each phrasal verb. Write _C_ if the verb is used in a command. Write _S_ if it is used in a statement.

1. The trucks take off.   _____

2. Get in!   _____

3. Hurry up!   _____

4. The trucks back away.   _____

B. Underline each phrasal verb. Then write it as a command.

1. The trucks keep out of quiet areas. _____

2. They move along the road. _____

3. They come back to the factory. _____

4. Then they line up at the garage. _____

Name _____

Some **phrasal verbs** can be used as commands.

Trucking

The trucks take off at dawn.

"Hurry up!" says the boss.

The drivers line up along the road.

"Move over!" says one driver to another.

"You need to watch out for my truck."

"Listen up!" calls the boss.

"Quiet down, everyone!"

The drivers open up their windows.

They hang up their phones and move out.

1. **Underline each phrasal verb. Circle the phrasal verbs that are used as commands.**

2. **Choose two phrasal verbs from the story that are not used as commands. Use them to write two commands.**

_____

_____

TEACHER: Read the directions and questions to students. Guide students to complete the exercise, providing support as needed.

Name _____

> A **pronoun** is a word used to replace a noun. Use **singular pronouns** to replace singular nouns. Use **plural pronouns** to replace plural nouns.
>
> **Singular:** I, you, he, she, it, me, him, her
>
> **Plural:** we, you, they, us, them

A. Draw a line to match each pronoun to the words it could replace.

1. her   a. Dad and I

2. we   b. our pets

3. it   c. the turtle

4. they   d. that girl

B. Read each sentence. Underline the singular pronouns. Circle the plural pronouns.

1. Molly and I visited the pet shop.

2. The shop owner knows us well.

3. He sold Molly two little turtles.

4. Molly keeps them in a small tank.

TEACHER: Read the directions and questions in Part A and Part B to students. Guide students to complete each exercise, providing support as needed.

Name _____

> A **pronoun** is a word used to replace a noun. Use **singular pronouns** to replace singular nouns. Use **plural pronouns** to replace plural nouns.
>
> **Singular:** I, you, he, she, it, me, him, her
>
> **Plural:** we, you, they, us, them

A. Read each sentence. Underline the singular pronoun. Circle the plural pronoun.

1. He sold us two little turtles.

2. Molly and I put them in a tank.

3. They looked up at me sadly.

4. We found the food and gave it to the turtles.

5. Molly said that she would feed them twice a day.

B. Circle the letter of the sentence that uses a plural pronoun.

1. a. We feed the turtles dry food.

   b. The turtles seem to like it.

   c. One turtle swims toward me.

2. a. I named one turtle Joey.

   b. Don't they look alike?

   c. Joey is smaller, and he has a red stripe.

TEACHER: Read the directions and questions in Part A and Part B to students. Guide students to complete each exercise, providing support as needed.

Name _____

> A **pronoun** is a word used to replace a noun. Use **singular pronouns** to replace singular nouns. Use **plural pronouns** to replace plural nouns.

Pet Turtles

Molly and I visit the pet shop.

The owner knows us very well.

He sells us two tiny turtles.

At home, we put them in a tank.

We feed them dry turtle food. They seem to like it very much.

Molly asks me to help her.

Together, we take the tank and put it on a shelf.

1. **Underline each singular pronoun. Circle each plural pronoun.**

2. **Write *singular* or *plural* to complete each sentence correctly.**

She is a _____ pronoun.

Us is a _____ pronoun.

TEACHER: Guide students to complete the exercise, providing support as needed.

Name _____

> Every pronoun should clearly refer to a noun.
>
> **INCORRECT:** Put your phone by the lamp and turn it on.
>
> **CORRECT:** Put your phone by the lamp and turn the lamp on.

**Underline each pronoun. Write *C* if the sentence is correct as it is.
Write *I* if the pronoun is not clear or incorrect.**

1. Jen has a cold, and she feels bad. _____

2. Jen uses tissues, and it helps. _____

3. Marta will get soup or salad because it is delicious. _____

4. Jen ate the soup, and it was delicious. _____

5. Jen takes her dishes and puts them away. _____

TEACHER: Guide students to complete the exercise, providing support as needed.

Name _____

> Every pronoun should clearly refer to a noun.
>
> **INCORRECT:** Put your phone by the lamp and turn it on.
>
> **CORRECT:** Put your phone by the lamp and turn the lamp on.

A. Underline each pronoun. Circle the letters of the sentences that are correct and not vague.

1. **a.** Jen has a cold, and she feels bad.

   b. Jen uses tissues, and it helps.

   c. Take the used tissues and throw them away.

2. **a.** Get a bowl, and pour hot soup into it.

   b. Jen tastes the soup, but it is very hot.

   c. They should make special soup for sick people.

B. Rewrite each sentence to make the meaning clearer.

1. My soup bowl is empty because I finished it.

   _____

2. Mom called the doctor's office, and they answered.

   _____

3. It says in the paper that flu season is here.

   _____

TEACHER: Guide students to complete each exercise in Part A and Part B, providing support as needed.

Name _____

> Every pronoun should clearly refer to a noun.
>
> **INCORRECT:** Put your phone by the lamp and turn it on.
>
> **CORRECT:** Put your phone by the lamp and turn the lamp on.

This passage contains some vague pronoun references. Read the passage. Then rewrite the passage more clearly on the lines below.

1. It says in the paper that flu season is here. Jen felt bad at school, but she kept her symptoms to herself. Now she is home, and it is worse. The tissue box is nearly empty, because Jen has used it all. Mom called the doctor's office, and they answered.

_____

_____

_____

_____

_____

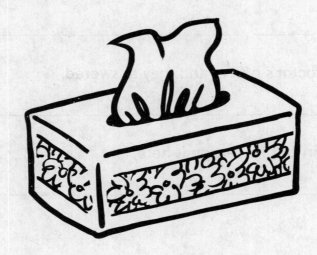

TEACHER: Guide students to complete the exercise, providing support as needed.

Name _____

> The subject of a sentence is the word or words that tell what the sentence is about. Sometimes, the subject is a pronoun. **Subject pronouns** can be singular or plural.
>
> **Singular:** I, you, he, she, it   **Plural:** we, you, they

A. Write a pronoun in the second sentence to replace the underlined subject in the first sentence.

1. <u>Mary</u> had a little lamb.

   _____ had a little lamb.

2. <u>The lamb</u> followed Mary to school.

   _____ followed Mary to school.

3. <u>The children</u> laughed.

   _____ laughed.

B. Underline the subject pronoun in each sentence.

1. We read nursery rhymes in an old book.

2. You may read along, too.

3. He gave that book of rhymes to the library.

4. Janelle and I like this old book.

5. She liked the rhyme about Jack the best.

TEACHER: Read the directions and questions in Part A and Part B to students. Guide students to complete each exercise, providing support as needed.

Name _____

> The subject of a sentence is the word or words that tell what the sentence is about. Sometimes, the subject is a pronoun. **Subject pronouns** can be singular or plural.
>
> **Singular:** I, you, he, she, it   **Plural:** we, you, they

A. Rewrite each sentence using a pronoun in place of the subject.

1. Mary had a little lamb.

   _____

2. The little lamb followed Mary to school.

   _____

3. The children laughed and played.

   _____

B. Write the plural form of each singular subject pronoun on the line.

1. it _____

2. I _____

3. he _____

4. you _____

TEACHER: Read the directions and questions in Part A and Part B to students. Guide students to complete each exercise, providing support as needed.

Name _____

> The subject of a sentence is the word or words that tell what the sentence is about. Sometimes, the subject is a pronoun. **Subject pronouns** can be singular or plural.

A. Underline the subject pronoun in each sentence. Write it on the line.

1. I am reading a book of nursery rhymes. _____

2. It was written long ago. _____

3. He gave this book to us. _____

4. Now we may read it at any time. _____

5. You would enjoy this book. _____

B. Choose three pronouns that you wrote above. Use them in three new sentences. Write the sentences on the lines.

1. _____

_____

2. _____

_____

3. _____

_____

TEACHER: Guide students to complete each exercise in Part A and Part B, providing support as needed.

Name _____

> Direct and indirect objects follow the action verb in a sentence. Sometimes, the objects are pronouns. **Object pronouns** can be singular or plural.
>
> **Singular:** me, you, him, her, it   **Plural:** us, you, them

A. Write a pronoun in the second sentence to replace the underlined object in the first sentence.

1. Please pass <u>Carl</u> the beans.

   Please pass _____ the beans.

2. Mom soaked <u>the beans</u> in water for hours.

   Mom soaked _____ in water for hours.

3. Carl filled <u>his plate</u> with beans.

   Carl filled _____ with beans.

B. Circle the object pronoun in each sentence.

1. Carl invited you to dinner.

2. Mama cooked us a lovely meal.

3. The family thanked her.

4. Carl served me a nice dessert.

TEACHER: Read the directions and questions in Part A and Part B to students. Guide students to complete each exercise, providing support as needed.

Name _____

> Direct and indirect objects follow the action verb in a sentence. Sometimes, the objects are pronouns. **Object pronouns** can be singular or plural.
>
> **Singular:** me, you, him, her, it   **Plural:** us, you, them

A. Rewrite each sentence using a pronoun in place of the underlined object.

1. Please pass <u>Carl</u> the beans.

    _____

2. Mama soaked <u>the beans</u> for hours.

    _____

3. Carl filled <u>his plate</u> with beans.

    _____

B. Write the plural form of each singular object pronoun on the line.

1. it _____

2. me _____

3. her _____

4. you _____

TEACHER: Guide students to complete each exercise in Part A and Part B, providing support as needed.

Name _____

> Direct and indirect objects follow the action verb in a sentence. Sometimes, the objects are pronouns. **Object pronouns** can be singular or plural.

A. Circle the object pronoun in each sentence. Write it on the line.

1. Please pass him the beans. _____

2. Mama soaked them for ages. _____

3. She invited you to stay. _____

4. You brought us a nice dessert. _____

5. The whole family enjoyed it. _____

B. Choose three pronouns that you wrote above. Use them in three new sentences. Write the sentences on the lines.

1. _____

   _____

2. _____

   _____

3. _____

   _____

TEACHER: Read the directions and questions in Part A and Part B to students. Guide students to complete each exercise, providing support as needed.

Name _____

> Use *that* if the information is necessary to understand the sentence.
>
> We need a map <u>that</u> shows the main roads.
>
> Use *which* if the information is not necessary to understand the sentence. Use a comma or commas when you use *which*.
>
> I went to the library, <u>which</u> is new.

A. Underline the relative pronoun. Write *Y* if it is used correctly. Write *N* if it is not used correctly.

1. We sat in the stands, that were crowded. _____

2. The game that we watched was exciting. _____

3. The score was 14 to 10, which is a very close game. _____

4. The popcorn which I ate was salty. _____

B. Decide if the sentence is punctuated correctly. Add or cross off a comma to correct each incorrect sentence.

1. The garden that I planted has grown.

2. The basil which comes from a small seed, is ready to pick.

3. The flowers, that are six feet tall are sunflowers.

4. The shorter flowers are hyacinths, which smell sweet.

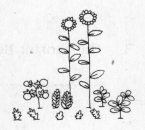

TEACHER: Read the directions and questions in Part A and Part B to students. Guide students to complete each exercise, providing support as needed.

Name _____

Use *that* if the information is necessary to understand the sentence.

We need a map <u>that</u> shows the main roads.

Use *which* if the information is not necessary to understand the sentence. Use a comma or commas when you use *which*.

I went to the library, <u>which</u> is new.

A. Read each sentence. Write *Y* if the relative pronoun is used correctly. Write *N* if it is not used correctly.

1. We sat in the stands, that were crowded. _____

2. The game that we watched was exciting. _____

3. The popcorn which I ate was salty. _____

B. Write *that* or *which* to complete each sentence. Add any commas that are needed.

1. The garden _____ I planted has grown.

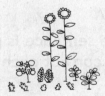

2. The flowers, _____ are six feet tall are sunflowers.

3. The shorter flowers are hyacinths, _____ smell sweet.

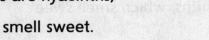

TEACHER: Read the directions and questions in Part A and Part B to students. Guide students to complete each exercise, providing support as needed.

Name _____

> Use *that* if the information is necessary to understand the sentence.
>
> Use *which* if the information is not necessary to understand the sentence. Use a comma or commas when you use *which*.

A. Use *that* or *which* in the parentheses () to combine the two sentences. Write the new sentence on the line.

1. We sat in the stands. The stands were crowded. (which)

   _____

2. We watched the game. The game was exciting. (that)

   _____

3. I ate popcorn. It was salty. (that)

   _____

B. Complete each sentence with the correct relative pronoun. Add any commas that are needed.

1. The garden _____ I planted has grown.

   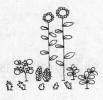

2. The flowers _____ are six feet tall are sunflowers.

3. The shorter flowers are hyacinths _____ smell sweet.

TEACHER: Guide students to complete each exercise in Part A and Part B, providing support as needed.

Name _____

Use *who* when the relative clause tells more about the subject of the sentence.

Use *whom* when the relative clause tells more about the object of the sentence.

Use *whose* to show possession.

Choose the relative pronoun to complete each sentence.

1. He is the man (who, whom) coaches the robotics

   team. _____

2. This writer is the one (whose, who) book became

   famous. _____

3. The teacher (whose, whom) I talked to was very

   nice. _____

4. Marguerite is the artist (whom, who) made that

   sculpture. _____

5. The firefighter (whose, who) arm was burned is getting

   a medal. _____

TEACHER: Guide students to complete the exercise, providing support as needed.

Name _____

> Use *who* when the relative clause tells more about the subject of the sentence.
>
> Use *whom* when the relative clause tells more about the object of the sentence.
>
> Use *whose* to show possession.

A. Choose the relative pronoun that best completes each sentence.

1. He is the man (who, whom) coaches the robotics team. _____

2. This writer is the one (whose, who) book became famous. _____

3. The teacher (whose, whom) I talked to was very nice. _____

B. Read the sentence. If the relative pronoun is correct, write *C* on the line. If the relative pronoun is incorrect, write the correct pronoun on the line.

1. Marguerite is the artist whom made that sculpture.

   _____

2. The firefighter who arm was burned is getting a medal.

   _____

3. The piano teacher with whom I take lessons is very strict.

   _____

TEACHER: Guide students to complete each exercise in Part A and Part B, providing support as needed.

Name _____

> Use *who* when the relative clause tells more about the subject of the sentence.
>
> Use *whom* when the relative clause tells more about the object of the sentence.
>
> Use *whose* to show possession.

A. Read the sentence. If the relative pronoun is correct, write *C* on the line. If the relative pronoun is incorrect, write the corrected sentence on the line.

1. Marguerite is the artist whom made that sculpture.

   _____

2. The firefighter who arm was burned is getting a medal.

   _____

3. The piano teacher with whom I take lessons is very strict.

   _____

B. Write *who, whom,* or *whose* to complete each sentence.

1. That is the man _____ coaches the robotics team.

2. This writer is the one _____ book became famous.

3. The teacher _____ I talked to was very nice.

TEACHER: Read the directions and questions in Part A and Part B to students. Guide students to complete each exercise, providing support as needed.

Name _____

> **Interrogative pronouns** are *who, whom, what, whose,* and *which*. These pronouns help you ask questions about a person, place, thing, or idea.
>
> <u>Who</u> is on the team?   <u>Whose</u> mittens are these?
> <u>Which</u> color is your favorite?

A. Circle the interrogative pronoun that completes the question.

1. (Who, Whose) is your math teacher? Mrs. Thomas is our math teacher.

2. (Which, What) did you learn about in math class today? We learned about fractions in math class.

3. (Which, Who) is your favorite class—math or spelling? Math is my favorite class.

4. (Who, Whose) turn is it to solve a problem? It is Ling's turn to solve a problem.

5. To (Who, Whom) should I give this apple? I should give this apple to my teacher.

B. Complete each question with an interrogative pronoun.

1. _____ bike is in the driveway?

2. _____ color will you paint the house?

3. _____ time will we get home?

TEACHER: Read the directions and questions in Part A and Part B to students. Guide students to complete each exercise, providing support as needed.

Name _____

> **Interrogative pronouns** are *who, whom, what, whose,* and *which.* These pronouns help you ask questions about a person, place, thing, or idea.
>
> <u>Who</u> is on the team?   <u>Whose</u> mittens are these?
>
> <u>Which</u> color is your favorite?

A. Complete each question with an interrogative pronoun.

1. _____ is your math teacher? Mrs. Thomas is our math teacher.

2. _____ did you learn about in math class today? We learned about fractions in math class.

3. _____ class is your favorite—math or spelling? Math is my favorite class.

4. _____ turn is it to solve a problem? It is Ling's turn to solve a problem.

B. Circle the correct word in parentheses to complete each sentence.

1. (Who, Whose, Whom) bike is in the driveway?

2. (Whose, Who, Which) color will you paint the house?

3. (Whom, What, Who) time will we get home?

4. To (Who, Whom, Which) should I give the newspaper?

TEACHER: Read the directions and questions in Part A and Part B to students. Guide students to complete each exercise, providing support as needed.

Name _____

> **Interrogative pronouns** are *who, whom, what, whose,* and *which*. These pronouns help you ask questions about a person, place, thing, or idea.

A. Circle the correct word in parentheses to complete each sentence.

1. (Who, Whose, Whom) bike is in the driveway?

2. (Whose, Who, Which) color will you paint the house?

3. (Whom, What, Who) time will we get home?

B. Complete each question with an interrogative pronoun.

1. _____ class is your favorite—math or spelling? Math class is my favorite.

2. _____ did you learn about in math class today? We learned about fractions in math class.

3. To _____ should I give this apple? I should give it to my teacher.

C. Read each statement. Then write a question that would be answered by the statement. Use an interrogative pronoun to begin your question.

1. Mrs. Thomas is our math teacher.

   _____

   _____

2. It is Ling's turn to solve a problem.

   _____

   _____

TEACHER: Read the directions and questions in Part A, Part B, and Part C to students. Guide students to complete each exercise, providing support as needed. Grades 4-6 **219**

Name _____

> **Indefinite pronouns** replace nouns that are not specific.
>
> There are indefinite pronouns that are considered singular, such as *somebody, everyone,* and *anything.*
>
> There are indefinite pronouns that are plural, such as *both, many,* and *several.*

A. Circle the word that completes each sentence. Then write the word.

1. Someone _____ playing the cello.

    are   is

2. Both _____ wonderful dancers.

    is   are

3. Nobody _____ doing the dishes.

    are   is

4. Everybody _____ going to the beach.

    is   are

5. Many _____ standing in line.

    are   is

B. Read the sentence. Circle the indefinite pronouns.

1. Something must be done quickly, or else everything will fall apart.

2. Many volunteered to work, but nobody came!

3. Anything you can do to help will be appreciated by everyone.

TEACHER: Read the directions and questions in Part A and Part B to students. Guide students to complete each exercise, providing support as needed.

Name _____

> **Indefinite pronouns** replace nouns that are not specific.
>
> There are indefinite pronouns that are considered singular, such as *somebody, everyone,* and *anything.*
>
> There are indefinite pronouns that are plural, such as *both, many,* and *several.*

A. Write *is* or *are* to complete each sentence.

1. Someone _____ playing the cello.

2. Both _____ wonderful dancers.

3. Nobody _____ doing the dishes.

B. Read the sentence. Circle the indefinite pronoun. Then use the indefinite pronoun in a new sentence.

1. Everyone seems happy to go to the beach.

   _____

2. Nobody volunteered for the park cleanup project.

   _____

3. Anything you can do to help will be appreciated.

   _____

TEACHER: Guide students to complete each exercise, providing support as needed.

Name _____

> **Indefinite pronouns** replace nouns that are not specific.
>
> There are indefinite pronouns that are considered singular, such as *somebody, everyone,* and *anything.*
>
> There are indefinite pronouns that are plural, such as *both, many,* and *several.*

A. Write *is* or *are* to complete each sentence.

1. Someone _____ playing the cello in the concert hall.

2. Both _____ wonderful ballroom dancers.

3. Nobody _____ doing the dishes, because everyone is outside.

B. Read the sentence. Circle the indefinite pronouns.

1. Something must be done quickly, or else everything will fall apart.

2. Many volunteered to work, but nobody came!

3. Anything you can do to help will be appreciated by everyone.

C. Read the sentences. Circle the indefinite pronouns. Then use the indefinite pronouns to write a new sentence or sentences.

1. Does anyone else hear the phone? I thought something was making a noise.

_____

2. She looked for anything that would be a good present. She found two shirts. Both were too expensive.

_____

TEACHER: Guide students to complete the exercises in each part, providing support as needed.

Name _____

A **reflexive pronoun** replaces an object when the object is the same person, place, or thing as the subject. The reflexive pronouns are:

myself, yourself, himself, herself, itself, themselves, ourselves, yourselves

Circle the subject of each sentence. Choose the reflexive pronoun that completes each sentence.

1. She burned _____ on the hot pan.

2. Moira and Kate made _____ sandwiches.

3. Cedar bought _____ a new camera.

4. We found _____ a new team member.

5. I saw _____ in the mirror.

TEACHER: Read the directions and questions to students. Guide students to complete the exercise, providing support as needed.

Grades 4-6 **223**

Name _____

> A **reflexive pronoun** replaces an object when the object is the same person, place, or thing as the subject. The reflexive pronouns are:
>
> myself, yourself, himself, herself, itself, themselves, ourselves, yourselves

A. Circle the subject of each sentence. Choose the reflexive pronoun that completes each sentence.

1. She burned _____ on the hot pan.

2. Moira and Kate made _____ sandwiches.

3. We found _____ a new team member.

B. The subject of a sentence is shown. Write a sentence about the subject, using a reflexive pronoun.

1. The man

_____

2. David and Mario

_____

3. I

_____

TEACHER: Guide students to complete the exercises in Part A and Part B, providing support as needed.

Name _____

> A **reflexive pronoun** replaces an object when the object is the same person, place, or thing as the subject. The reflexive pronouns are:
>
> myself, yourself, himself, herself, itself, themselves, ourselves, yourselves

A. The subject of a sentence is shown. Write a sentence about the subject, using a reflective pronoun.

1. The man

_____

2. David and Mario

_____

3. I

_____

4. She

_____

5. We

_____

B. Write two original sentences that use reflexive pronouns.

1. _____

_____

2. _____

_____

Name _____

> **Intensive pronouns** are the same words as reflexive pronouns but are used to emphasize the subject of the sentence.
>
> I <u>myself</u> made that cake!   I made the cake <u>myself.</u>

A. Circle the intensive pronoun that completes each sentence correctly.

1. I walked all the way to school (herself / myself).

2. She earned the money (himself / herself) to buy the earrings.

3. He (himself / themselves) picked out his new shoes.

4. They shopped for a gift (themselves / ourselves).

5. We paid for our selections (themselves / ourselves).

B. Circle the intensive pronoun in each sentence.

1. The students themselves picked the paint color.

2. We will finish the job ourselves.

3. I painted the table myself.

TEACHER: Guide students to complete each exercise in Part A and Part B, providing support as needed.

Name _____

> **Intensive pronouns** are the same words as reflexive pronouns but are used to emphasize the subject of the sentence.
>
> I made the cake <u>myself.</u>

A. Choose the correct intensive pronoun to complete each sentence.

1. I walked all the way to the mall (herself / myself).

2. The girl washed all the dishes (himself / herself).

3. He (himself / themselves) picked out his new shoes.

4. They shopped for a gift (themselves / ourselves).

B. Write an intensive pronoun to complete each sentence.

1. We painted the room _____.

2. I painted the door _____.

3. We _____ will finish the job tomorrow.

4. The students _____ picked the paint color.

TEACHER: Read the directions and questions in Part A and Part B to students. Guide students to complete each exercise, providing support as needed.

Name _____

> **Intensive pronouns** are the same words as reflexive pronouns but are used to emphasize the subject of the sentence.

A. Rewrite each sentence using an intensive pronoun.

1. She earned the money to buy the earrings.

   _____

2. He picked out his new shoes.

   _____

3. They shopped for a gift.

   _____

B. Write an intensive pronoun to complete each sentence.

1. We painted the room _____.

2. I painted the window frames _____.

3. The students _____ picked the paint color.

TEACHER: Guide students to complete Part A and Part B, providing support as needed.

Name _____

Reciprocal pronouns are *each other* and *one another*.

Each other is used to talk about two people or animals.

One another is used for groups of three or more.

Look at the picture. Write *each other* or *one another* to complete the sentence.

1. The girls smile at _____.

2. The students have fun with _____.

3. The friends gave gifts to _____.

4. They played chess with _____.

5. We read books to _____ in the park.

TEACHER: Read the directions and questions to students. Guide students to complete the exercise, providing support as needed.

Grades 4-6   229

Name _____

> **Reciprocal pronouns** are *each other* and *one another*.
>
> *Each other* is used to talk about two people or animals.
>
> *One another* is used for groups of three or more.

A. Circle the correct reciprocal pronoun to complete the sentence.

1. The two girls smile at (each other, one another).

2. All of the students have fun with
   (each other, one another).

3. The two boys played chess with
   (each other, one another).

4. Mom and I read stories to (each other,
   one another) in the park.

B. Write *each other's* or *one another's* to complete the sentence.

1. The two sisters picked out _____
   costumes for the party.

2. Adam and Miguel always go to _____
   parties.

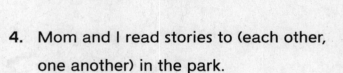

3. The guests complimented _____ costumes.

**TEACHER: Read the directions and questions in Part A and Part B to students. Guide
students to complete each exercise, providing support as needed.**

Name _____

> **Reciprocal pronouns** are *each other* and *one another*.
>
> *Each other* is used to talk about two people or animals.
>
> *One another* is used for groups of three or more.

A. Write *each other* or *one another* to complete the sentence.

1. The two girls smile at _____.

2. The students in our class have fun with _____.

3. Suzie and Tamara played chess with _____.

B. Write *C* on the line if the reciprocal pronoun is correct. If it is not, write the correct reciprocal pronoun for the sentence.

1. The two sisters picked out one another's costumes. _____

2. Adam and Miguel always go to each other's parties. _____

3. The group of friends gave gifts to each other. _____

C. Identify the complete subject of the sentence. Use the subject to write a new sentence that uses a reciprocal pronoun.

1. The five teachers planned a field trip.

   _____

2. The two dogs played.

   _____

Name _____

> **Possessive pronouns** show ownership, or possession, of something.
>
> The possessive pronouns *my, your, his, her, its, our,* and *their* come before a noun in a sentence.
>
> The possessive pronouns *yours, his, hers, its, ours, theirs,* and *mine* can stand alone in a sentence.

A. Circle the possessive pronoun that completes each sentence.

1. This computer is _____.
   my   mine

2. That is _____ mother's car.
   their   theirs

3. What is _____ phone number?
   yours   your

4. Come over to _____ house after school.
   our   ours

5. Do you want a piece of _____ pizza?
   my   mine

B. Underline the possessive pronoun in each sentence.

1. I'm not sure if this is his book.

2. Is this violin hers?

3. What is its expiration date?

TEACHER: Read the directions and questions in Part A and Part B to students. Guide students to complete each exercise, providing support as needed.

Name _____

> **Possessive pronouns** show ownership, or possession, of something.
>
> The possessive pronouns *my, your, his, her, its, our,* and *their* come before a noun in a sentence.
>
> The possessive pronouns *yours, his, hers, its, ours, theirs,* and *mine* can stand alone in a sentence.

A. Write a possessive pronoun to complete each sentence.

1. I own this computer. This computer is _____.

2. The boys are getting in the car. That is _____ mother's car.

3. I'll call you later. What is _____ phone number?

B. Underline the possessive pronoun in each sentence. Then use the pronoun in a new sentence.

1. Come over to our house after school.

   _____

2. Do you want a piece of my pizza?

   _____

3. I'm not sure if this is his book.

   _____

TEACHER: Read the directions and questions in Part A and Part B to students. Guide students to complete each exercise, providing support as needed.

Name _____

> **Possessive pronouns** show ownership, or possession, of something.
>
> The possessive pronouns *my, your, his, her, its, our,* and *their* come before a noun in a sentence.
>
> The possessive pronouns *yours, his, hers, its, ours, theirs,* and *mine* can stand alone in a sentence.

A. Write a possessive pronoun to complete each sentence.

1. I own this computer. This computer is _____.

2. The boys are getting in the car. That is _____ mother's car.

3. I'll call you later. What is _____ phone number?

B. Underline the possessive pronoun in each sentence.

1. Come over to our house after school.

2. Would you like a piece of our pizza?

3. I'm not sure if this is his book.

C. Underline the possessive pronoun in each sentence. Use it in a new sentence.

1. The soccer players listened to their coach.

   _____

2. My art teacher showed us his painting.

   _____

TEACHER: Read the directions and questions in Part A, Part B, and Part C to students. Guide students to complete each exercise, providing support as needed.

Name _____

> A pronoun must match, or agree with, its antecedent.
>
> **Incorrect:** The boy put on <u>their</u> jacket.   **Correct:** The boy put on <u>his</u> jacket.

A.   Draw a line to connect the pronoun with a matching antecedent.

1.   The woman   **a.**   their

2.   The students   **b.**   his

3.   A man   **c.**   its

4.   The book   **d.**   her

B.   Circle the correct pronoun to complete each sentence.

1.   Chloe put on (her, their) shoes.

2.   Mariana and Roberto worked hard on (our, their) project.

3.   The sun gives off (his, its) light.

4.   We enjoyed (their, our) trip to the city.

5.   The teacher helped (his, their) students with ideas.

6.   Gabe and Annie painted a mural for (her, their) school.

Name _____

A pronoun must match, or agree with, its antecedent.

The <u>boy</u> put on <u>his</u> jacket.

A. Circle the correct pronoun to complete each sentence.

1. Chloe put on (her, their) shoes.

2. Mariana and Roberto worked hard on (our, their) project.

3. The sun gives off (his, its) light.

B. Rewrite each sentence to tell about a different subject. Change the underlined subject of the sentence. Then change the pronoun to match.

1. <u>The actress</u> held up her award.

   _____

   _____

2. <u>The puppies</u> chewed their food.

   _____

   _____

3. <u>The boy</u> ran to meet his friend.

   _____

   _____

TEACHER: Read the directions and questions in Part A and Part B to students. Guide students to complete each exercise, providing support as needed.

Name _____

> A pronoun must match, or agree with, its antecedent.

A. Rewrite each sentence to tell about a different subject. Change the underlined subject of the sentence. Then change the pronoun to match.

1. <u>The actress</u> held up her award.

   _____

2. <u>The puppies</u> chewed their food.

   _____

3. <u>The boy</u> ran to meet his friend.

   _____

B. Read each sentence. If the pronoun is correct, write *C* on the line. If it is incorrect, write the correct pronoun on the line.

1. Chloe put on their shoes. _____

2. Mariana and Roberto worked hard on their

   project. _____

3. The sun gives off his light. _____

TEACHER: Read the directions and questions in Part A and Part B to students. Guide students to complete each exercise, providing support as needed.

Name _____

> An antecedent may appear in a previous sentence or paragraph.
>
> <u>Nettie</u> went to the dentist. Then <u>she</u> went home.
>
> *Nettie* is the antecedent of the pronoun *she*.

A. Identify the antecedent of the underlined pronoun.

1. Trina and Elliott went sledding on the big hill. <u>They</u> had fun.

   a. Trina **b.** sledding **c.** the big hill **d.** Trina and Elliot

2. Marcus bought a cup of tea. <u>He</u> also bought a muffin for his friend Samuel.

   a. tea **b.** a muffin **c.** Marcus **d.** Samuel

3. The farmer planted the field. <u>He</u> used a tractor.

   a. The farmer **b.** the field **c.** tractor **d.** planted

B. Read the sentences. Circle the pronoun and underline its antecedent.

1. The campers went swimming. They played a game at the pool.

2. The waiter brought the salad. Then he brought the sandwiches.

3. Lee went to the hair salon. She wanted a new haircut.

TEACHER: Read the directions and questions in Part A and Part B to students. Guide students to complete each exercise, providing support as needed.

Name _____

> An antecedent may appear in a previous sentence or paragraph.
>
> <u>Nettie</u> went to the dentist. Then <u>she</u> went home.
>
> *Nettie* is the antecedent of the pronoun *she*.

A. Complete each pair of sentences with the correct pronoun.

1. Trina and Elliott went sledding on the big hill.

   _____ had fun.

2. Marcus bought a cup of tea. _____
   also bought a muffin for his friend Samuel.

3. The woman planted corn in the field.

   _____ used a tractor.

B. Read the sentences. Rewrite the sentences with the correct pronoun.

1. The campers went swimming. She played a game at the pool.

   _____

2. The waiter brought the salad. Then they brought the sandwiches.

   _____

3. The woman went to the hair salon. We wanted a new haircut.

   _____

TEACHER: Guide students to complete each exercise, providing support as needed.

Name _____

> An antecedent may appear in a previous sentence or paragraph.
>
> <u>Nettie</u> went to the dentist. Then <u>she</u> went home.

Rewrite the paragraphs below. Correct any mistakes in pronoun-antecedent agreement.

1. The day was very hot. The campers wanted to cool down! So, it went swimming. She played a game at the pool.

_____

_____

2. My friend and I were hungry. They ordered food at the restaurant. The waiter brought the salad. Then it brought the sandwiches.

_____

_____

3. Trina and Elliott went sledding on the big hill. He had fun. Then, they got cold. She decided to make hot chocolate for themselves.

_____

_____

TEACHER: Read the directions and questions to students. Guide students to complete the exercise, providing support as needed.

Name _____

> Add –s to the verb after the pronouns *he, she,* and *it*.
>
> Do not add –s to the verb after the other pronouns *I, you, we,* and *they*.
>
> He/She/It <u>likes</u> bananas.   I/You/We/They <u>like</u> bananas.

A.   Underline the pronoun and circle the verb in each sentence.

1.   I go to Willow School.

2.   We get good grades.

3.   She makes sandwiches.

4.   He knows English.

5.   It sleeps all day.

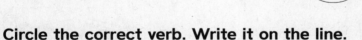

B.   Circle the correct verb. Write it on the line.

1.   She _____ a new bike.
              want   wants

2.   He _____ funny stories.
              tell   tells

3.   They _____ fast.
              run   runs

TEACHER: Guide students to complete each exercise, providing support as needed.

Grades 4-6   **241**

Name _____

> Add –s to the verb after the pronouns *he*, *she*, and *it*.
>
> Do not add –s to the verb after the other pronouns *I, you, we,* and *they*.
>
> He/She/It <u>likes</u> bananas.   I/You/We/They <u>like</u> bananas.

A.   Circle the correct verb. Write it on the line.

1.   She (want, wants) _____ a new bike

2.   He (tell, tells) _____ funny stories.

3.   They (run, runs) _____ fast.

B.   Complete the sentences with the verb in parentheses ( ).

1.   I _____ school. (enter)

2.   We _____ good grades. (get)

3.   She _____ sandwiches. (make)

TEACHER: Read the directions and questions in Part A and Part B to students. Guide students to complete each exercise, providing support as needed.

Name _____

> Add –s to the verb after the pronouns *he*, *she*, and *it*.
>
> Do not add –s to the verb after the other pronouns *I, you, we,* and *they*.
>
> He/She/It <u>likes</u> bananas.   I/You/We/They <u>like</u> bananas.

A. Fill in the blanks with the correct form of the verb in parentheses ( ).

1. I _____ the Willow School. (enter)

2. The student _____ good grades. (get)

3. She _____ sandwiches. (make)

B. Complete each sentence with a pronoun (*He/She/It* or *I/You/We/They*). Some questions may have more than one correct answer.

1. _____ wants a new bike.

2. _____ tells funny stories.

3. _____ run fast.

Name _____

> The pronouns *he, she,* and *it* agree with *is/was* and *has/had*.
>
> The pronouns *you, we,* and *they* agree with *are/were* and *have/had*.
>
> The pronoun *I* agrees with *am/was* and *have/had*.

A. **Underline the pronoun and circle the verb in each sentence. Write *past* or *present* on the line.**

1. I am twelve years old. _____

2. We had a delicious lunch. _____

3. She has two brothers. _____

4. We are from Russia. _____

5. You were a cowboy for Halloween. _____

B. **Circle the correct verb. Write it on the line.**

1. She _____ a new bike.
          has   have

2. He _____ funny.
         is   were

3. They _____ new shoes.
         has   have

TEACHER: Read the directions and questions in Part A and Part B to students. Guide students to complete each exercise, providing support as needed.

Name _____

> The pronouns _he, she,_ and _it_ agree with _is/was_ and _has/had._
>
> The pronouns _you, we,_ and _they_ agree with _are/were_ and _have/had._
>
> The pronoun _I_ agrees with _am/was_ and _have/had._

A. Circle the correct verb. Write it on the line.

1. She (has, have) _____ a new bike.

2. He (is, were) _____ funny.

3. They (has, have) _____ new shoes.

B. Fill in the blanks with _am, is, are, was, were, have, has,_ or _had._

1. I _____ twelve years old now.

2. We _____ a delicious lunch yesterday.

3. She _____ two brothers now.

TEACHER: Read the directions and questions in Part A and Part B to students. Guide students to complete each exercise, providing support as needed.

Name _____

The pronouns *he, she,* and *it* agree with *is/was* and *has/had*.

The pronouns *you, we,* and *they* agree with *are/were* and *have/had*.

The pronoun *I* agrees with *am/was* and *have/had*.

A. Fill in the blanks with *am, is, are, was, were, have, has,* or *had*.

1. I _____ twelve years old now.

2. We _____ a delicious lunch yesterday.

3. She _____ two brothers.

B. Complete each sentence with a pronoun (*He/She/It* or *I/You/We/They*). Some questions can have more than one correct answer.

1. _____ has a new bike.

2. _____ is funny.

3. _____ have new shoes.

TEACHER: Read the directions and questions in Part A and Part B to students. Guide students to complete each exercise, providing support as needed.

Name _____

A **contraction** can be the short form of a pronoun combined with a verb.

he, she, it + is = he's, she's, it's

you, we, they + are = you're, we're, they're

I + am = I'm

A. Circle the contraction in each sentence. Then write the pronoun and verb.

1. I'm twelve years old. _____

2. We're twelve years old. _____

3. She's my sister. _____

4. You're welcome! _____

5. It's not raining. _____

B. Write the contraction on the line.

1. you + are = _____

2. he + is = _____

3. I + am = _____

TEACHER: Read the directions and questions in Part A and Part B to students. Guide students to complete each exercise, providing support as needed.

Grades 4-6   247

Name _____

> A **contraction** can be the short form of a pronoun combined with a verb.
>
> he, she, it + is = he's, she's, it's
>
> you, we, they + are = you're, we're, they're
>
> I + am = I'm

A.   Write the missing word on the line.

1.   you + are = _____

2.   _____ + is = he's

3.   I + _____ = I'm

4.   _____ + are = we're

B.   Write the correct form of the present-tense verb *be* on each line. Then write the contraction on the line after the sentence.

1.   I _____ twelve years old. _____

2.   We _____ twelve years old. _____

3.   She _____ my sister. _____

4.   You _____ welcome! _____

TEACHER: Read the directions and questions in Part A and Part B to students. Guide students to complete each exercise, providing support as needed.

Name _____

> A **contraction** can be the short form of a pronoun combined with a verb.
>
> he, she, it + is = he's, she's, it's
>
> you, we, they + are = you're, we're, they're
>
> I + am = I'm

A. Write the missing word on each line.

1. you're = _____ + _____

2. _____ = we + are

3. I'm = _____ + _____

4. _____ = she + is

B. Circle the letter of the sentence that is written correctly.

1. **a.** They're a twelve-year-old child.

   b. He's a twelve-year-old child.

2. **a.** They're twelve-year-old children.

   b. He's twelve-year-old children.

3. **a.** You're my sister.

   b. We're my sister.

4. **a.** It's not a big tree.

   b. They're not a big tree.

Name _____

> Some possessive pronouns sound like pronoun-verb contractions but are spelled differently:
>
> *your* and *you're*   *its* and *it's*
>
> *their* and *they're*   *whose* and *who's*

A.   Circle the contraction to complete each sentence.

1. _____ the best soccer player?
   Who's   Whose

2. _____ a beautiful day.
   Its   It's

3. _____ a great student.
   You're   Your

4. _____ my favorite shoes.
   There   They're

B.   Circle the correct word in parentheses.

1. (They're, Their) bikes are new.

2. (Who's, Whose) cat is that?

3. (It's, Its) Saturday!

TEACHER: Read the directions and questions in Part A and Part B to students. Guide students to complete each exercise, providing support as needed.

Name _____

> Some possessive pronouns sound like pronoun-verb contractions but are spelled differently:
>
> *your* and *you're*   *its* and *it's*
>
> *their* and *they're*   *whose* and *who's*

A. Choose the correct word in parentheses to complete each sentence. Write it on the line.

1. _____ bikes are new. (They're, Their)

2. _____ cat is that? (Who's, Whose)

3. _____ Saturday! (It's, Its)

B. Write the correct possessive pronoun or contraction in each blank.

1. _____ a beautiful day.

2. _____ the best soccer player?

3. _____ answers are correct.

Name _____

> Some possessive pronouns sound like pronoun-verb contractions but are
> spelled differently:
>
> *your* and *you're*   *its* and *it's*
>
> *their* and *they're*   *whose* and *who's*

**Write the correct possessive pronoun or contraction in each blank. Choose
from the words in the box. Use each word once.**

Whose	They're	It's	There	You're
Its	Their	Your	Who's	

1. _____ the best soccer player?

2. _____ a beautiful day.

3. _____ hat is very nice.

4. _____ is your pencil.

5. _____ bikes are new.

6. _____ cat is that?

7. _____ name is the Great Wall of China.

8. _____ a great student!

9. _____ my favorite cousins.

**TEACHER: Read the directions and questions to students. Guide students to complete
the exercise, providing support as needed.**

Name _____

> Some adjectives are normally placed before nouns.
>
> **Examples:** <u>main</u> idea, <u>former</u> president, <u>indoor</u> pool
>
> Some adjectives are normally placed after linking verbs.
>
> **Examples:** is <u>asleep</u>, feels <u>alive</u>, looks <u>ready</u>, feels <u>sorry</u>

A. Circle the letter of the phrase that completes the sentence correctly.

1. I am _____

   a. an only child.   **b.** a child who is only.

2. This _____

   a. idea is the main.   **b.** is the main idea.

3. She is _____

   a. ready   **b.** a ready person.

B. Circle the adjective in each sentence.

1. She is the main singer.

2. My sister is asleep.

3. He is our former principal.

4. I was sick.

TEACHER: Guide students to complete each exercise in Part A and Part B, providing support as needed.

Name _____

> Some adjectives are normally placed before nouns.
>
> **Examples:** <u>main</u> idea, <u>former</u> president, <u>indoor</u> pool
>
> Some adjectives are normally placed after linking verbs.
>
> **Examples:** is <u>asleep</u>, feels <u>alive</u>, looks <u>ready</u>, feels <u>sorry</u>

A. Circle the correct word in parentheses to complete each sentence.

1. She is the (alive, main) singer.

2. My sister is (asleep, only).

3. That is our (former, finished) principal.

4. I was (sick main) last week.

5. This is an (alone, outdoor) stadium.

B. Circle the letter of the sentence that is correct. Underline the adjective in each correct sentence.

1. **a.** I am an only child.
   b. I am a child who is only.

2. **a.** This idea is the main.
   b. This is the main idea.

TEACHER: Read the directions and questions in Part A and Part B to students. Guide students to complete each exercise, providing support as needed.

Name _____

> Some adjectives are normally placed before nouns.
>
> **Examples:** <u>main</u> idea, <u>former</u> president, <u>indoor</u> pool
>
> Some adjectives are normally placed after linking verbs.
>
> **Examples:** is <u>asleep</u>, feels <u>alive</u>, looks <u>ready</u>, feels <u>sorry</u>

Complete each sentence with a word from the box. Write the word on the line.

sorry	north	future	is	child
main	asleep	well	ready	outdoor

1. I am an only _____.

2. This is the _____ idea.

3. The man _____ alone.

4. She is _____ to climb.

5. That is our _____ home.

6. Go in the _____ entrance.

7. My sister is _____.

8. I am _____.

9. I was _____ all weekend.

10. This is an _____ stadium.

TEACHER: Read the directions and questions to students. Guide students to complete the exercise, providing support as needed.

Grades 4-6   255

Name _____

> Adjectives usually appear in this order. (Examples are in parentheses.)
>
> **1.** general opinion (good) **2.** specific opinion (delicious) **3.** size (large)
>
> **4.** shape (round) **5.** condition (cracked) **6.** age (old)
>
> **7.** color (red) **8.** nationality (Canadian) **9.** material (metal)

A. Choose the correct group for each set of adjectives.

1. red – blue – yellow – green

    a. general opinion **b.** age **c.** color **d.** condition

2. square – diamond – triangle – rectangle

    a. specific opinion **b.** shape **c.** condition **d.** size

3. bad – beautiful – lovely – nice

    a. general opinion **b.** size **c.** age **d.** condition

B. Choose the correct order for the words in parentheses. Write the words on the lines.

1. Let's eat some _____ _____ food. (Indian, delicious)

2. I love this _____, _____ book. (funny, old)

3. That is a _____, _____ balloon. (red, huge)

4. I want that _____, _____ shirt. (cotton, soft)

TEACHER: Read the directions and questions in Part A and Part B to students. Guide students to complete each exercise, providing support as needed.

Name _____

> Adjectives usually appear in this order. (Examples are in parentheses.)
> 1. general opinion (good)   2. specific opinion (delicious)   3. size (large)
> 4. shape (round)   5. condition (cracked)   6. age (old)
> 7. color (red)   8. nationality (Canadian)   9. material (metal)

A. Choose the correct group for each set of adjectives.

1. young – new – elderly – 12-year-old
   a. general opinion   b. age   c. color   d. condition

2. leather – cotton – paper – plastic
   a. specific opinion   b. shape   c. material   d. condition

3. bad – strange – lovely – important
   a. general opinion   b. size   c. age   d. condition

B. Underline the sentence that is written correctly.

1. That is a striped, gigantic balloon.
   That is a gigantic, striped balloon.

2. I want to buy that soft, silk shirt.
   I want to buy that silk, soft shirt.

3. Let's eat some nice, spicy Indian food.
   Let's eat some spicy, nice Indian food.

TEACHER: Read the directions and questions in Part A and Part B to students. Guide students to complete each exercise, providing support as needed.

Name _____

Adjectives usually appear in this order. (Examples are in parentheses.)
1. general opinion (good)   **2.** specific opinion (delicious)   **3.** size (large)
4. shape (round)   **5.** condition (cracked)   **6.** age (old)
7. color (red)   **8.** nationality (Canadian)   **9.** material (metal)

A. Write the name of the group each set of adjectives belong to.

1. gold – cotton – paper – clay _____

2. wonderful – strange – lovely – important _____

3. curly – sharp – pointed – triangle _____

B. Choose the correct order for the words. Write them on the line.

1. striped – balloon – giant _____

2. soft – silk – shirt _____

3. spicy – Indian – food – nice _____

4. pillow – fluffy – white _____

5. wooden – old – boat _____

TEACHER: Read the directions and questions in Part A and Part B to students. Guide students to complete each exercise, providing support as needed.

Name _____

> Many proper adjectives have these suffixes, or endings:
>
> • –ian/–ean/–an: Brazilian (Brazil), Korean (Korea), German (Germany)
>
> • –ish: Irish (Ireland)   • –i: Afghani (Afghanistan)   • –ese: Chinese (China)

A.   Read the words. Draw a line to match each proper noun to its proper adjective.

1. Scotland   a. Iraqi

2. Vietnam   b. Vietnamese

3. Turkey   c. Scottish

4. Iraq   d. Turkish

5. Russia   e. Russian

B.   Read each proper noun. Circle the correct proper adjective.

1. Mexico   Mexicani   Mexican

2. Pakistan   Pakistanian   Pakistani

3. Japan   Japanese   Japanish

4. Spain   Spanish   Spainian

5. Africa   Africani   African

Name _____

Many proper adjectives have these suffixes, or endings:
- –ian/–ean/–an: Brazilian (Brazil), Korean (Korea), German (Germany)
- –ish: Irish (Ireland)   • –i: Afghani (Afghanistan)   • –ese: Chinese (China)

A.   Change each proper noun to a proper adjective.

1.   Mexico + –n = _____

2.   Pakistan + –i = _____

3.   Japan + –ese = _____

4.   Spain + –ish = _____

5.   Canada + –ian = _____

B.   Circle the proper adjective in each sentence. On the line, write the proper noun for the proper adjective.

1.   Let's visit the Scottish Highlands.   _____

2.   I have a Vietnamese hat.   _____

3.   Swedish meatballs are delicious.   _____

4.   The Iraqi people are friendly.   _____

TEACHER: Read the directions and questions in Part A and Part B to students. Guide students to complete each exercise, providing support as needed.

Name _____

> Many proper adjectives have these suffixes, or endings:
> • –ian/–ean/–an: Brazilian (Brazil), Korean (Korea), German (Germany)
> • –ish: Irish (Ireland)   • –i: Afghani (Afghanistan)   • –ese: Chinese (China)

Choose the correct word to complete each sentence. Write the word on the line.

1. I love to visit _____ beaches.
   Mexican   Mexico

2. _____ food is very spicy.
   Pakistani   Pakistanian

3. Let's eat some _____ sushi!
   Japan   Japanese

4. Madrid is the capital of _____.
   Spain   Spanish

5. The _____ capital is Ankara.
   Turkey   Turkish

6. Let's visit the Highlands of _____.
   Scotland   Scottish

TEACHER: Read the directions and questions to students. Guide students to complete the exercise, providing support as needed.

Name _____

> Remember these basic rules for articles (*a, an,* and *the*):
>
> - *a/an*: with countable, singular nouns only; "a" before consonant sounds; "an" before vowel sounds
> - *the*: with countable or uncountable nouns; with singular or plural nouns; before consonant or vowel sounds

A. Choose the correct article in parenthese and write in on the line.

1. Josh ate (the, an) apples. _____

2. Cara picked (a, an) apple. _____

3. Ahmed wants (a, an) red apple. _____

4. I want (the, an) water. _____

5. Sara has (a, an) old computer. _____

B. Circle the articles (*a, an, the*) in each sentence.

1. The children took a bus to an aquarium.

2. They saw a baby fish in a tank.

3. They saw an adult fish with the baby.

TEACHER: Read the directions and questions in Part A and Part B to students. Guide students to complete each exercise, providing support as needed.

Name _____

Remember these basic rules for articles (*a, an,* and *the*):

- *a/an*: with countable, singular nouns only; "a" before consonant sounds; "an" before vowel sounds

- *the*: with countable or uncountable nouns; with singular or plural nouns; before consonant or vowel sounds

A. Choose the correct article in parentheses and write it on the line.

1. Josh ate (the, a, an) apples. _____

2. Ahmed wants (a, an) red apple. _____

3. I want (the, a, an) water. _____

4. Sara has (a, an) old computer. _____

B. Write the correct article (*a, an, the*) in each space. Some spaces have more than one correct answer.

1. _____ children took a bus to an aquarium.

2. They saw _____ baby fish in a tank.

3. They saw _____ adult fish with _____ baby.

TEACHER: Read the directions and questions in Part A and Part B to students. Guide students to complete each exercise, providing support as needed.

Name _____

Remember these basic rules for articles (*a, an,* and *the*):

- *a/an*: with countable, singular nouns only; "a" before consonant sounds; "an" before vowel sounds

- *the*: with countable or uncountable nouns; with singular or plural nouns; before consonant or vowel sounds

---

A. **Write the correct article (*a, an, the*) in each space. Some spaces have more than one correct answer.**

1. Josh ate _____ apples.

2. Ahmed wants _____ red apple.

3. I want to swim in _____ water.

4. Antonio bought _____ computer.

5. Sara has _____ old computer.

B. **Write the correct article (*a, an, the*) before the word or words. Some spaces have more than one correct answer.**

1. _____ air

2. _____ school

3. _____ university

4. _____ elementary school

5. _____ sugar

6. _____ baby fish

7. _____ adult fish

8. _____ paint

TEACHER: Read the directions and questions in Part A and Part B to students. Guide students to complete each exercise, providing support as needed.

Name _____

> **General adjectives**—such as *nice*—can describe many types of things.
>
> **Concrete adjectives** describe specific things, such as how something feels (*smooth*), tastes (*salty*), looks (*bright*), smells (*fruity*), and sounds (*loud*).

A.   Circle the concrete adjective under each sentence. Write it on the line.

1.   The carrots taste _____.
                  great   delicious

2.   My sweater feels _____.
                  itchy   terrible

3.   The sky looks _____.
                  dark   bad

4.   These flowers smell _____.
                  sweet   wonderful

5.   What is that _____ noise?
                  awful   growling

B.   Read each adjective. Write *concrete* or *general* on the line.

1.   spicy _____

2.   excellent _____

3.   noisy _____

Name _____

> **General adjectives**—such as *nice*—can describe many types of things.
>
> **Concrete adjectives** describe specific things, such as how something feels (*smooth*), tastes (*salty*), looks (*bright*), smells (*fruity*), and sounds (*loud*).

A.   Circle the concrete adjective under each sentence. Write it on the line.

1.   The carrots are _____.
     great   sweet

2.   My sweater is _____.
     scratchy   terrible

3.   The sky is _____.
     dark   bad

4.   These flowers are _____.
     fragrant   wonderful

B.   Read each concrete adjective. Decide which sense it is for. Write *feel*, *taste*, *look*, *smell*, or *sound* on the line.

1.   spicy _____

2.   sparkling _____

3.   soft _____

TEACHER: Read the directions and questions in Part A and Part B to students. Guide students to complete each exercise, providing support as needed.

Name _____

> **General adjectives**—such as *nice*—can describe many types of things.
>
> **Concrete adjectives** describe specific things, such as how something feels (*smooth*), tastes (*salty*), looks (*bright*), smells (*fruity*), and sounds (*loud*).

A. Read each sentence. Circle the adjective. On the line, describe the adjective with one of these words: general, feel, taste, look, smell, sound.

1. The carrots are sweet. _____

2. My sweater is scratchy. _____

3. The sky is dark. _____

4. These flowers are wonderful. _____

5. What is that growling noise? _____

B. Rewrite each sentence on the line below it. Replace the general adjective with the concrete adjective in parentheses.

1. I don't like the bad taste of this juice. (sour)

   _____

   _____

2. Who is making that wonderful music? (harmonious)

   _____

   _____

TEACHER: Read the directions and questions in Part A and Part B to students. Guide students to complete each exercise, providing support as needed.

Name _____

> The ordinal numbers for 1 through 10 are:
>
> 1st (first)   2nd (second)   3rd (third)   4th (fourth)   5th (fifth)
>
> 6th (sixth)   7th (seventh)   8th (eighth)   9th (ninth)   10th (tenth)

Circle the word that completes each sentence. Then write it on the line.

1. I am in _____ grade.

          six   sixth

2. This is my _____ pair of shoes this year.

        second   two

3. The _____ thing I do is say, "Good morning."

     first   one

4. I will be the _____ person in my family to go to college!

     fifth   five

5. Turn right at the _____ traffic light.

     three   third

6. We're ready to start the _____ quarter.

     four   fourth

TEACHER: Read the directions and questions to students. Guide students to complete the exercise, providing support as needed.

Name _____

The ordinal numbers for 1 through 10 are:

1st (first)	2nd (second)	3rd (third)	4th (fourth)	5th (fifth)
6th (sixth)	7th (seventh)	8th (eighth)	9th (ninth)	10th (tenth)

Circle the word that completes each sentence. Then write it on the line.

1. six   sixth   I am in _____ grade.

2. second   twice   This is my _____ pair of shoes this year.

3. first   once   The _____ thing I do is say, "Good morning."

4. fifth   5   I will be the _____ person in my family to go to college!

5. three   third   Turn right at the _____ traffic light.

6. 4   fourth   We're ready to start the _____ quarter.

TEACHER: Read the directions and questions to students. Guide students to complete the exercise, providing support as needed.

Name _____

> The ordinal numbers for 1 through 10 are:
>
> 1st (first)   2nd (second)   3rd (third)   4th (fourth)   5th (fifth)
>
> 6th (sixth)   7th (seventh)   8th (eighth)   9th (ninth)   10th (tenth)

Write the ordinal number that matches the number in parentheses. Spell the ordinal number (first, tenth, etc.).

1. I am in _____ grade. (6)

2. This is my _____ pair of shoes this year. (2)

3. I finished the race in _____ place. (9)

4. I will be the _____ person in my family to go to college! (5)

5. Turn right at the _____ traffic light. (3)

6. We're ready to start the _____ quarter of the basketball game. (4)

7. She said, "My birthday is December _____." (10)

8. We stayed in a _____ -class hotel! (1)

9. My mother's office is on the _____ floor. (7)

10. This is the _____ house that my parents have lived in. (8)

TEACHER: Read the directions and questions to students. Guide students to complete the exercise, providing support as needed.

Name _____

> The words *that, this, these,* and *those* may act as adjectives or pronouns. They are called **demonstrative adjectives and pronouns.**
>
> They may answer the question "Which one?" about a noun: <u>That</u> dog looks like a toy.
>
> They may take the place of a noun in a sentence: <u>That</u> looks like a toy.

Underline each demonstrative adjective or demonstrative pronoun. Write *A* if the word is an adjective. Write *P* if it is a pronoun.

1. This is a wonderful dog show. _____

2. These dogs are used for hunting. _____

3. Those are used as guard dogs. _____

4. A lady brushed this animal's fur. _____

5. Look at that prize-winning dog! _____

TEACHER: Guide students to complete the exercise, providing support as needed.

Name _____

> The words *that, this, these,* and *those* may act as adjectives or pronouns. They are called **demonstrative adjectives and pronouns.**
>
> They may answer the question "Which one?" about a noun: <u>That</u> dog looks like a toy.
>
> They may take the place of a noun in a sentence: <u>That</u> looks like a toy.

Complete each sentence by adding a word from the box. Then write the sentence correctly. Use each word only once.

> This   That   These   Those

1. _____ dog in my arms will win a prize.

   _____

2. _____ dogs over there are guard dogs.

   _____

3. _____ are the animals I like best.

   _____

4. _____ is the dog who won last year.

   _____

TEACHER: Read the directions and questions to students. Guide students to complete the exercise, providing support as needed.

Name _____

> The words *that, this, these,* and *those* may act as adjectives or pronouns. They are called **demonstrative adjectives and pronouns.**
>
> They may answer the question "Which one?" about a noun: <u>That</u> dog looks like a toy.
>
> They may take the place of a noun in a sentence: <u>That</u> looks like a toy.

A. Underline the demonstrative adjective or demonstrative pronoun. Write *A* if the word is an adjective. Write *P* if it is a pronoun.

1. I attended this dog show last year. _____

2. That was last year's winning dog. _____

3. We all wonder who will win this year. _____

4. Those curly-haired dogs are unusual. _____

5. These are special dogs from China. _____

B. Choose one demonstrative adjective and one demonstrative pronoun from the sentences in Part A. Use each word in a new sentence. Write your sentences on the lines.

1. _____

_____

2. _____

_____

Name _____

> Adjectives may be used to compare two or more things. With longer adjectives, we use *more* to compare two things. We use *most* to compare three or more things.
>
> That race was <u>more exciting</u> than a football game.
> That was the <u>most exciting</u> race I've ever seen.

Circle the phrase that completes each sentence correctly. Then write the it on the line.

1. Tamara is _____ than Wu is.

   more flexible   most flexible

2. Wu is the _____ runner on the team.

   more athletic   most athletic

3. He runs on the _____ trails in town.

   more difficult   most difficult

4. She is _____ about running than I am.

   more passionate   most passionate

TEACHER: Read the directions and questions to students. Guide students to complete the exercise, providing support as needed.

Name _____

> Adjectives may be used to compare two or more things. With longer adjectives, we use **more** to compare two things. We use **most** to compare three or more things.
>
> That race was <u>more exciting</u> than a football game.
> That was the <u>most exciting</u> race I've ever seen.

A. Write the correct form of each adjective.

Compare Two Things   Compare More Than Two things

1. flexible   _____   _____

2. athletic   _____   _____

3. difficult   _____   _____

4. passionate   _____   _____

B. Write the correct form of the adjective in parentheses to complete each sentence.

1. Wu is the (enthusiastic) _____ runner on the team.

2. His gold medals are (numerous) _____ than mine.

3. He is a (dedicated) _____ athlete than I am.

TEACHER: Read the directions and questions in Part A and Part B to students. Guide students to complete each exercise, providing support as needed.

Grades 4-6   275

Name _____

> Adjectives may be used to compare two or more things. With longer adjectives, we use *more* to compare two things. We use *most* to compare three or more things.

Read the passage. Circle each mistake in comparison. Then rewrite the passage correctly on the lines below.

1. Wu is the more dedicated athlete I know. He is the enthusiasticest runner on our team. He is most passionate about running than about schoolwork. He loves to jog on the difficulter trails in town.

_____

_____

_____

_____

_____

TEACHER: Read the directions and questions to students. Guide students to complete the exercise, providing support as needed.

Name _____

> Adjectives may be used to compare two or more things. Most short adjectives add the suffix *-er* to compare two things. They add the suffix *-est* to compare three or more things.
>
> The parrot has <u>brighter</u> colors than the lovebird.
> The macaw has the <u>brightest</u> colors of all the birds.

Circle the verb that completes each sentence correctly.
Then write the verb.

1. Those feathers are _____ than the sky.
   bluer   bluest

2. Which bird is the _____ of all?
   smarter   smartest

3. Parrots are _____ than parakeets.
   bigger   biggest

4. This bird is the _____ one in the store.
   lovelier   loveliest

TEACHER: Read the directions and questions to students. Guide students to complete the exercise, providing support as needed.

Name _____

Adjectives may be used to compare two or more things. Most short adjectives add the suffix *-er* to compare two things. They add the suffix *-est* to compare three or more things.

The parrot has <u>brighter</u> colors than the lovebird.
The macaw has the <u>brightest</u> colors of all the birds.

A. Write the correct form of each adjective.

Compare Two Things   Compare More Than Two things

1. smart   _____   _____

2. blue   _____   _____

3. big   _____   _____

4. lovely   _____   _____

B. Write the correct form of the adjective in parentheses to complete each sentence.

1. That parrot is the (mean) _____ bird in the shop.

2. The lovebird is (pretty) _____ than the parakeet is.

3. Is an owl really (wise) _____ than a parrot is?.

TEACHER: Read the directions and questions in Part A and Part B to students. Guide students to complete each exercise, providing support as needed.

Name _____

> Adjectives may be used to compare two or more things. Most short adjectives add the suffix *-er* to compare two things. They add the suffix *-est* to compare three or more things.

Read the passage. Circle each mistake in comparison. Then rewrite the passage correctly on the lines below.

1. That parrot has the bluer feathers I have ever seen. It is pretty than the parakeet and smart than the lovebird. It is also the bigger and meaner bird in the store!

_____

_____

_____

_____

_____

Name _____

> Some adjectives follow different rules to compare.
>
> | Adjective | Comparative | Superlative |
> |-----------|-------------|-------------|
> | good | better | best |
> | bad | worse | worst |
> | many/much | more | most |

A. Write the word that is missing in each set.

1.   good   _____   best

2.   many   _____   most

3.   bad   _____   worse

B. Write the form of the word in parentheses that best completes each sentence.

1. Your story was the (good) _____ one I read.

2. Your writing last year was (bad) _____ than it is now.

3. You wrote the (many) _____ stories of anyone in class.

4. Each story was (good) _____ than the last.

TEACHER: Read the directions and questions in Part A and Part B to students. Guide students to complete each exercise, providing support as needed.

Name _____

Some adjectives follow different rules to compare.

Adjective	Comparative	Superlative
good	better	best
bad	worse	worst
many/much	more	most

A. Circle the letter of each sentence with a comparative adjective. Make an X on the letter of each sentence with a superlative adjective.

1. **a.** You wrote the best story of all.

    b. Your writing is better now than it was last year.

    c. I think that you are a very good writer.

2. **a.** You wrote many good stories this year.

    b. You wrote more stories than Jeff did.

    c. In fact, you wrote the most stories of all!

B. Circle the correct adjective in parentheses. Then write the sentence correctly on the line.

1. Last year, your writing was (worse, worst) than it is now.

    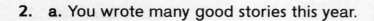

2. Are you the (better, best) story writer in our class?

    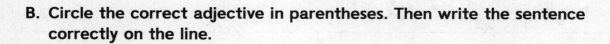

3. You got (more, most) A's in English than in math.

_____

TEACHER: Guide students to complete each exercise, providing support as needed.

Name _____

> Some adjectives follow different rules to compare.
>
> | Adjective | Comparative | Superlative |
> |-----------|-------------|-------------|
> | good | better | best |
> | bad | worse | worst |
> | many/much | more | most |

Rewrite the sentences below, correcting any mistakes in comparison.

1. Yours was the better story I read this week.

   _____

   _____

2. Did you write the more stories of all?

   _____

   _____

3. Your earlier stories were badder than this one

   _____

   _____

TEACHER: Read the directions and questions to students. Guide students to complete the exercise, providing support as needed.

Name _____

> When you use *as* or *too* to compare two or more things, the adjective does not change.
>
> The hill looked <u>as big as</u> a mountain.   It seemed <u>too high</u> to climb.

Underline the comparisons in each sentence.

1. My backpack is too heavy for me.

2. That tree is as huge as a giant.

3. The trail is as long as a road.

4. This hike may be too hard for us.

5. My stick is as tall as I am.

6. I may be too tired to go on.

TEACHER: Read the directions and questions to students. Guide students to complete the exercise, providing support as needed.

Name _____

When you use *as* or *too* to compare two or more things, the adjective does not change.

The hill looked <u>as big as</u> a mountain.   It seemed <u>too high</u> to climb.

Write the correct form of the adjective in parentheses on the line.

1. My backpack is too _____ for me. (heavy, heavier)

2. My hiking stick is as _____ as I am. (tall, taller)

3. This hike may be too _____ for us. (hard, hardest)

4. The trail is as _____ as a highway. (long, longer)

5. I may be too _____ to go on. (tired, more tired)

6. This tree is as _____ as a giant. (huge, huger)

TEACHER: Read the directions and questions to students. Guide students to complete the exercise, providing support as needed.

Name _____

When you use *as* or *too* to compare two or more things, the adjective does not change.

Think of an adjective that could complete each sentence. Write your sentence on the line.

1. The trail is as _____ as a highway.

   _____

   _____

2. My backpack is too _____ for me.

   _____

   _____

3. That tree is as _____ as a giant.

   _____

   _____

TEACHER: Read the directions and questions to students. Guide students to complete the exercise, providing support as needed.

Name _____

Some adjectives are formed from other words plus a suffix. The suffix
–*ish* can mean "like."

> Marta has a <u>girlish</u> laugh.

The suffix –*y* can mean "having" or "tending to."

> Marta ate a <u>juicy</u> plum.   Marta has a <u>chirpy</u> voice.

A.   Add the given suffix. Then write the adjective.

1.   dust + y   _____

2.   leaf + y   _____

3.   fool + ish   _____

4.   baby + ish   _____

**B.   Write the adjective form of the word in parentheses to complete
each sentence.**

1. Do you feel (itch) _____?

2. Don't be (child). _____?

3. Maybe you are just (thirst) _____?

TEACHER: Read the directions and questions in Part A and Part B to students. Guide
students to complete each exercise, providing support as needed.

Name _____

> Some adjectives are formed from other words plus a suffix. The suffix –*ish* can mean "like."
>
> Marta has a <u>girlish</u> laugh.
>
> The suffix –*y* can mean "having" or "tending to."
>
> Marta ate a <u>juicy</u> plum.   Marta has a <u>chirpy</u> voice.

A. Look for the adjective. Then write a word to finish the sentence.

1. *Dusty* means "having _____."

2. *Leafy* means "having _____."

3. *Foolish* means "like a _____."

4. *Babyish* means "like a _____."

B. Write the adjective form of the word in parentheses to complete each sentence. Check your spelling.

1. Your game is too (noise) _____.

2. Don't be so (child) _____

3. Those pants are too (bag) _____.

4. Don't be (self) _____ with your toys.

Copyright © McGraw-Hill Education

TEACHER: Guide students to complete each exercise, providing support as needed.

Name _____

> Some adjectives are formed from other words plus a suffix. The suffix *–ish* can mean "like."
>
> The suffix *-y* can mean "having" or "tending to."

Add the given suffix. Check your spelling. Then use each adjective you made in a sentence of your own.

1. baby + ish

   _____

   _____

2. noise + y

   _____

   _____

3. fool + ish

   _____

   _____

TEACHER: Read the directions and questions to students. Guide students to complete the exercise, providing support as needed.

Name _____

> Two suffixes that can change nouns to adjectives are –*ful* and –*less*. The suffix –*ful* means "full of." The suffix –*less* means "without."
>
> Be <u>careful</u> with those glasses. Do not be <u>careless</u> and drop them.

A. Add the given suffix. Then write the adjective.

1.   grace + ful   _____

2.   sleeve + less   _____

3.   color + ful   _____

4.   shoe + less   _____

B. Add –*less* or –*ful* to the word in parentheses to complete each sentence and make it true.

1. A bad fall may be (pain) _____.

2. Most insects are (harm) _____.

3. A puppy can be very (play) _____.

4. A net is (use) _____ for carrying water.

TEACHER: Read the directions and questions in Part A and Part B to students. Guide students to complete each exercise, providing support as needed.

Name _____

> Two suffixes that can change nouns to adjectives are *–ful* and *–less*. The suffix *–ful* means "full of." The suffix *–less* means "without."
>
> Be <u>careful</u> with those glasses. Do not be <u>careless</u> and drop them.

A. Look for the adjective. Then write a noun to finish the sentence.

1. *Graceful* means "full of _____."

2. *Sleeveless* means "without _____."

3. *Colorful* means "full of _____."

4. *Shoeless* means "without _____."

B. Add *–less* or *–ful* to the word in parentheses to complete each sentence and make it true.

1. A net is (use) _____ for carrying water.

2. The woods are (peace) _____ in the early morning.

3. A movie that is dull may seem (end) _____ .

4. Everyone enjoys a (thought) _____ gift.

TEACHER: Read the directions and questions in Part A and Part B to students. Guide students to complete each exercise, providing support as needed.

Name _____

> Two suffixes that can change nouns to adjectives are *-ful* and *-less*. The suffix *-ful* means "full of." The suffix *-less* means "without."

Add the suffix. Then use each adjective you made in a sentence of your own.

1. color + ful

_____

_____

2. peace + ful

_____

_____

3. grace + ful

_____

_____

TEACHER: Read the directions and questions to students. Guide students to complete the exercise, providing support as needed.

Grades 4-6 **291**

Name _____

You can use suffixes to change nouns to adjectives. The suffix –*ous* means "full of" or "characterized by." The suffix –*ic* means "like" or "characterized by." The suffix –*like* means "like."

Switzerland is <u>mountainous</u>.   The mountains are <u>majestic</u>.
This painting is quite <u>lifelike</u>.

A. Draw a line to match each noun to the suffix that turns it into an adjective.

1. artist   a. ous

2. cat   b. ic

3. adventure   c. like

B. Read each definition. Circle the correct adjective with that meaning.

1. full of courage   courageic   courageous

2. like a cube   cubic   cubeous

3. characterized by danger dangerlike   dangerous

4. characterized by acid   acidic   acidous

5. like a dream   dreamlike   dreamous

TEACHER: Read the directions and questions in Part A and Part B to students. Guide students to complete each exercise, providing support as needed.

Name _____

You can use suffixes to change nouns to adjectives. The suffix –ous means "full of" or "characterized by." The suffix –ic means "like" or "characterized by." The suffix –like means "like."

Switzerland is <u>mountainous</u>.   The mountains are <u>majestic</u>.
This painting is quite <u>lifelike</u>.

Add –ous, -ic, or –like to the noun in bold. Write the new word. Use a dictionary to check your work.

1. **base**   We study _____ math.

2. **danger**   Fire can be _____.

3. **fish**   An eel is _____.

4. **acid**   Lemon juice is _____.

5. **workman** He did a _____ job.

6. **nerve**   I felt _____ before the show.

TEACHER: Read the directions and questions to students. Guide students to complete the exercise, providing support as needed.

Grades 4-6   293

Name _____

You can use suffixes to change nouns to adjectives. The suffix *–ous* means "full of" or "characterized by." The suffix *–ic* means "like" or "characterized by." The suffix *–like* means "like."

A. Add *–ous, -ic,* or *–like* to the noun in parentheses. Write the new word. Use a dictionary to check your work.

1. We are studying (base) _____ science.

2. An eel is a (fish) _____ creature.

3. We learned that lemon juice is (acid) _____.

4. Our brain is part of the (nerve) _____ system.

5. Working with electricity may be (hazard) _____.

B. Choose two adjectives that you made from nouns above. Use them in two new sentences. Write the sentences on the lines.

1. _____

_____

_____

2. _____

_____

_____

TEACHER: Read the directions and questions in Part A and Part B to students. Guide students to complete each exercise, providing support as needed.

Name _____

> An **adverb** is a word that modifies a verb, an adjective, or another adverb. Adverbs may appear at the beginning, middle, or end of a sentence. Many adverbs that modify verbs end in –*ly*.
>
> We rapped on the door <u>loudly</u>. We <u>loudly</u> rapped on the door.

Underline the adverb in each sentence.

1. We dressed quickly in our costumes.

2. Excitedly, we hurried down the sidewalk.

3. Mr. Barnes opened his door cautiously.

4. "Trick or treat!" we joyfully yelled.

5. Mr. Barnes divided the treats equally.

6. Luckily, our neighbors are generous!

TEACHER: Read the directions and questions to students. Guide students to complete the exercise, providing support as needed.

Name _____

> An **adverb** is a word that modifies a verb, an adjective, or another adverb. Adverbs may appear at the beginning, middle, or end of a sentence. Many adverbs that modify verbs end in *-ly*.
>
> We rapped on the door <u>loudly</u>. We <u>loudly</u> rapped on the door.

A. Separate each underlined adverb into an adjective plus a suffix.

1. We dressed <u>quickly</u>.   _____ + _____

2. <u>Excitedly</u>, we hurried.   _____ + _____

3. Mr. Barnes answered <u>cautiously</u>.   _____ + _____

4. He divided our treats <u>equally</u>.   _____ + _____

B. Complete each sentence with the adverb form of the word in parentheses. Check your spelling.

1. Mr. Barnes greeted us (kind) _____.

2. He (generous) _____ filled our treat bags.

3. Of course, we thanked him (polite) _____.

4. Then we ran (happy) _____ to the next house.

5. The moon shone (bright) _____ in the sky.

TEACHER: Read the directions and questions in Part A and Part B to students. Guide students to complete each exercise, providing support as needed.

Name _____

> An **adverb** is a word that modifies a verb, an adjective, or another adverb. Adverbs may appear at the beginning, middle, or end of a sentence. Many adverbs that modify verbs end in -*ly*.

The writer below used adjectives instead of adverbs. Find the words that are used incorrectly. Change them to adverbs. Then write the paragraph correctly.

1. On Beggar's Night, we dressed rapid in our costumes. We ran happy down the sidewalk. Ms. Barnes opened her door cautious. She generous filled our bags with treats. We thanked her polite.

_____

_____

_____

_____

_____

Name _____

Adverbs may answer one of these questions about a verb:

When? I visited you <u>yesterday</u>.　　**Where?** I visited you <u>there</u>.

How? I visited you <u>gladly</u>.　　**To what extent?** I visited you <u>briefly</u>.

A. Write *when, where, how,* or *to what extent* to tell what question the bold adverb answers.

1.　**First** I took the bus. _____

2.　I rode **up** in the elevator. _____

3.　Your building is **very** tall. _____

B. Underline the adverb in each sentence. Then circle the question it answers.

1.　I traveled far to see you.　　　　　how　　　　　to what extent

2.　We moved away last year.　　　　where　　　　　when

3.　I hug you happily.　　　　　　　　how　　　　　to what extent

4.　You always greet me with a smile.　where　　　　　when

TEACHER: Read the directions and questions in Part A and Part B to students. Guide students to complete each exercise, providing support as needed.

Name _____

> **Adverbs** may answer one of these questions about a verb:
>
> **When?** I visited you <u>yesterday</u>.   **Where?** I visited you <u>there</u>.
>
> **How?** I visited you <u>gladly</u>.   **To what extent?** I visited you <u>briefly</u>.

Underline the adverb. Then write *when, where, how,* or *to what extent* to tell what question the adverb answers.

1. First I took the bus. _____

2. I rode up in the elevator. _____

3. Your building is very tall. _____

4. I traveled far to see you. _____

5. We moved away last year. _____

6. You greet me happily. _____

Name _____

Adverbs may answer one of these questions about a verb:

When? I visited you <u>yesterday</u>.   **Where?** I visited you <u>there</u>.

How? I visited you <u>gladly</u>.   **To what extent?** I visited you <u>briefly</u>.

**Read the list of adverbs below. Decide which question each adverb answers.
Sort the words into the correct lists.**

immediately	too	here	backward
slowly	afterward	barely	gently
underneath	very	soon	fiercely
extremely	lazily	everywhere	finally

WHEN?

1. _____

2. _____

3. _____

4. _____

HOW?

5. _____

6. _____

7. _____

8. _____

WHERE?

9. _____

10. _____

11. _____

12. _____

TO WHAT EXTENT?

13. _____

14. _____

15. _____

16. _____

**TEACHER: Read the directions and questions to students. Guide students to complete
the exercise, providing support as needed.**

Name _____

> Some **adverbs** express **frequency.** These include *always, usually, frequently, often, sometimes, occasionally, seldom, rarely,* and *never.*

Choose the adverb that best completes each sentence.

1. The students enjoy playing volleyball.
   They (often, never) play games with friends.

2. The zookeeper feeds the animals.
   She (rarely, frequently) feeds them.

3. She dislikes turnips. She (always, seldom) buys them.

4. I (usually, never) take my dog for a walk in the morning,
   because I like to see the sunrise.

5. She (often, rarely) wears boots, because she thinks
   they are uncomfortable.

TEACHER: Read the directions and questions to students. Guide students to complete the exercise, providing support as needed.

Grades 4-6   **301**

Name _____

> Some **adverbs** express **frequency.** These include *always, usually, frequently, often, sometimes, occasionally, seldom, rarely,* and *never.*

A. Choose the adverb that best completes each sentence.

1. The students enjoy playing volleyball.
   They (often, never) play games with friends.

2. The zookeeper feeds the animals.
   She (rarely, frequently) feeds them.

3. She dislikes turnips. She (always, seldom) buys them.

B. Underline the adverb in each sentence. Then use the adverb in a new sentence.

1. I usually take my dog for a walk in the morning, because I like to see the sunrise.

   _____

2. He rarely wears boots, because he thinks they are uncomfortable.

   _____

3. I always go to music rehearsal right after school.

   _____

TEACHER: Guide students to complete each exercise in Part A and Part B, providing support as needed.

Name _____

> Some **adverbs** express **frequency.** These include *always, usually, frequently, often, sometimes, occasionally, seldom, rarely,* and *never.*

A. Write an adverb of frequency to complete each sentence.

1. The students enjoy playing volleyball. They _____ play games with friends.

2. She dislikes turnips. She _____ buys them.

B. Circle the words that best complete each sentence.

1. I (go always/always go) to music rehearsal right after school.

2. (Never go/Go never) close to the edge of the cliff!

C. Underline the adverb in each sentence. Then use the adverb in a new sentence.

1. I usually take my dog for a walk in the morning, because I like to see the sunrise.

    _____

    _____

2. He rarely wears boots, because he thinks they are uncomfortable.

    _____

    _____

TEACHER: Read the directions and questions in Parts A, B, and C to students. Guide students to complete each exercise, providing support as needed.

Grades 4-6   303

Name _____

> **Intensifiers** are words that make an adjective stronger or weaker.
>
> The mountain path is <u>extremely</u> dangerous. (stronger)
>
> The mountain path is <u>rather</u> dangerous. (weaker)

A. Circle the intensifier that best completes each sentence.

1. The building was _____ old, so it needed repairs.
   somewhat   very

2. This juice is _____ fresh, and it tastes great.
   too   extremely

3. Don't eat that bread. It is _____ old.
   too   just

4. He is _____ tall that he has to bend
   rather   so

   down to go through doors!

5. I am _____ tired, but not tired enough to
   extremely   somewhat

   miss the movie.

B. Read sentences 1 and 2. Circle the intensifier in each sentence. Then circle the word that makes sentence 3 true.

1. The piglet is extremely small.

2. The lamb is rather small.

3. The piglet is (smaller/larger) than the lamb.

TEACHER: Read the directions and questions in Part A and Part B to students. Guide students to complete each exercise, providing support as needed.

Name _____

> **Intensifiers** are words that make an adjective stronger or weaker.
>
> The mountain path is <u>extremely</u> dangerous. (stronger)
>
> The mountain path is <u>rather</u> dangerous. (weaker)

A. Circle the letter of the choice that uses the intensifier correctly.

1. **a.** The building was very old, so it needed repairs.

    b. The building was old extremely, so it needed repairs.

    c. The building was just old, so it needed repairs.

    d. The building rather was old, so it needed repairs.

2. **a.** This juice is fresh, and it tastes great.

    b. This juice is too fresh, and it tastes great.

    c. This juice is extremely fresh, and it tastes great.

    d. This juice is fresh somewhat, and it tastes great.

B. Read each sentence. Choose an intensifier from the box to complete the sentence.

> too   just   rather   extremely   so   quite

1. Don't eat that bread. It is _____ old.

2. He is _____ tall that he has to bend down to go through doors!

3. I am _____ tired, but not tired enough to miss the movie.

4. The piglet is _____ small enough to fit in the cup.

Name _____

> **Intensifiers** are words that make an adjective stronger or weaker.

A. Circle the intensifier that best completes each sentence.

1. The building was (somewhat/very) old, so it needed repairs.

2. This juice is (too/extremely) fresh, and it tastes great.

3. Don't eat that bread. It is (too/just) old.

4. He is (rather/so) tall that he has to bend down to go through doors!

5. I am (extremely/somewhat) tired, but not tired enough to miss the movie.

B. Choose two intensifiers that you circled above. Use them in two new sentences. Write the sentences on the lines.

1. _____

   _____

2. _____

   _____

TEACHER: Read the directions and questions in Part A and Part B to students. Guide students to complete each exercise, providing support as needed.

Name _____

Relative adverbs include the words *where, when,* and *why.*

Where is used after nouns that are places. *When* refers to times.
Why tells a reason for something, and may come after the noun *reason.*

Circle the relative adverb that completes each sentence.

1. You will explain _____ you are late to class.
    why   when

2. We saw the Statue of Liberty _____ we visited
    New York City.   where   when

3. 1972 is the year _____ our house was built.
    why   when

4. My dog likes the park _____ we throw the
    Frisbee.   where   when

5. What is the reason _____ Jeanie looks angry?
    why   when

6. The hospital _____ we visited Grandma was
    very nice.   why   where

**TEACHER: Read the directions and questions to students. Guide students to complete
the exercise, providing support as needed.**

Name _____

> **Relative adverbs** include the words *where, when,* and *why.*
>
> *Where* is used after nouns that are places. *When* refers to times.
> *Why* tells a reason for something, and may come after the noun *reason.*

A. Circle the relative adverb that completes each sentence.

1. You will explain (why/when) you are late to class.

2. We saw the Statue of Liberty (where/when) we
visited New York City.

3. 1972 is the year (why/when) our house was built.

B. Write a relative adverb to complete each sentence.

1. The hospital _____ we visited Grandma was very nice.

2. I can't understand _____ our experiment is not working.

3. Les will need the shoes _____ he goes to soccer practice.

**TEACHER: Read the directions and questions in Part A and Part B to students. Guide
students to complete each exercise, providing support as needed.**

Name _____

> **Relative adverbs** include the words *where, when,* and *why*.
>
> *Where* is used after nouns that are places. *When* refers to times.
> *Why* tells a reason for something, and may come after the noun *reason*.

A. Circle the relative adverb that completes each sentence.

1. You will explain (why/when) you are late to class.

2. We saw the Statue of Liberty (where/when) we visited New York City.

3. 1972 is the year (why/when) our house was built.

B. Write a relative adverb to complete each sentence.

1. What is the reason _____ Jeanie looks angry?

2. The hospital _____ we visited Grandma was very nice.

3. I can't understand _____ our experiment is not working.

C. Combine the sentences using a relative adverb.

1. My dog likes the park. We throw the Frisbee.

   _____

2. Les will need the shoes. He goes to soccer practice.

   _____

Name _____

> **Adverbs** can modify adjectives. An adjective is a word that tells more about a noun.
>
> Your haircut is <u>simply</u> marvelous! (The adverb *simply* modifies the adjective *marvelous*.)
>
> I was <u>too</u> tired to stay awake! (The adverb *too* modifies the adjective *tired*.)

Circle the adjective and underline the adverb that modifies it in each sentence.

1. Grandpa said he was too tired to dance!

2. He became terribly sad at the news.

3. The weather is pleasantly warm.

4. The professor's lesson was fairly short.

5. They were too small to go on the roller coaster.

6. The music was dramatically loud.

TEACHER: Read the directions and questions to students. Guide students to complete the exercise, providing support as needed.

Name _____

> **Adverbs** can modify adjectives. An adjective is a word that tells more about a noun.
>
> Your haircut is <u>simply</u> marvelous!
> (The adverb *simply* modifies the adjective *marvelous*.)
>
> I was <u>too</u> tired to stay awake!
> (The adverb *too* modifies the adjective *tired*.)

A. Circle the adjective and underline the adverb that modifies it in each sentence.

1. The professor's lesson was fairly short.

2. They were too small to go on the roller coaster.

3. The music was dramatically loud.

B. Look at the picture. Circle an adverb to complete the sentence.

1. Grandpa said he was not (too/fairly) tired to dance!

2. He became (simply/terribly) sad at the news.

3. The weather is (pleasantly/terribly) warm.

TEACHER: Guide students to complete each exercise in Part A and Part B, providing support as needed.

Grades 4-6   **311**

Name _____

> **Adverbs** can modify adjectives. An adjective is a word that tells more about a noun.
>
> Your haircut is <u>simply</u> marvelous!
> (The adverb *simply* modifies the adjective *marvelous*.)
>
> I was <u>too</u> tired to stay awake!
> (The adverb *too* modifies the adjective *tired*.)

A. Expand each sentence by adding an adverb to modify the adjective. Write the new sentence on the line.

1. The professor's lesson was short.

   _____

2. They are small.

   _____

3. The music was loud.

   _____

B. Look at the picture. Circle an adverb to complete the sentence.

1. Grandpa said he was not (too/fairly) tired to dance!

2. He became (simply/terribly) sad at the news.

3. The weather is (pleasantly/terribly) warm.

TEACHER: Guide students to complete each exercise in Part A and Part B, providing support as needed.

Name _____

To compare with short adverbs, add -er or -est.

When an adverb ends in -ly, add more or most to the adverb to compare.

Complete each sentence with the correct form of the adverb in parentheses.

1. The teacher talked (loudly) _____ than the student.

2. The winner ran (fast) _____ of all the runners in the race.

3. The child was dressed (warmly) _____ than her sister.

4. He skates the (quickly) _____ of all his friends.

5. Liz paints (carefully) _____ than her brother.

TEACHER: Read the directions and questions to students. Guide students to complete the exercise, providing support as needed.

Name _____

> To compare with short adverbs, add -*er* or -*est*.
>
> When an adverb ends in -*ly*, add *more* or *most* to the adverb to compare.

A. Complete each sentence with the correct form of the adverb in parentheses.

1. The teacher talked (loudly) _____ than the student.

2. The winner ran (fast) _____ of all the runners in the race.

3. The child was dressed (warmly) _____ than her sister.

B. Decide if the underlined form of the adverb is correct. If it is correct, write *C* on the line. If it is incorrect, write the correct form.

1. He skates the <u>quickly</u> of all his friends. _____

2. Liz paints <u>more carefully</u> than her brother. _____

3. Roy speaks <u>most confidently</u> than Tim. _____

TEACHER: Guide students to complete each exercise in Part A and Part B, providing support as needed.

Name _____

> To compare with short adverbs, add -er or -est.
>
> When an adverb ends in -ly, add more or most to the adverb to compare.

A.   Read the sentences. Rewrite them as one sentence that compares, using the correct form of the adverb.

1.   The teacher talked loudly. The student talked softly.

_____

2.   The winner ran fast. The other runners did not run as fast.

_____

3.   The child was dressed warmly. Her sister was not dressed warmly.

_____

B.   Decide if the underlined form of the adverb is correct. If it is correct, write C on the line. If it is incorrect, write the correct form.

1.   He skates quickly of all his friends. _____

2.   Liz paints more carefully than her brother. _____

3.   Roy speaks most confidently than Tim. _____

TEACHER: Read the directions and questions in Part A and Part B to students. Guide students to complete each exercise, providing support as needed.

Name _____

You can compare using the **irregular adverbs** *well* and *badly*:

well	badly
better	worse
best	worst

A. Circle the word that completes each sentence. Then write the word.

1. The home team played _____ than the
   visiting team.   worse   worst

2. This magician performed _____ than the
   one we saw on TV.   better   best

3. You ski the _____ of all the team members.
                  better   best

4. The skunk smells the _____ of the animals
   at the zoo.   worse   worst

5. The winning chef cooked the _____ of all
   the contestants.   better   best

B. Circle the word that completes each sentence correctly.

1. They row the boat (well/good).

2. The trained dog obeys (well/good).

3. That is a (well/good) restaurant.

TEACHER: Guide students to complete each exercise, providing support as needed.

Name _____

> You can compare using the **irregular adverbs** *well* and *badly*:
>
> | well | badly |
> |--------|--------|
> | better | worse |
> | best | worst |

A. Write *better*, *best*, *worse*, or *worst* to complete each sentence.

1. The home team played _____ than the visiting team. That's why the home team lost the game.

2. This magician performed even _____ than the one we saw on TV. He really fooled me!

3. You ski the _____ of all the team members. You will probably win the trophy.

B. Circle the word that completes the sentence.

1. The rowing team rows the boat (well/good).

2. Wow, your trained dog obeys so (well/good)!

3. That is a (well/good) restaurant. I love the food there.

TEACHER: Read the directions and questions in Part A and Part B to students. Guide students to complete each exercise, providing support as needed.

Name _____

> You can compare using the **irregular adverbs** *well* and *badly*:
>
> | well | badly |
> |--------|-------|
> | better | worse |
> | best | worst |

A. Use the information in the sentences to write a new sentence on the line. The new sentence should use *better, best, worse,* or *worst.*

1. The home team played badly. The visiting team won the game.

   _____

2. This magician performed well. The one we saw on TV was not as amazing!

   _____

3. You ski well. All the other skiers are slower than you are.

   _____

B. Write *well* or *good* to complete each sentence.

1. The rowing team rows the boat _____.

2. Wow, your trained dog obeys so _____!

3. That is a _____ restaurant. I love the food there.

TEACHER: Guide students to complete each exercise, providing support as needed.

Name _____

> Use only one **negative** in a sentence.
>
> **Incorrect:** She <u>never</u> asked for <u>nothing</u>.
> **Correct:** She <u>never</u> asked for anything.

A. Read each sentence. Circle the letter of the sentence that is incorrect.

1. Which sentence is incorrect?

    a. I will not ask for anything at the store.

    b. They never wanted no money.

    c. The city has no one to clean up the park.

    d. Nobody will come to help.

2. Which sentence is incorrect?

    a. The parents planned a party for the child.

    b. They never expected so many guests.

    c. The parents didn't get any cake.

    d. There wasn't no more cake left for them.

B. Circle the word that correctly forms a <u>negative</u> sentence.

1. Kate cannot find her books (anywhere/nowhere).

2. I will be able to see (anything/nothing) in this fog.

3. I won't go (anywhere/nowhere) without my phone.

4. Please take (no one/anyone) outside in the heat.

Name _____

Use only one negative in a sentence.

Incorrect: She <u>never</u> asked for <u>nothing</u>.
Correct: She <u>never</u> asked for anything.

A. Circle the word that correctly completes the sentence.

1. The city hasn't hired (no one/anyone) to clean up the park.

2. There (is/isn't) no more cake left.

3. She can't drive (anywhere/nowhere) with her leg in a cast.

B. If the sentence is correct, write *C* on the line. If the sentence is incorrect, write the corrected sentence on the line.

1. Kate can't find her books nowhere.

_____

2. I won't be able to see nothing in this fog.

_____

3. I won't go anywhere without my phone.

_____

TEACHER: Guide students to complete each exercise in Part A and Part B, providing support as needed.

Name _____

> Use only one **negative** in a sentence.
>
> **Incorrect:** She <u>never</u> asked for <u>nothing</u>.
> **Correct:** She <u>never</u> asked for anything.

A. Circle the word that correctly completes the sentence.

1. The city hasn't hired (no one/anyone) to clean up the park.

2. There (is/isn't) no more cake left.

3. She can't drive (anywhere/nowhere) with her leg in a cast.

B. Complete each sentence with a word that makes it negative.

1. I won't be able to see _____ in this fog.

2. There are _____ parking spots anywhere!

C. If the sentence is correct, write _C_ on the line. If the sentence is incorrect, write the corrected sentence on the line.

1. Kate can't find her books nowhere.

_____

2. I won't go anywhere without my phone.

_____

TEACHER: Read the directions and questions in Part A, Part B, and Part C to students. Guide students to complete each exercise, providing support as needed.

Name _____

Use *do not, did not, am not, is not, are not* or their contractions to form a **negative** statement:

They <u>do not</u> enjoy skating.   They <u>don't</u> enjoy skating.

Circle the word or words that make each sentence negative.

1. I (am not/did not) have fun at camp.

2. My mother (is not/does not) enjoy scary movies.

3. They (doesn't/don't) have their hats on.

4. That (isn't/doesn't) the right way to put the puzzle together.

5. Justin and Selena (are not/do not) playing a game.

TEACHER: Read the directions and questions to students. Guide students to complete the exercise, providing support as needed.

Name _____

> Use *do not, did not, am not, is not, are not* or their contractions to form a **negative** statement:
>
> They <u>do not</u> enjoy skating.   They <u>don't</u> enjoy skating.

A. Circle the word or words that make each sentence negative.

1. I (am not/did not) have fun at camp.

2. My mother (is not/does not) enjoy scary movies.

3. Justin and Selena (are not/do not) playing a game.

B. Rewrite each sentence to be negative.

1. They have their hats on.

   _____

2. That is the right way to put the puzzle together.

   _____

3. She helped her sister with math homework.

   _____

TEACHER: Read the directions and questions in Part A and Part B to students. Guide students to complete each exercise, providing support as needed.   Grades 4-6   **323**

Name _____

Use *do not, did not, am not, is not, are not* or their contractions to form a **negative** statement.

A. Circle the word or words that make each sentence negative.

1. I (am not/did not) have fun at camp.

2. My mother (is not/does not) enjoy scary movies.

3. Justin and Selena (are not/do not) playing a game.

B. Circle the word that completes each sentence.

1. She does not (knit/knits) very well.

2. Lars did not (dance/danced) at the party.

3. They didn't (studied/study) for the test.

C. Rewrite each sentence to be negative.

1. That is the right way to put the puzzle together.

   _____

   _____

2. She helped her sister with math homework.

   _____

   _____

TEACHER: Read the directions and questions in Part A, Part B, and Part C to students. Guide students to complete each exercise, providing support as needed.

Name _____

> Use *already* to say that an action happened before it was expected to happen.
>
> Use *still* to say that an action continues to happen.
>
> Use *yet* to say that an action is expected to happen in the future.
>
> Use *anymore* to say that an action used to happen but does not continue to happen.

Circle the adverb that correctly completes the sentence. Then write the word on the line.

1. We _____ ate dinner. We saved you a plate of food.
   already   still

2. Is he _____ sleeping? School starts soon!
   still   anymore

3. I don't like to ski _____ . Last time I did not have fun.
   anymore   already

4. The doctor is not in her office _____ . We are too early.
   yet   still

5. Are you _____ done with your homework?
   yet   already

6. The birds are _____ eating the food.
   anymore   still

TEACHER: Read the directions and questions to students. Guide students to complete the exercise, providing support as needed.

Name _____

> Use *already* to say that an action happened before it was expected to happen.
>
> Use *still* to say that an action continues to happen.
>
> Use *yet* to say that an action is expected to happen in the future.
>
> Use *anymore* to say that an action used to happen but does not continue to happen.

A.   Circle the sentence that correctly uses the adverb.

1.   **a.** We ate dinner anymore. We saved you a plate of food.

    b. We ate dinner still. We saved you a plate of food.

    c. We ate dinner yet. We saved you a plate of food.

    d. We ate dinner already. We saved you a plate of food.

2.   **a.** Is he sleeping yet? School starts soon!

    b. Is he still sleeping? School starts soon!

    c. Is already he sleeping? School starts soon!

    d. Is he not sleeping anymore? School starts soon!

B.   Choose an adverb from the box to complete each sentence.

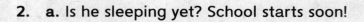

| already | still | anymore | yet |

1.   I don't like to ski _____ Last time I did not have fun.

2.   The doctor is not in her office _____. We are too early.

3.   Are you _____ done with your homework?

TEACHER: Read the directions and questions in Part A and Part B to students. Guide students to complete each exercise, providing support as needed.

Name _____

> Use *already* to say that an action happened before it was expected to happen.
>
> Use *still* to say that an action continues to happen.
>
> Use *yet* to say that an action is expected to happen in the future.
>
> Use *anymore* to say that an action used to happen but does not continue to happen.

A. Circle the adverb that correctly completes the sentence.

1. We (already/still) ate dinner. We saved you a plate of food.

2. Is he (anymore/still) sleeping? School starts soon!

3. I don't like to ski (anymore/already). Last time I did not have fun.

B. Write *yet, already,* or *still* to complete each sentence.

1. The doctor is not in her office _____. We are too early.

2. Are you _____ done with your homework?

3. The birds are _____ eating the food. They have been eating for a long time!

C. Write a pair of sentences that use the given adverb or adverbs.

1. still; yet

    _____

2. already; yet

    _____

Name _____

> The **conjunctive adverb** *also* means "in addition to" and is used to give an additional fact or example.
>
> The conjunctive adverb *therefore* shows that one thing is the result of another thing.
>
> Use a semi-colon before the conjunctive adverb and a comma after it.

A.   Complete the sentence by writing *also* or *therefore*.

1.   She missed the bus; _____, she will walk to school.

2.   My mother is smart; _____, my mother is kind.

3.   The dog barked; _____, the dog growled.

4.   He forgot to study; _____, he was worried about the test.

5.   Matthew worked hard to learn the dance. _____, he performed well.

B.   Add the correct punctuation to the sentence.

1.   The class cleaned up the classroom therefore they got a reward.

2.   My baby sister likes books also she likes toys.

3.   The dog was covered in mud Therefore we gave him a bath.

TEACHER: Read the directions and questions in Part A and Part B to students. Guide students to complete each exercise, providing support as needed.

Name _____

> The **conjunctive adverb** *also* means "in addition to" and is used to give an additional fact or example.
>
> The conjunctive adverb *therefore* shows that one thing is the result of another thing.
>
> Use a semi-colon before the conjunctive adverb and a comma after it.

A. Complete the sentence by writing *also* or *therefore*.

1. She missed the bus; _____, she will walk to school.

2. My mother is smart; _____, my mother is kind.

3. The dog barked; _____, the dog growled.

B. Rewrite the two sentences as one sentence that uses a conjunctive adverb.

1. The class cleaned up the classroom. They got a reward.

   _____

2. My baby sister likes books. She likes toys.

   _____

3. The dog was covered in mud. We gave him a bath.

   _____

TEACHER: Read the directions and questions in Part A and Part B to students. Guide students to complete each exercise, providing support as needed.

Name _____

> The **conjunctive adverb** *also* means "in addition to" and is used to give an additional fact or example.
>
> The conjunctive adverb *therefore* shows that one thing is the result of another thing.
>
> Use a semi-colon before the conjunctive adverb and a comma after it.

A. Complete the sentence by writing *also* or *therefore*.

1. She missed the bus; _____, she will walk to school.

2. My mother is smart; _____, my mother is kind.

3. Matthew worked hard to learn the dance. _____, he performed well.

B. Add the correct punctuation to the sentence.

1. The class cleaned up the classroom therefore they got a reward.

2. My baby sister likes books also she likes toys.

3. The dog was covered in mud Therefore we gave him a bath.

C. Rewrite the two sentences as one sentence that uses a conjunctive adverb.

1. The dog barked. The dog growled.

    _____

2. He forgot to study. He was worried about the test.

    _____

TEACHER: Read the directions and questions in Part A, Part B, and Part C to students. Guide students to complete each exercise, providing support as needed.

Name _____

> **Prepositions** combine with other words to show direction, location, and time.
>
> Here are some examples of prepositions:
>
> after   at   for   on   up
>
> around   between   in   to   with

Circle the prepositions in each sentence. Some sentences have more than one preposition.

1. She walked up the stairs.

2. We ran on a path at the park.

3. I wake up at 7:00 on Saturdays.

4. She leaned against the wall.

5. The bird flew over his head.

TEACHER: Read the directions and questions to students. Guide students to complete the exercise, providing support as needed.

Name _____

> **Prepositions** combine with other words to show direction, location, and time.
>
> Here are some examples of prepositions:
>
> after   at   for   on   up
>
> around   between   in   to   with

Circle the prepositions in each sentence. Some sentences have more than one preposition.

1. She walked up the stairs.

2. We ran on a path at the park.

3. I wake up at 7:00 on Saturdays.

4. She leaned against the wall.

5. The bird flew over his head.

6. I walked around the table to get my pencil.

7. My shoes are under my bed.

8. She walked across the street to see her friend.

TEACHER: Read the directions and questions to students. Guide students to complete the exercise, providing support as needed.

Name _____

> **Prepositions** combine with other words to show direction, location, and time.
>
> Here are some examples of prepositions:
>
> | after | at | for | on | up |
> |---|---|---|---|---|
> | around | between | in | to | with |

A. Circle the prepositions in each sentence. Some sentences have more than one preposition.

1. She walked up the stairs.

2. We ran on a path at the park.

3. I wake up at 7:00 on Saturdays.

B. Circle the correct prepositions in parentheses to complete the sentence.

1. I walked (around, in) the table (for, to) get my pencil.

2. My shoes are (up, under) my bed.

3. She walked (across, after) the street (to, for) see her friend.

C. Complete each sentence with a preposition that makes sense.

1. She leaned _____ the wall.

   _____

2. The bird flew _____ his head.

   _____

TEACHER: Read the directions and questions in Part A, Part B, and Part C to students. Guide students to complete each exercise, providing support as needed.

Name _____

> **Prepositional phrases** contain prepositions and one or more other words. They do not contain the subject of the sentence or the main verb.
>
> | subject | verb | prepositional phrase |
> |---------|------|----------------------|
> | My pencil | is | on the table. |

Circle the prepositional phrase in each sentence.

1. I ran with my sister.

2. We played until sunset.

3. They traveled to Paris.

4. The airplane is above the clouds.

5. School starts at 8:00 a.m.

TEACHER: Read the directions and questions to students. Guide students to complete the exercise, providing support as needed.

Name _____

> **Prepositional phrases** contain prepositions and one or more other words. They do not contain the subject of the sentence or the main verb.
>
> | subject | verb | prepositional phrase |
> |---------|------|----------------------|
> | My pencil | is | on the table. |

Circle the prepositional phrases. Some sentences have more than one prepositional phrase.

1. I ran with my sister.

2. We played until sunset.

3. The ball is beneath the bench in the park.

4. They traveled to Paris.

5. The airplane is above the clouds.

6. School starts at 8:00 in the morning.

7. Amir looks like his brother.

TEACHER: Read the directions and questions to students. Guide students to complete the exercise, providing support as needed.

Name _____

> **Prepositional phrases** contain prepositions and one or more other words.
> They do not contain the subject of the sentence or the main verb.

A. Draw a line through the subject and main verb of each sentence. Circle the prepositional phrases. Some sentences have more than one prepositional phrase.

1. I ran with my sister.

2. We played until sunset.

3. The ball is beneath the bench in the park.

4. They traveled to Paris.

5. The airplane is above the clouds.

B. Write a sentence using the prepositional phrase listed.

1. in the morning _____

   _____

   _____

2. near a lake _____

   _____

   _____

TEACHER: Read the directions and questions in Part A and Part B to students. Guide students to complete each exercise, providing support as needed.

Name _____

> **Prepositions** can be used to indicate time.
>
> *At* is for clock time: <u>at</u> 9:00   *By* means before or on: <u>by</u> Friday
>
> *On* is for calendar time: <u>on</u> Sunday   *In* means during a time: <u>in</u> July

A. **Circle the letter of the sentence that correctly uses a preposition to indicate time.**

1. Which sentence uses the preposition correctly?

   a. My birthday is on August.

   b. My birthday is in August.

   c. My birthday is at August.

   d. My birthday is by August.

2. Which sentence uses the preposition correctly?

   a. My birthday party is on 2:00.

   b. My birthday party is in 2:00.

   c. My birthday party is at 2:00.

   d. My birthday party is by 2:00.

B. **Circle the preposition that correctly completes each sentence.**

1. School ends (at, in) 3:00 every day.

2. We do not have school (on, by) Sundays.

3. We do not have school (by, in) August.

4. School usually starts (at, by) September 5th.

TEACHER: Read the directions and questions in Part A and Part B to students. Guide students to complete each exercise, providing support as needed.

Name _____

Prepositions can be used to indicate time.

At is for clock time: <u>at</u> 9:00   *By* means before or on: <u>by</u> Friday

On is for calendar time: <u>on</u> Sunday   *In* means during a time: <u>in</u> July

---

Circle the correct preposition in each sentence.

1. My birthday is (on, in, at) August.

2. My birthday is (on, in, by) August 22ⁿᵈ.

3. My birthday party is (on, in, at) Saturday.

4. My birthday party is (on, in, at) 2:00.

5. My birthday party will be over (on, in, by) 5:00.

6. School ends (on, in, at) 3:00 every day.

AUGUST

1	2	3	4	5	6	
7	8	9	10	11	12	13
14	15	16	17	18	19	20
21	22	23	24	25	26	27
28	29	30	31			

TEACHER: Read the directions and questions to students. Guide students to complete the exercise, providing support as needed.

Name _____

> **Prepositions** can be used to indicate time.
>
> *At* is for clock time: <u>at</u> 9:00   *By* means before or on: <u>by</u> Friday
>
> *On* is for calendar time: <u>on</u> Sunday   *In* means during a time: <u>in</u> July

Write the correct preposition to complete each sentence. Use *at, on, by,* or *in*. Some questions have more than one possible answer.

1. My birthday is _____ August.

2. My birthday is _____ August 22nd.

3. My birthday party is _____ Saturday.

4. My birthday party is _____ 2:00.

5. My birthday party will be over _____ 5:00.

6. We do not have school _____ August.

TEACHER: Read the directions and questions to students. Guide students to complete the exercise, providing support as needed.

Name _____

> **Prepositions** can be used to indicate place.
>
> *In* can mean "inside" or "within" a thing or place. *On* can mean "on top of" or "along a street." *At* is often used with addresses and general locations.

Circle the correct preposition in each sentence.

1. The dog is (on, at) the sofa.

2. The dog is (on, in) its doghouse.

3. Let's meet (on, at) the park.

4. Sally lives (on, in) Centerville.

5. The restaurant is (on, at) First Avenue.

TEACHER: Read the directions and questions to students. Guide students to complete the exercise, providing support as needed.

Name _____

> **Prepositions** can be used to indicate place.
>
> *In* can mean "inside" or "within" a thing or place. *On* can mean "on top of" or "along a street." *At* is often used with addresses and general locations.

Write the correct preposition on the line.

1. The dog is (on, at) the sofa. _____

2. The dog is (on, in) its doghouse. _____

3. Let's meet (on, at) the park. _____

4. Sally lives (on, in) Centerville. _____

5. The restaurant is (on, at) First Avenue. _____

6. I am (on, at) home right now. _____

7. They have many books (on, at) their shelves. _____

TEACHER: Read the directions and questions to students. Guide students to complete the exercise, providing support as needed.

Name _____

Prepositions can be used to indicate place.

In can mean "inside" or "within" a thing or place. *On* can mean "on top of" or "along a street." *At* is often used with addresses and general locations.

Write the correct preposition to complete each sentence. Use *at, on,* or *in*. Some items have more than one possible answer.

1. Let's meet _____ the park.

2. Sally lives _____ Centerville.

3. The restaurant is _____ First Avenue.

4. I am _____ home right now.

5. They have many books _____ their shelves.

6. Rahim is _____ the dentist's office.

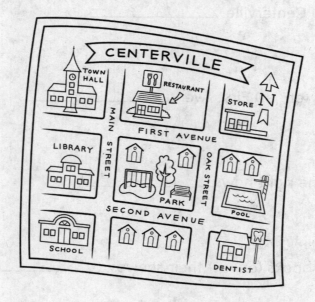

TEACHER: Read the directions and questions to students. Guide students to complete the exercise, providing support as needed.

Name _____

Some **prepositions** can indicate movement in a sentence.

- *to* = moving in the direction of a specific place and arriving

- *toward* = moving in the direction of a specific place but not arriving

- *in* and *into* = something is moving inside something else

- *across* = moving from one side to the other of something while outside it

- *through* = moving from one side to the other of something by going inside it

Circle the correct preposition in parentheses ().

1. Juan is walking (to, toward) the door.

2. Juan walked (to, toward) the door.

3. I put the key (into, to) the lock.

4. Svetlana skated (across, through) the ice.

5. The dog ran (across, through) a hole in the fence.

TEACHER: Read the directions and questions to students. Guide students to complete the exercise, providing support as needed.

Grades 4-6

Name _____

Some **prepositions** can indicate movement in a sentence.

- *to* = moving in the direction of a specific place and arriving
- *toward* = moving in the direction of a specific place but not arriving
- *in* and *into* = something is moving inside something else
- *across* = moving from one side to the other of something while outside it
- *through* = moving from one side to the other of something by going inside it

Circle the correct preposition in parentheses ().

1. Juan is walking (to, into, toward) the door.

2. Juan walked (to, into, toward) the door.

3. I put the key (into, to, across) the lock.

4. Svetlana skated (across, through, toward) the ice.

5. The dog ran (across, through, to) a hole in the fence.

6. The teacher walked (across, in, toward) the classroom.

7. The airplane flew (to, through, toward) the sky.

TEACHER: Read the directions and questions to students. Guide students to complete the exercise, providing support as needed.

Name _____

Some **prepositions** can indicate movement in a sentence.

- *to* = moving in the direction of a specific place and arriving
- *toward* = moving in the direction of a specific place but not arriving
- *in* and *into* = something is moving inside something else
- *across* = moving from one side to the other of something while outside it
- *through* = moving from one side to the other of something by going inside it

Write the correct preposition in each space. Use *to, toward, in, into, across,* or *through*.

1. Juan is walking _____ the door.

2. I put the key _____ the lock.

3. Svetlana skated _____ the ice.

4. The dog ran _____ a hole in the fence.

5. The teacher walked _____ the classroom.

6. The dog is running _____ the cat.

TEACHER: Read the directions and questions to students. Guide students to complete the exercise, providing support as needed.

Name _____

> Some **prepositions** are used to indicate direction. These include *up*, *down*, *under*, *over*, *around*, and *past*.

Circle the correct preposition in parentheses to complete each sentence.

1. Phillipe walked (past, over) the bakery.

2. The cat ran (around, under) the mouse.

3. Andrea climbed (past, up) the mountain.

4. The racers climbed (over, around) the wall.

5. The worker went (down, around) the hole.

TEACHER: Read the directions and questions to students. Guide students to complete the exercise, providing support as needed.

Name _____

Some **prepositions** are used to indicate direction. These include *up, down, under, over, around,* and *past.*

Circle the correct preposition in parentheses.

1. Phillipe walked (past, over, around) the bakery.

2. The cat ran (past, around, under) the mouse.

3. Andrea climbed (past, up, around) the mountain.

4. The racers climbed (over, around, under) the wall.

5. The worker went (down, around, under) the hole.

6. The mouse ran (past, around, under) the chair.

7. The ball went (under, around, over) her hands.

TEACHER: Read the directions and questions to students. Guide students to complete the exercise, providing support as needed.

Name _____

> Some **prepositions** are used to indicate direction. These include *up, down, under, over, around,* and *past.*

A. Rewrite each sentence with the correct preposition to match the picture. Some items can have more than one answer.

1. Phillipe walked up the bakery.

   _____

2. The cat ran under the mouse.

   _____

3. Andrea climbed past the mountain.

   _____

B. Complete each sentence with the correct preposition to match the picture. Some items can have more than one answer.

1. The racers climbed _____ the wall.

2. The worker went _____ the hole.

3. The mouse ran _____ the chair.

TEACHER: Read the directions and questions in Part A and Part B to students. Guide students to complete each exercise, providing support as needed.

Name _____

> Some **prepositions** are used to indicate location. These include *behind, in front of, between, beside, next to, near,* and *by.*

Circle the correct preposition in parentheses.

1. The dog is (in front of, between) the two girls.

2. The car is (in front of, between) the house.

3. The park bench is (behind, beside) the tree.

4. Oscar is (behind, beside) the park bench.

5. The post office is (next to, between) the bakery.

TEACHER: Read the directions and questions to students. Guide students to complete the exercise, providing support as needed.

Grades 4-6   **349**

Name _____

Some **prepositions** are used to indicate location. These include *behind, in front of, between, beside, next to, near,* and *by.*

Circle the correct preposition in parentheses to complete each sentence.

1. The dog is (in front of, between, behind) the two girls.

2. The car is (in front of, between, behind) the house.

3. The park bench is (between, behind, beside) the tree.

4. Oscar is (between, behind, beside) the park bench.

5. The post office is (next to, in front of, between) the bakery.

6. The bakery is (next to, in front of, between) the post office and the flower shop.

7. The flower shop is (beside, in front of, between) the bakery.

TEACHER: Read the directions and questions to students. Guide students to complete the exercise, providing support as needed.

Name _____

> Some **prepositions** are used to indicate location. These include *behind, in front of, between, beside, next to, near,* and *by.*

Write the correct preposition in each space. Use *behind, in front of, between, next to,* or *beside*. *Next to* and *beside* are interchangeable.

1. The dog is _____ the two girls.

2. The car is _____ the house.

3. The park bench is _____ the tree.

4. Oscar is _____ the park bench.

5. The post office is _____ the bakery.

6. The bakery is _____ the post office and the flower shop.

7. The flower shop is _____ the bakery.

TEACHER: Read the directions and questions to students. Guide students to complete the exercise, providing support as needed.

Name _____

> **Quantifiers** for count nouns: *a good number of; a great number of*
>
> Quantifiers for uncountable nouns: *a bit of; a good deal of; a great deal of*
>
> Quantifiers for all nouns: *plenty of; a lot of*

Circle the quantifier in each sentence. In the space, write *count* or *uncountable* for the underline noun.

1. There is a great deal of <u>rain</u> today. _____

2. Amanda has a good number of <u>bananas</u>. _____

3. I drink plenty of <u>milk</u>. _____

4. I would like a bit of that <u>gold</u>. _____

5. Our school has (a lot of, a bit of) <u>classrooms</u>. _____

TEACHER: Read the directions and questions to students. Guide students to complete the exercise, providing support as needed.

Name _____

> **Quantifiers** for count nouns: *a good number of; a great number of*
>
> Quantifiers for uncountable nouns: *a bit of; a good deal of; a great deal of*
>
> Quantifiers for all nouns: *plenty of; a lot of*

A. Read each sentence. Circle the letter of the sentence with the correct quantifier.

1. **a.** There is a good number of rain today.

   b. There is a great deal of rain today.

   c. There is a great number of rain today.

   d. There is just a bit of rain today.

2. **a.** Amanda has a great deal of bananas.

   b. Amanda has a good deal of bananas.

   c. Amanda has a good number of bananas.

   d. Amanda has a bit of bananas.

B. Circle the correct quantifier in parentheses to complete each sentence.

1. Our school has (a lot of, a bit of) classrooms.

2. Our classroom has (a good deal of, a good number of) students.

3. Victor's sister has (a great deal of, a great number of) hair.

4. I drink (plenty of, a good number of) milk.

TEACHER: Read the directions and questions in Part A and Part B to students. Guide students to complete each exercise, providing support as needed.

Name _____

> **Quantifiers** for count nouns: *a good number of; a great number of*
>
> Quantifiers for uncountable nouns: *a bit of; a good deal of; a great deal of*
>
> Quantifiers for all nouns: *plenty of; a lot of*

A. Circle the correct quantifier in parentheses to complete each sentence.

1. Our school has (a lot of, a bit of, a good deal of) classrooms.

2. Our classroom has (a bit of, a good deal of, a good number of) students.

3. Victor's sister has (a great deal of, a great number of, a good number of) hair.

4. I drink (plenty of, a good number of, a great number of) milk.

B. Read each sentence. Circle the letter of the sentence with the correct quantifier.

1. a. There is a good number of rain today.

   b. There is a great deal of rain today.

   c. There is a great number of rain today.

   d. There is just a bit of rain today.

2. a. Amanda has a great deal of bananas.

   b. Amanda has a good deal of bananas.

   c. Amanda has a good number of bananas.

   d. Amanda has a bit of bananas.

TEACHER: Read the directions and questions in Part A and Part B to students. Guide students to complete each exercise, providing support as needed.

Name _____

> Some **prepositions** can connect sentences: *after, as, before, since, until.*
>
> *After, as, before,* and *until* are for time. *Since* gives a reason.
>
> We ate dinner. You came home. (after) ➜ We ate dinner <u>after</u> you came home.

A. Circle the preposition that best connects the sentences and write it on the line.

1. I set the table _____ we ate dinner.
   before   after

2. I listened to music _____ I did my homework.
   as   until

3. I ran _____ I got tired.
   after   until

4. I went to bed _____ I was sleepy.
   since   until

5. I washed the dishes _____ we ate dinner.
   before   after

B. Circle the preposition.

1. I brushed my teeth before I went to bed.

2. I woke up early since I had morning practice.

Name _____

> Some **prepositions** can connect sentences: *after, as, before, since, until.*
>
> *After, as, before,* and *until* are for time. *Since* gives a reason.
>
> We ate dinner. You came home. (after) ➜ We ate dinner <u>after</u> you came home.

A.   Complete each sentence with the correct preposition.

1.   I set the table _____ we ate dinner.

2.   I listened to music _____ I did my homework.

3.   I ran _____ I got tired.

B.   Combine the two sentences with the preposition in parentheses. Write the new sentence on the line.

1.   I went to bed. I was sleepy. (since)

_____

2.   We ate dinner. Then I washed the dishes. (after)

_____

TEACHER: Read the directions and questions in Part A and Part B to students. Guide students to complete each exercise, providing support as needed.

Name _____

> Some **prepositions** can **connect sentences:** *after, as, before, since, until.*
>
> - **After, as, before,** and **until** are for time.
> - **Since** gives a reason.
>
> Example: We ate dinner. You came home. (after) → We ate dinner **after** you came home.

Use one of the prepositions in the box to combine the two sentences. Write the new sentence on the line. Use each preposition one time.

> until   before   since   after   as

1. I set the table. Then we ate dinner.

   _____

2. I listened to music. At the same time, I did my homework.

   _____

3. I studied for my test. I studied up to 10:00.

   _____

4. I went to bed. I was sleepy.

   _____

5. We ate dinner. I washed the dishes.

   _____

Name _____

> *Since* indicates beginning time. *Until* indicates ending time.
>
> *For* indicates support of something. *Against* indicates non-support.
>
> *Onto* indicates movement to a particular place or position.

A. Circle the preposition in each sentence.

1. The voting place has been open since 7:00.

2. She stuck an "I voted!" sticker onto her coat.

3. Many people voted for the new president.

4. Some people voted against the new president.

B. Circle the preposition in parentheses that completes each sentence correctly.

1. I will read here (since, until) the library closes.

2. Please move these books (until, onto) the shelf.

3. I'm reading about a march (onto, for) civil rights.

4. Martin Luther King fought (since, against) injustice.

TEACHER: Read the directions and questions in Part A and Part B to students. Guide students to complete each exercise, providing support as needed.

Name _____

Since indicates beginning time. Until indicates ending time.

For indicates support of something. Against indicates non-support.

Onto indicates movement to a particular place or position.

Circle the correct preposition to complete each sentence.

1.   The voting place has been open (since, until, onto) 7:00.

2.   She stuck an "I voted!" sticker (since, until, onto) onto her coat.

3.   Many people voted (onto, for, until) the new president.

4.   Some people voted (onto, since, against) the new president.

5.   I will read here (for, since, until) the library closes.

6.   Please move these books (since, until, onto) the shelf.

7.   I'm reading about a march (onto, for, since) civil rights.

8.   Martin Luther King fought (since, against, until) injustice.

Name _____

Since indicates beginning time. *Until* indicates ending time.

For indicates support of something. *Against* indicates non-support.

Onto indicates movement to a particular place or position.

Write the correct preposition to complete each sentence. Use *since, until, for, against,* or *onto*. Some questions have more than one possible answer.

1. The voting place has been open _____ 7:00.

2. She stuck an "I voted!" sticker _____ her coat.

3. Many people voted _____ the new president.

4. Some people voted _____ the new president.

5. I will read here _____ the library closes.

6. Please move these books _____ the shelf.

TEACHER: Read the directions and questions to students. Guide students to complete the exercise, providing support as needed.

Name _____

> Some English phrases are made up of a verb and a preposition used with a special meaning.
>
> We <u>depend on</u> the subway.   We <u>complain about</u> the crowds.

Circle the phrase that best completes each sentence. Then write the phrase on the line.

1. We _____ our ride.
   pay for   pay at

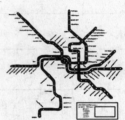

2. We _____ a destination.
   decide of   decide on

3. You _____ my plan.
   agree for   agree with

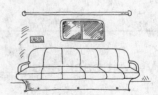

4. I _____ a seat.
   search for   search on

5. We _____ a long ride.
   prepare of   prepare for

Copyright © McGraw-Hill Education

Name _____

Some English phrases are made up of a verb and a preposition used with a special meaning.

We <u>depend on</u> the subway.

Complete each sentence by adding a phrase from the box. Then write the sentence correctly. Use each phrase only once.

| prepare for | refer to | pay for | warn about | insist on |

1. We _____ a ticket at the booth.

_____

2. You _____ paying me back.

_____

3. We _____ the map to find our stop.

_____

4. Signs _____ the dangers of standing too close.

_____

5. We sit back and _____ a long ride to Brooklyn.

_____

Name _____

> Some English phrases are made up of a verb and a preposition used with a special meaning.

Circle the verb-preposition combination in each sentence. Then rewrite the passage so that each verb goes with the correct preposition.

1. We pay on a ticket at the booth. You insist at paying me back. I refer on a map to find our stop. Signs warn to the dangers of standing too close to the edge. Finally, we arrive for our destination

_____

_____

_____

_____

_____

_____

TEACHER: Read the directions and questions to students. Guide students to complete the exercise, providing support as needed.

Grades 4-6   363

Name _____

Some English phrases are made up of an adjective and a preposition used with a special meaning. The combination follows a form of the verb *to be*.

We are <u>pleased with</u> our new house.   It is <u>protected from</u> the rain.

Circle the phrase that completes each sentence. Then write the phrase.

1. Dad is _____ his building skills.

   known for   known about

2. Our treehouse is _____ wood.

   made of   made on

3. Are you _____ heights?

   afraid for   afraid of

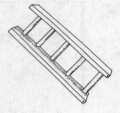

4. I am _____ building, too.

   interested in   interested of

5. Soon our house will be _____ friends.

   filled of   filled with

TEACHER: Read the directions and questions to students. Guide students to complete the exercise, providing support as needed.

Name _____

> Some English phrases are made up of an adjective and a preposition used with a special meaning. The combination follows a form of the verb *to be*.
>
> We are <u>pleased with</u> our new house.

Complete each sentence by adding a phrase from the box. Then write the sentence correctly. Use each phrase only once.

> afraid of   related to   patient with   made of   known for

1. Manny is _____ his fine building skills.

   _____

2. Are you _____ climbing tall ladders?

   _____

3. Manny is _____ me on my mother's side.

   _____

4. Our treehouse will be _____ scrap wood.

   _____

5. Be _____ Manny as he finishes the job.

   _____

TEACHER: Read the directions and questions to students. Guide students to complete the exercise, providing support as needed.

Name _____

> Some English phrases are made up of an adjective and a preposition used with a special meaning. The combination follows a form of the verb *to be*.

Circle the adjective-preposition combination in each sentence. Then rewrite the passage so that each adjective goes with the correct preposition.

1. Manny is related for me on my mother's side. He is known with his fine building skills. Are you afraid with climbing tall ladders? Don't be worried to Manny. He is equipped about safety gear.

_____

_____

_____

_____

_____

_____

TEACHER: Read the directions and questions to students. Guide students to complete the exercise, providing support as needed.

Name _____

A coordinating conjunction joins words or groups of words of the same kind.

ADDITION: Maria <u>and</u> Sara visited the nurse.

CONTRAST: Maria had a headache, <u>but</u> Sara felt fine.

CHOICE: The nurse told Maria to lie down <u>or</u> go home.

Circle the conjunction. Write _N_ if it connects nouns. Write _V_ if it connects verbs. Write _S_ if it connects sentences.

1. Ron tripped or fell on the playground. _____

2. He hurt himself, but the nurse helped him. _____

3. His arm and leg are bandaged now. _____

4. He will rest and go back to class. _____

5. Sara or Jane will carry his books. _____

Name _____

A coordinating conjunction joins words or groups of words of the same kind.

ADDITION: Maria <u>and</u> Sara visited the nurse.

CONTRAST: Maria had a headache, <u>but</u> Sara felt fine.

CHOICE: The nurse told Maria to lie down <u>or</u> go home.

Finish each sentence with the conjunction *or, and,* or *but*. Use the clue to choose the correct conjunction.

1. **choice**   Ron tripped _____ fell on the playground.

2. **contrast**   He hurt himself, _____ the nurse helped him.

3. **addition**   His arm _____ leg are bandaged now.

4. **addition**   He will rest _____ go back to class.

5. **choice**   Sara _____ I will carry his books.

6. **contrast**   Ron is brave, _____ his leg hurts.

TEACHER: Read the directions and questions to students. Guide students to complete the exercise, providing support as needed.

Name _____

> A coordinating conjunction joins words or groups of words of the same kind.

Ron's Accident

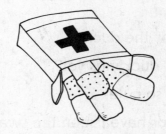

Ron fell or tripped on the playground.	1
He hurt himself, but the nurse helped him.	2
She bandaged his leg and arm.	3
He was brave, but his leg hurt a lot.	4
The nurse called Ron's mother and told her what happened.	5
Ron will rest and then head back to class.	6
Sara or another friend will carry his books.	7
We are sorry he was hurt but glad he feels better.	8

1. **Circle all of the coordinating conjunctions.**

2. **Answer each question with the line numbers from the story.**

   Which sentences show a contrast? _____

   Which sentences show a choice? _____

   Which sentences show an addition? _____

Name _____

> The words *nor, so, for,* and *yet* may be used as conjunctions that connect sentences.
>
> The sun was shining, <u>so</u> we went to the park.

A. Circle the letter of the sentence that contains a conjunction.

1. **a.** I brought some bread for the ducks.

    b. Have you seen the baby ducklings yet?

    c. Their fluffy feathers are so cute!

    d. I have not seen them, nor have I seen the swans.

2. **a.** I can swing so high up in the sky!

    b. You fear heights, yet you love to swing.

    c. Some swings are for younger children.

    d. So many children enjoy swinging!

B. Circle the conjunction in parentheses that completes each sentence correctly.

1. The park is nearby, (so/yet) we can walk there.

2. You won't need your jacket, (for/nor) will I need boots.

3. The weather is warm, (yet/for) spring is here at last!

4. It is early May, (nor/yet) it feels like late June.

TEACHER: Read the directions and questions in Part A and Part B to students. Guide students to complete each exercise, providing support as needed.

Name _____

> The words *nor, so, for,* and *yet* may be used as conjunctions that connect sentences.
>
> The sun was shining, <u>so</u> we went to the park.

A. Circle the letter of each sentence with a conjunction.

1. **a.** Have you seen the baby ducklings yet?

   b. I have not seen them, nor have I seen the swans.

   c. The ducklings are cute, for their feathers are fluffy.

2. **a.** You fear heights, yet you love to swing.

   b. Are those small swings for younger children?

   c. You are small, so you can swing there, too.

B. Circle the conjunction in parentheses that completes each sentence correctly. Then write the sentence correctly on the line.

1. The park is nearby, (so/yet) we can walk there.

   _____

2. The weather is warm, (nor/for) spring is here at last!

   _____

3. It is early May, (yet/nor) it feels like late June.

   _____

TEACHER: Read the directions and questions in Part A and Part B to students. Guide students to complete each exercise, providing support as needed.

Name _____

> The words *nor, so, for,* and *yet* may be used as conjunctions that connect sentences.
>
> The sun was shining, <u>so</u> we went to the park.

Make each sentence make sense by adding *nor, so, for,* or *yet*. Then rewrite the sentences correctly.

1. The ducklings look cute, _____ their feathers are fluffy.

   _____

   _____

2. The swans are beautiful, _____ they scare me a little.

   _____

   _____

3. They pecked me once, _____ now I stay away from them.

   _____

   _____

TEACHER: Read the directions and questions to students. Guide students to complete the exercise, providing support as needed.

Name _____

Sometimes **conjunctions** come in pairs and are used together.

<u>Both</u> rivers <u>and</u> lakes are bodies of water.

Our local streams flow <u>either</u> east <u>or</u> west.

That river <u>neither</u> floods <u>nor</u> dries up.

Underline the conjunctions in each sentence.

1. This fish is neither too big nor too small.

2. I will need both my hat and my sunglasses.

3. I will fish either for trout or for perch.

4. People fish either from the pier or from a boat.

5. Neither a turtle nor a fish tugged on my line.

6. The sun made me both sleepy and hot.

TEACHER: Read the directions and questions to students. Guide students to complete
the exercise, providing support as needed.

Name _____

Sometimes **conjunctions** come in pairs and are used together.

<u>Both</u> rivers <u>and</u> lakes are bodies of water.

Our local streams flow <u>either</u> east <u>or</u> west.

That river <u>neither</u> floods <u>nor</u> dries up.

Write the missing part of each conjunction in the blank.

1. This fish is neither too big _____ too small.

2. I will need both my hat _____ my sunglasses.

3. I will fish either for trout _____ for perch.

4. People fish _____ from the pier or from a boat.

5. _____ a turtle nor a fish tugged on my line.

6. The sun made me _____ sleepy and hot.

TEACHER: Read the directions and questions to students. Guide students to complete the exercise, providing support as needed.

Name _____

> Sometimes **conjunctions** come in pairs and are used together.
>
> <u>Both</u> rivers <u>and</u> lakes are bodies of water.
>
> Our local streams flow <u>either</u> east <u>or</u> west.
>
> That river <u>neither</u> floods <u>nor</u> dries up.

Rewrite each sentence on the lines using appropriate conjunctions to fill in the blanks.

1. A stream is _____ as long _____ as wide as a river.

   _____

   _____

2. All oceans _____ have tides _____ are salty.

   _____

   _____

3. A pond may be _____ natural _____ manmade.

   _____

   _____

TEACHER: Read the directions and questions to students. Guide students to complete the exercise, providing support as needed.

Grades 4-6

Name _____

> Sometimes conjunctions come in pairs and are used together.
>
> <u>Not only</u> is the play sad, <u>but</u> it is <u>also</u> confusing.
>
> I don't know <u>whether</u> to laugh <u>or</u> cry.

Underline the conjunctions in each sentence.

1. That character is not only odd-looking but also loud.

2. Whether he is the hero or the villain is hard to tell.

3. I am not only confused, but I am also bored.

4. Not only is this a mystery, but it is also a comedy.

5. Whether you like it or hate it, you will find it strange.

6. I am not sure whether to recommend it or not.

TEACHER: Read the directions and questions to students. Guide students to complete the exercise, providing support as needed.

Name _____

> Sometimes conjunctions come in pairs and are used together.
>
> <u>Not only</u> is the play sad, <u>but</u> it is <u>also</u> confusing.
>
> I don't know <u>whether</u> to laugh <u>or</u> cry.

Write the missing part of each conjunction in the blank.

1. That character is not only odd-looking _____ loud.

2. Whether he is the hero _____ the villain is hard to tell.

3. I am _____ confused, but I am also bored.

4. _____ is this a mystery, but it is also a comedy.

5. _____ you like it or hate it, you will find it strange.

6. I am not sure _____ to recommend it or not.

Name _____

> Sometimes conjunctions come in pairs and are used together.
>
> Not only is the play sad, but it is also confusing.
>
> I don't know whether to laugh or cry.

Rewrite each sentence on the lines using appropriate conjunctions to fill in the blanks.

1. That character is _____ odd-looking _____ loud.

   _____

   _____

2. _____ he is the hero _____ the villain is hard to tell.

   _____

   _____

3. _____ is this a mystery, _____ it is _____ a comedy.

   _____

   _____

TEACHER: Read the directions and questions to students. Guide students to complete the exercise, providing support as needed.

Name _____

> A **subordinating conjunction** introduces an adverb clause. It connects that clause to the rest of the sentence.
>
> <u>Because</u> it is spring, I am planting my garden.
>
> I plant peas <u>even though</u> I don't like them.
>
> <u>Although</u> I will not eat them, my family will.

Underline the adverb clause. Circle the subordinating conjunction that introduces the clause.

1. Peas are great because they grow fast.

2. Although I love carrots, they are hard to grow.

3. Because they are dry, I will water my plants.

4. Even though it is hot, everything is growing well.

5. Although it is too soon, I want to taste my crop.

6. I picked a tomato even though it was not ripe.

TEACHER: Read the directions and questions to students. Guide students to complete the exercise, providing support as needed.

Name _____

> A **subordinating conjunction** introduces an adverb clause. It connects that clause to the rest of the sentence.
>
> <u>Because</u> it is spring, I am planting my garden.
>
> I plant peas <u>even though</u> I don't like them.
>
> <u>Although</u> I will not eat them, my family will.

A. Circle the letter of each sentence with a subordinating conjunction. Then underline the subordinating conjunction.

1. **a.** Peas are great because they grow fast.

    b. The green pods dangle from the vines.

    c. Although they look ready, they are not ripe.

2. **a.** The sun is bringing heat and light to the garden.

    b. Even though it is hot, my plants are growing well.

    c. Because they are dry, I will water my plants.

B. Add an adverb clause to each sentence. Start with the word(s) in parentheses. Use commas correctly. Write the new sentence on the line.

1. _____ I like carrots. (Even though)

    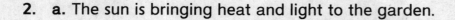

2. _____ I planted some flowers. (Because)

    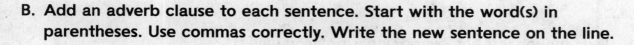

TEACHER: Read the directions and questions in Part A and Part B to students. Guide students to complete each exercise, providing support as needed.

Name _____

A **subordinating conjunction** introduces an adverb clause. It connects that clause to the rest of the sentence.

<u>Because</u> it is spring, I am planting my garden.

I plant peas <u>even though</u> I don't like them.

<u>Although</u> I will not eat them, my family will.

Read each sentence. Add an adverb clause that begins with the subordinating conjunction in parentheses. Write the new sentence.

1.   I like carrots. (even though)

_____

_____

2.   I planted some flowers. (because)

_____

_____

3.   My garden looks lovely. (although)

_____

_____

TEACHER: Read the directions and questions to students. Guide students to complete the exercise, providing support as needed.

Name _____

> **Subordinating conjunctions** introduce adverb clauses. The clauses may appear at the beginning or end of a sentence. Each clause contains a subject and a verb.
>
> It has been six months <u>since</u> I saw the dentist.
> <u>While</u> I wait, I read a magazine.

Circle the word or phrase that correctly describes how the underline word is being used.

1. <u>After</u> my appointment, we will go shopping.

    conjunction   not a conjunction

2. <u>By the time</u> I finish here, it will be lunchtime.

    conjunction   not a conjunction

3. Mom waits <u>while</u> the dentist works on me.

    conjunction   not a conjunction

4. Nurse Jane took X-rays <u>after</u> she cleaned my teeth.

    conjunction   not a conjunction

5. <u>Since</u> last year, I have seen Doctor Ruiz once.

    conjunction   not a conjunction

6. I may need braces <u>by the time</u> I turn 12.

    conjunction   not a conjunction

TEACHER: Read the directions and questions to students. Guide students to complete the exercise, providing support as needed.

Name _____

> **Subordinating conjunctions** introduce adverb clauses. The clauses may appear at the beginning or end of a sentence. Each clause contains a subject and a verb.
>
> It has been six months <u>since</u> I saw the dentist.
> <u>While</u> I wait, I read a magazine.

A. Circle the letter of each sentence with a subordinating conjunction. Then underline the subordinating conjunction.

1. a. Nurse Jane took X-rays after she cleaned my teeth.

    b. After my appointment, we will go shopping.

    c. After we shop, it will be time for lunch.

2. a. Since last year, I have seen Dr. Ruiz once.

    b. Since I lost my baby teeth, I have had no cavities.

    c. My gums have been healthy since I started flossing.

B. Add an adverb clause to each sentence. Start with the word or words in parentheses. Use commas correctly. Write the new sentence on the line.

1. _____ I may need braces. (By the time)

_____

_____

2. _____ Mom waits for me. (While)

_____

_____

TEACHER: Read the directions and questions in Part A and Part B to students. Guide students to complete each exercise, providing support as needed.

Name _____

> **Subordinating conjunctions** introduce adverb clauses. The clauses may appear at the beginning or end of a sentence. Each clause contains a subject and a verb.
>
> It has been six months <u>since</u> I saw the dentist.
> <u>While</u> I wait, I read a magazine.

Read each sentence. Add an adverb clause that begins with the subordinating conjunction in parentheses. Write the new sentence.

1. The nurse takes x-rays. (after)

   _____

   _____

2. I may need braces. (by the time)

   _____

   _____

3. Mom sits in the waiting room. (while)

   _____

   _____

TEACHER: Read the directions and questions to students. Guide students to complete the exercise, providing support as needed.

Name _____

> A **conjunctive adverb** may connect ideas in a sentence or between sentences. When a conjunctive adverb comes in the middle of a sentence, a semicolon comes before it, and a comma comes after it.
>
> The wind was fierce; <u>however,</u> it had not begun to rain.

Underline the conjunctive adverb in each sentence.

1. I ran to the barn; meanwhile, Dad closed the windows.

2. Thunder boomed; however, the lightning was far away.

3. My horse whinnied; also, the cows mooed unhappily.

4. The wind was wild; however, this was not a tornado.

5. The lights went out; meanwhile, Dad lit a fire.

6. The animals were safe; likewise, we were protected.

TEACHER: Read the directions and questions to students. Guide students to complete the exercise, providing support as needed.

Name _____

A **conjunctive adverb** may connect ideas in a sentence or between sentences. When a conjunctive adverb comes in the middle of a sentence, a semicolon comes before it, and a comma comes after it.

The wind was fierce; however, it had not begun to rain.

A. Rewrite each sentence, punctuating it correctly.

1. I ran to the barn meanwhile Dad closed the windows.

   _____

2. Thunder boomed however the lightning was far away.

   _____

3. My horse whinnied also the cows mooed unhappily.

   _____

4. The animals were safe likewise we were protected.

   _____

B. Complete each sentence with an appropriate conjunctive adverb. Choose from *however, likewise,* and *meanwhile*. Use each adverb only once.

1. The wind was strong; _____, this was not a tornado.

2. We heard a crash; _____, the power went out.

3. We lost two trees; _____, our neighbors lost a tree.

TEACHER: Read the directions and questions in Part A and Part B to students. Guide students to complete each exercise, providing support as needed.

Name _____

> A **conjunctive adverb** may connect ideas in a sentence or between
> sentences. When a conjunctive adverb comes in the middle of a sentence,
> a semicolon comes before it, and a comma comes after it.

Circle the conjunctive adverbs in this paragraph. Then rewrite the paragraph, punctuating it correctly.

1. Thunder boomed however the lightning was far away. We heard a crash meanwhile the power went out. My horse whinnied in the barn also the cows mooed unhappily. The animals were safe likewise we were protected. We lost a few trees however it could have been worse.

_____

_____

_____

_____

_____

TEACHER: Read the directions and questions to students. Guide students to complete the exercise, providing support as needed.

Grades 4-6   **387**

Name _____

> **Conjunctive adverbs** may be used to connect ideas in a sentence or between sentences.
>
> then = after that   moreover = in addition
> finally = at last   nevertheless = even so

A.   Circle the conjunctive adverb. Then write it in the blank.

1.   I dusted the furniture; moreover, I dusted the piano.

_____

2.   The piano was heavy; nevertheless, we moved it.

_____

3.   I swept behind it; then, we moved the piano back.

_____

B.   Underline the conjunctive adverb in each sentence. Then circle its meaning

1.   I washed the dishes; moreover, I scrubbed the pots.

   even so   in addition

2.   You dried the dishes; finally, you put them away.

   at last   after that

3.   The room was clean; nevertheless, we had more to do.

   even so   in addition

4.   We took a break; then, we swept the porch outside.

   at last   after that

TEACHER: Read the directions and questions in Part A and Part B to students. Guide students to complete each exercise, providing support as needed.

Name _____

> **Conjunctive adverbs** may be used to connect ideas in a sentence or between sentences.
>
> then = after that   moreover = in addition
> finally = at last   nevertheless = even so

Complete each sentence with the correct conjunctive adverb.

1. I dusted the furniture; _____, I dusted the piano.

2. The piano was heavy; _____, we moved it.

3. We pushed and pulled; _____, the piano rolled away.

4. The piano is old; _____, it hadn't been moved in years.

5. It was dusty back there; _____, I did my best.

6. I swept behind it; _____ we moved the piano back.

TEACHER: Read the directions and questions to students. Guide students to complete the exercise, providing support as needed.

Name _____

> **Conjunctive adverbs** may be used to connect ideas in a sentence or between sentences.
>
> | then = after that | moreover = in addition |
> |---|---|
> | finally = at last | nevertheless = even so |

A. Complete each sentence with a conjunctive adverb that has the meaning given in parentheses.

1. I dusted the furniture; _____, I dusted the piano. (in addition)

2. The piano was heavy; _____, we moved it. (even so)

3. We pushed and pulled; _____, the piano rolled away. (at last)

4. The piano is old; _____, it had been there for a long time. (in addition)

5. I swept behind it; _____ we moved the piano back. (after that)

B. Choose three conjunctive adverbs from your work above. Use them in three new sentences. Be sure to punctuate the sentences correctly.

1. _____

   _____

2. _____

   _____

3. _____

   _____

TEACHER: Read the directions and questions in Part A and Part B to students. Guide students to complete each exercise, providing support as needed.

Name _____

> The expressions *as well as, of course, on the other hand, in order to*, and *as soon as* show different types of relationships in a text.
>
> *As soon as* shows order of events. *As well as* shows addition. *In order to* shows cause and effect. *On the other hand* shows contrasting options or ideas. *Of course* shows that something is clear or obvious.

Circle the transitional phrase that correctly completes each sentence.

1. We practiced hard (as soon as/in order to) win the soccer game.

2. I would like to visit California on my vacation. (As well as/On the other hand), I might want to visit Maine.

3. Dar will mow the lawn (as soon as/as well as) she is done with her homework.

4. Kerry and Will performed flawlessly in the singing competition. (On the other hand/Of course), they had spent many hours practicing.

5. I am sure you will like the green tea (in order to/ as well as) the black tea.

TEACHER: Read the directions and questions to students. Guide students to complete the exercise, providing support as needed.

Name _____

The expressions *as well as, of course, on the other hand, in order to,* and *as soon as* show different types of relationships in a text.

As soon as shows order of events. *As well as* shows addition. *In order to* shows cause and effect. *On the other hand* shows contrasting options or ideas. *Of course* shows that something is clear or obvious.

A. Circle the transitional phrase that best completes each sentence.

1. We practiced hard (as soon as/in order to) win the soccer game.

2. I would like to visit California on my vacation. (As well as/On the other hand), I might want to visit Maine.

3. Kerry and Will performed flawlessly in the singing competition. (On the other hand/Of course), they had spent many hours practicing.

B. Write the transitional phrase that best completes each sentence.

1. Dar will mow the lawn _____ she is done with her homework.

2. I am sure you will like the green tea _____ the black tea.

3. Sandwiches sound yummy. _____ , I might choose a green salad.

TEACHER: Read the directions and questions in Part A and Part B to students. Guide students to complete each exercise, providing support as needed.

Name _____

> The expressions *as well as, of course, on the other hand, in order to,* and *as soon as* show different types of relationships in a text.
>
> *As soon as* shows order of events. *As well as* shows addition. *In order to* shows cause and effect. *On the other hand* shows contrasting options or ideas. *Of course* shows that something is clear or obvious.

A. Write the transitional phrase that completes each sentence.

1. We practiced hard _____ win the soccer game.

2. I would like to visit California on my vacation. _____, I might want to visit Maine.

3. Kerry and Will performed flawlessly in the singing competition. _____, they had spent many hours practicing.

4. Dar will mow the lawn _____ she is done with her homework.

5. I am sure you will like the green tea _____ the black tea.

B. Choose two of the transitional phrases you wrote above. Use them in two new sentences.

1. _____

_____

2. _____

_____

Name _____

> The expressions *consequently, in conclusion, in the same way,* and *by the time* show different types of relationships in a text.
>
> *In the same way* shows a similarity in actions.
>
> *By the time* shows order of events.
>
> *Consequently* shows a logical result.
>
> *In conclusion* is used to sum up many points.

Write the transitional phrase that correctly begins each sentence.

1. _____ Mary noticed the sink was leaking, there was a puddle on the floor. (By the time/Consequently)

2. It was sunny and warm out. We went to the beach. We made a sandcastle. _____, it was a perfect summer day. (In the same way/In conclusion)

3. I forgot to water the garden. _____, the plants wilted. (In conclusion/Consequently)

4. Learning an instrument takes hard work. _____, learning a new language takes time and patience. (In conclusion/In the same way)

5. Kate brought an umbrella. _____, she didn't get wet when it began to rain. (In conclusion/Consequently)

TEACHER: Read the directions and questions to students. Guide students to complete the exercise, providing support as needed.

Name _____

> The expressions *consequently, in conclusion, in the same way,* and *by the time* show different types of relationships in a text.
>
> *In the same way* shows a similarity in actions.
>
> *By the time* shows order of events.
>
> *Consequently* shows a logical result.
>
> *In conclusion* is used to sum up many points.

A. Circle the transitional phrase that best begins each sentence.

1. (By the time/Consequently) Mary noticed the sink was leaking, there was a puddle on the floor.

2. It was sunny and warm out. We went to the beach. We made a sandcastle. (In the same way/In conclusion), it was a perfect summer day.

3. I forgot to water the garden. (In conclusion/ Consequently), the plants wilted.

B. Write the transitional phrase that best begins each sentence.

1. Learning an instrument takes hard work.

    _____, learning a new language takes time and patience.

2. Kate brought an umbrella. _____, she didn't get wet when it began to rain.

3. _____ we put up the tent, it was time to cook dinner.

TEACHER: Read the directions and questions in Part A and Part B to students. Guide students to complete each exercise, providing support as needed.

Name _____

> The expressions *consequently, in conclusion, in the same way,* and *by the time* show different types of relationships in a text.
>
> > *In the same way* shows a similarity in actions.
> >
> > *By the time* shows order of events.
> >
> > *Consequently* shows a logical result.
> >
> > *In conclusion* is used to sum up many points.

A. **Circle the transitional phrase that best begins each sentence.**

1. (By the time/Consequently) Mary noticed the sink was leaking, there was a puddle on the floor.

2. It was sunny and warm out. We went to the beach. We made a sandcastle. (In the same way/In conclusion), it was a perfect summer day.

3. I forgot to water the garden. (In conclusion/Consequently), the plants wilted.

B. **Write the transitional phrase that best begins each sentence.**

1. Learning an instrument takes hard work. _____ , learning a new language takes time and patience.

2. Kate didn't bring an umbrella. _____ , she got wet when it began to rain.

C. **Complete each paragraph.**

1. We fixed the roof. Next, we painted the walls. Then, we cleaned the windows and floors. In conclusion, _____ .

2. On the way to school, we got a flat tire. It took a long time to put the new tire on the car. Consequently, _____ .

TEACHER: Read the directions and questions in Part A, Part B, and Part C to students. Guide students to complete each exercise, providing support as needed.

Name _____

> Use *Who* to ask questions about a person or people.
>
> Use *Where* to ask questions about the location of a person, place, or thing.
>
> Use *What* to ask questions about a topic, such as an object or idea.
>
> Use *Why* to ask for a reason.

A. Circle the letter of the word that correctly completes each question.

1. _____ did you bring so many cookies to the meeting?

   a. Who   **b.** What   **c.** Where   **d.** Why

2. _____ is the best place to start looking for the keys?

   a. Who   **b.** What   **c.** Where   **d.** Why

3. _____ do you think will win the Spelling Bee?

   a. Who   **b.** What   **c.** Where   **d.** Why

B. Choose the word to correctly begin each question.

1. (Who/Where) is your favorite singer?

2. (When/Why) did you wear a coat on such a hot day?

3. (Who/When) will we fix the car?

4. (Who/Where) are my glasses?

Name _____

Use *Who* to ask questions about a person or people.

Use *Where* to ask questions about the location of a person, place, or thing.

Use *What* to ask questions about a topic, such as an object or idea.

Use *Why* to ask for a reason.

A. Circle the letter of the word that correctly completes each question.

1. _____ is your favorite singer?

   a. Who

   b. What

   c. Where

   d. Why

2. _____ did you wear a coat on such a hot day?

   a. Who

   b. What

   c. Where

   d. Why

B. Write a word from the box that correctly completes each question.

Who	Where	Why	When

1. _____ will we eat? I hope it is soon!

2. _____ did you bring so many cookies to the meeting?

3. _____ is the best place to start looking for the keys?

4. _____ do you think will win the Spelling Bee?

TEACHER: Read the directions and questions in Part A and Part B to students. Guide students to complete each exercise, providing support as needed.

Name _____

> Use *Who* to ask questions about a person or people.
>
> Use *Where* to ask questions about the location of a person, place, or thing.
>
> Use *What* to ask questions about a topic, such as an object or idea.
>
> Use *Why* to ask for a reason.

A. Circle the word that best completes each question.

1. (When/Who) is your favorite singer?

2. (Where/Why) did you wear a coat on such a hot day?

3. (Why/When) will we eat? I hope it is soon!

B. Write *Who, When, Why,* or *Where* to best complete each question.

1. _____ did you bring so many cookies to the meeting?

2. _____ is the best place to start looking for the keys?

3. _____ do you think will win the Spelling Bee?

C. Read each statement. Write a question that can be answered with the statement. Use *Who, When, Why,* or *Where* to begin your question.

1. Nan ate the last pickle.

   _____

2. We ate our picnic at Marshfield Park.

   _____

Name _____

> Use *how many* to ask about a specific number of items.
>
> How many dollars do you have?   How many cups of milk should I add?
>
> Use *how much* to ask about an amount of something you can't count as individual pieces.
>
> How much money do you have?   How much milk should I add?

Choose the words that correctly begin each question.

1. (How many/How much) gasoline do you need?

2. (How many/How much) pepper is in the peppershaker?

3. (How many/How much) children are in the pool?

4. (How many/How much) paper cups do we need?

5. (How many/How much) spaghetti should I make?

TEACHER: Read the directions and questions to students. Guide students to complete the exercise, providing support as needed.

Name _____

Use *how many* to ask about a specific number of items.

  <u>How many dollars</u> do you have?   <u>How many cups</u> of milk should I add?

Use *how much* to ask about an amount of something you can't count as individual pieces.

      <u>How much money</u> do you have?   <u>How much milk</u> should I add?

A. Circle *How many* or *How much* to correctly begin each question.

1. (How many/How much) gasoline do you need?

2. (How many/How much) pepper is in the peppershaker?

3. (How many/How much) children are in the pool?

B. Write *How many* or *How much* to correctly begin each question.

1. _____ spaghetti should I make?

2. _____ hats are on the hat rack?

3. _____ rolls are in the basket?

TEACHER: Read the directions and questions in Part A and Part B to students. Guide students to complete each exercise, providing support as needed.

Name _____

> Use *how many* to ask about a specific number of items.
>
> How many dollars do you have?   How many cups of milk should I add?
>
> Use *how much* to ask about an amount of something you can't count as individual pieces.
>
> How much money do you have?   How much milk should I add?

A. Circle *How many* or *How much* to correctly begin each question.

1. (How many/How much) gasoline do you need?

2. (How many/How much) pepper is in the peppershaker?

3. (How many/How much) paper cups do we need?

B. Write *How many* or *How much* to correctly begin each question.

1. _____ spaghetti should I make?

2. _____ hats are on the hat rack?

3. _____ rolls are in the basket?

C. Read each statement. Write a question that can be answered with the statement. Use *How many* or *How much* to begin your question.

1. There are fifteen children in the pool.

   _____

2. We should make two liters of lemonade.

   _____

TEACHER: Read the directions and questions in Part A, Part B, and Part C to students. Guide students to complete each exercise, providing support as needed.

Name _____

To form questions using the words *Was there, Were there, Is there,* and *Are there,* reverse the word order used in the question.

Question	*Yes* Answer	*No* Answer
Was there...	Yes, there was...	No, there wasn't...
Were there...	Yes, there were...	No, there weren't...
Is there...	Yes, there is...	No, there isn't...
Are there...	Yes, there are...	No, there aren't...

A. **Look at the picture. Then write the words that correctly answer the question.**

1. Are there eggs in the package? Yes,

   _____ eggs in the package.

2. Is there a coat in the closet? No,

   _____ a coat in the closet.

3. Were there many children in the art class? Yes,

   _____ many children in the art class.

B. **Choose the words that correctly complete each question.**

1. (Was there, Were there) any candy left? No, there wasn't any candy left.

2. (Is there, Were there) any problems with your computer? No, there weren't any problems with my computer.

3. (Are there, Was there) six pieces of pizza? No, there aren't. There are only four pieces of pizza.

TEACHER: Read the directions and questions in Part A and Part B to students. Guide students to complete each exercise, providing support as needed.

Grades 4-6   **403**

Name _____

To form questions using the words *Was there, Were there, Is there,* and *Are there,* reverse the word order used in the question.

Question	*Yes* Answer	*No* Answer
Was there...	Yes, there was...	No, there wasn't...
Were there...	Yes, there were...	No, there weren't...
Is there...	Yes, there is...	No, there isn't...
Are there...	Yes, there are...	No, there aren't...

A. Look at the picture. Then write the words that correctly answer the question.

1. Are there eggs in the package? Yes,

   _____ eggs in the package.

2. Is there a coat in the closet? No,

   _____ a coat in the closet.

3. Were there many children in the art class? Yes,

   _____ many children in the art class.

B. Rewrite each question and statement in the past tense. Change the underlined words.

1. <u>Are</u> there many people at the museum? Yes, there <u>are</u>.

   _____

2. <u>Are</u> there any problems with your computer? No, there <u>are not</u>.

   _____

3. <u>Is</u> there an empty seat on the bus? No, there <u>is not</u>.

   _____

TEACHER: Read the directions and questions in Part A and Part B to students. Guide students to complete each exercise, providing support as needed.

Name _____

> To form questions using the words *Was there*, *Were there*, *Is there*, and *Are there*, reverse the word order used in the question.

A. Circle the words that correctly complete each question.

1. (Was there, Were there) any candy left? No, there wasn't any candy left.

2. (Is there, Were there) any problems with your computer?
    No, there weren't any problems with my computer.

3. (Are there, Was there) six pieces of pizza? No, there aren't.
    There are only four pieces of pizza.

B. Write the words that complete the question.

1. Are there eggs in the package? Yes, _____ eggs in the package.

    _____

2. Is there a coat in the closet? No, _____ a coat in the closet.

    _____

**C. Rewrite each question and statement in the past tense.
    Change the underlined words.**

1. <u>Are</u> there many people at the museum? Yes, there <u>are</u>.

    _____

2. <u>Is</u> there an empty seat on the bus? No, there <u>is not</u>.

    _____

TEACHER: Read the directions and questions in Part A, Part B, and Part C to
students. Guide students to complete each exercise, providing support as needed.

Name _____

> To answer questions that begin with *Will there be, Has there been,* and *Have there been,* change the word order used in the question.
>
> | Question | *Yes* Answer | *No* Answer |
> |---|---|---|
> | Will there be... | There will be... | There won't be... |
> | Has there been... | There has been... | There hasn't been... |
> | Have there been... | There have been... | There haven't been... |

A. Look at the picture. Then circle the words that correctly complete the answer to the question.

1. Will there be food at the picnic? Yes, there (will/won't) be food at the picnic.

2. Have there been many storms this summer? No, there (hasn't/haven't) been many storms this summer.

3. Will there be any bread at the market? No, there (will/won't) be any bread at the market.

4. Has there been an accident on the road? No, there (hasn't/haven't) been an accident on the road.

B. Choose the words that correctly complete the question.

1. (Will there be, Have there been) a second movie?
    No, there won't be a second movie.

2. (Have there been, Has there been) any rain?
    No, there hasn't been any rain.

3. (Have there been, Has there been) many complaints?
    No, there haven't been many complaints.

TEACHER: Read the directions and questions in Part A and Part B to students. Guide students to complete each exercise, providing support as needed.

Name _____

To answer questions that begin with *Will there be, Has there been,* and *Have there been,* change the word order used in the question.

Question	*Yes* Answer	*No* Answer
Will there be…	There will be…	There won't be…
Has there been…	There has been…	There hasn't been…
Have there been…	There have been…	There haven't been…

A. Look at the picture and read the question. Write the words that correctly complete the answer.

1. Will there be ants at the picnic? Yes, _____ be ants at the picnic.

2. Have there been many storms this summer?

   No, there _____ been many storms this summer.

3. Will there be any bread at the market? No, there

   _____ be any bread at the market.

B. Write the words that correctly complete the questions.

1. _____ a line for the movie? Yes, there will be a line for the movie.

2. _____ any rain? No, there hasn't been any rain.

3. _____ many late planes? No, there haven't been many late planes.

TEACHER: Read the directions and questions in Part A and Part B to students. Guide students to complete each exercise, providing support as needed.

Name _____

> To answer questions that begin with *Will there be, Has there been,* and *Have there been,* change the word order used in the question.

A. Write the words that complete the question or the answer.

1. Will there be food at the picnic? Yes, _____ food at the picnic.

2. Have there been many storms this summer? No, _____ many storms this summer.

3. Will there be any bread at the market? No, _____ any bread at the market.

4. _____ a second movie today? No, there will not be a second movie today.

5. _____ any rain this month? No, there hasn't been any rain this month.

B. For number 1, write a question using *Will there be, Has there been,* or *Have there been*. For number 2, write an answer to your question.

1. _____

_____

_____

2. _____

_____

_____

TEACHER: Read the directions and questions in Part A and Part B to students. Guide students to complete each exercise, providing support as needed.

Name _____

> The helping verb *can* is used to ask about and express the ability to do an action.
>
> <u>Can</u> a pig fly? No, a pig <u>can't</u> fly.   <u>Can</u> a pig walk? Yes, a pig <u>can</u> walk.

Circle the words that complete each answer.

1. Can a bird cook? (Yes/No), a bird (can't/can) cook.

2. Can a dog bark? (Yes/No), a dog (can't/can) bark.

3. Can basketball players jump? (Yes/No), they (can't/can) jump.

4. Can cows dance? (Yes/No), cows (can't/can) dance.

5. Can a kitten read? (Yes/No), a kitten (can't/can) read.

TEACHER: Read the directions and questions to students. Guide students to complete the exercise, providing support as needed.

Name _____

> The helping verb *can* is used to ask about and express the ability to do an action.
>
> <u>Can</u> a pig fly? No, a pig <u>can't</u> fly.   <u>Can</u> a pig walk? Yes, a pig <u>can</u> walk.

A.   Circle the words that complete each answer.

1.   Can a bird cook? (Yes/No), a bird (can't/can) cook.

2.   Can a dog bark? (Yes/No), a dog (can't/can) bark.

3.   Can snowmen talk? (Yes/No), they (can't/can) talk.

B.   Write the words that complete each answer.

1.   Can cows dance? _____, cows _____ dance.

2.   Can a kitten read? _____, a kitten _____ read.

3.   Can basketball players jump? _____, they

_____ jump.

TEACHER: Read the directions and questions in Part A and Part B to students. Guide students to complete each exercise, providing support as needed.

Name _____

> The helping verb *can* is used to ask about and express the ability to do an action.
>
> <u>Can</u> a pig fly? No, a pig <u>can't</u> fly.   <u>Can</u> a pig walk? Yes, a pig <u>can</u> walk.

A. Answer each question. Write a complete sentence.

1. Can a bird cook?

_____

2. Can a dog bark?

_____

3. Can snowmen talk?

_____

B. Write the words that complete each answer.

1. Can cows dance? _____, cows _____ dance.

2. Can a kitten read? _____, a kitten _____ read.

3. Can basketball players jump? _____, they

_____ jump.

TEACHER: Read the directions and questions in Part A and Part B to students. Guide students to complete each exercise, providing support as needed.

Name _____

> Ask about the present and the past using *did, do,* or *does* along with a main verb.
>
> <u>Did</u> you <u>like</u> orange juice when you were little?
>
> <u>Do</u> you <u>like</u> orange juice now?   <u>Does</u> your sister <u>like</u> orange juice, too?

A. Circle the letter that answers the question.

1. Which sentence asks about something in the past?

   a. Does he like chocolate?

   b. Do you want to help me make cupcakes?

   c. Did you get him a book for his birthday?

   d. Do you think we should wrap the presents?

2. Which sentence asks about something in the past?

   a. Did you learn about Mozart in class?

   b. Does he know how to play the cello?

   c. Do you want to hear the orchestra?

   d. Do you enjoy classical music?

B. Circle the word or words that correctly complete the sentence.

1. Do you take the train? Yes, I (take/don't take) the train.

2. Does he need a ride? Yes, he (needs/doesn't need) a ride.

3. (Do/Did) we win the game? No, we didn't win the game.

4. (Does/Do) you live in the city? No, I don't live in the city.

TEACHER: Read the directions and questions in Part A and Part B to students. Guide students to complete each exercise, providing support as needed.

Name _____

> Ask about the present and the past using *did, do,* or *does* along with a main verb.
>
> <u>Did</u> you <u>like</u> orange juice when you were little?
>
> <u>Do</u> you <u>like</u> orange juice now?   <u>Does</u> your sister <u>like</u> orange juice, too?

A. Read each sentence. Circle the letter of the question that asks about the past.

1. **a.** Does he like chocolate?
   b. Do you want to help me make cupcakes?
   c. Did you get him a book for his birthday?
   d. Do you think we should wrap the presents?

2. **a.** Did you learn about Mozart in class?
   b. Does he know how to play the cello?
   c. Do you want to hear the orchestra?
   d. Do you enjoy classical music?

B. Choose the word or words from the box that complete the question or the answer. Write the word or words on the line.

> take   Did   didn't   needs   don't take   doesn't need   Do   Does

1. Do you take the train? Yes, I _____ the train.

2. Does he need a ride? No, he _____ a ride.

3. _____ we win last week's game? No, we didn't win the game.

4. _____ you live in the city? No, I don't live in the city.

TEACHER: Read the directions and questions in Part A and Part B to students. Guide students to complete each exercise, providing support as needed.   Grades 4-6

Name _____

> Ask about the present and the past using *did, do,* or *does* along with a main verb.

A. Write a word to complete each answer.

1. Do you take the train? Yes, I _____ the train.

2. Does he need a ride? Yes, he _____ a ride.

3. Did we win the game? No, we _____ win the game.

B. Write *Did, Do,* or *Does* to complete each question.

1. _____ you live in the city now? No, I don't live in the city.

2. _____ you get him a book for his birthday last week?

3. _____ he know how to play the cello?

C. Read each statement. Write a question that can be answered with the statement. Use *Did, Do* or *Does* to begin your question.

1. No, I don't like jazz music.

   _____

2. Yes, Zane went to the baseball game last night.

   _____

TEACHER: Read the directions and questions in Part A, Part B, and Part C to students. Guide students to complete each exercise, providing support as needed.

Name _____

> You can combine simple sentences using a coordinating conjunction such as *or, and,* or *but.* Put a comma before the coordinating conjunction.
>
> Liz likes kittens, <u>but</u> she doesn't like dogs.

A. Read the sentences. Circle the sentence that best combines them.

1. I would like to buy a new hat. It costs a lot of money.

   a. I would like to buy a new hat it costs a lot of money.

   b. I would like to buy a new hat, or it costs a lot of money.

   c. I would like to buy a new hat and it costs a lot of money.

   d. I would like to buy a new hat, but it costs a lot of money.

2. Wild animals will run away from danger. They will attack.

   a. Wild animals will run away from danger, but they will attack.

   b. Wild animals will run away from danger and they will attack.

   c. Wild animals will run away from danger, or they will attack.

   d. Wild animals will run away from danger they will attack.

B. Write the coordinating conjunction to combine the sentences.

1. Mr. Davis drove to the store, _____ he bought some oranges.

2. Maria wanted to go to the soccer game, _____ she had to do her chores.

3. You may have yogurt, _____ you may have a banana.

4. I would like to go swimming, _____ it is cold outside.

TEACHER: Read the directions and questions in Part A and Part B to students. Guide students to complete each exercise, providing support as needed.

Grades 4-6   415

Name _____

> You can combine simple sentences using a coordinating conjunction such as *or, and,* or *but.* Put a comma before the coordinating conjunction.
>
> Liz likes kittens<u>, but</u> she doesn't like dogs.

A. Read the sentences. Write *C* if the coordinating conjunction is the best one for the sentence. Write *X* if the coordinating conjunction is incorrect.

1. I would like to buy a new hat, or it costs a

    lot of money. _____

2. Wild animals will run away from danger, or

    they will attack. _____

3. The new puppy was cute, but he caused a

    lot of trouble. _____

4. Mr. Davis drove to the store, but then he

    bought some oranges. _____

B. Write the coordinating conjunction you would use to combine the sentences.

1. Maria wanted to go to the soccer game. She had to finish her chores.

    _____

2. You may have yogurt. You may have a banana. _____

3. I would like to go swimming. It is cold outside. _____

TEACHER: Read the directions and questions in Part A and Part B to students. Guide students to complete each exercise, providing support as needed.

Name _____

> You can combine simple sentences using a coordinating conjunction such as *or, and,* or *but.* Put a comma before the coordinating conjunction.

A. Read the sentences. Write *C* if the coordinating conjunction is the best one for the sentence. Write *X* if the coordinating conjunction is incorrect.

1. I would like to buy a new hat, or it costs a lot of money. _____

2. Wild animals will run away from danger, or they will attack. _____

3. The new puppy was cute, but he caused a lot of trouble. _____

B. Write the coordinating conjunction you would use to combine the sentences.

1. Maria wanted to go to the soccer game. She had to finish her chores.

_____

2. You may have yogurt. You may have a banana. _____

3. I would like to go swimming. It is cold outside. _____

C. The underlined coordinating conjunction is incorrect. Rewrite the sentence on the line, using the correct coordinating conjunction.

1. Mr. Davis drove to the store, but then he bought some oranges.

_____

2. The runner planned to compete in the Olympics, or she hurt her foot and could not race.

_____

TEACHER: Read the directions and questions in Part A and Part B to students. Guide students to complete each exercise, providing support as needed.

Name _____

> Simple sentences can be combined using a coordinating conjunction such as *and, or, but, yet,* or *so.* A comma is placed directly before the coordinating conjunction.
>
> The travelers were tired, so they walked slowly through the airport.

A. Read the simple sentences. Combine them into one sentence using the coordinating conjunction in parentheses.

1. She was excited. She was nervous. (yet)

    _____

2. The children liked animals. They had fun at the farm. (so)

    _____

3. We brought picnic food. We forgot to bring drinks. (but)

    _____

4. He worked hard. He won an award. (so)

    _____

5. Maynie visited the zoo. She visited the museum. (and)

    _____

B. Circle the correct coordinating conjunction to complete the compound sentence.

1. The oven is still warm, (and/so) you should be careful.

2. Katie lost the tennis match, (so/yet) she still felt good about trying her best.

3. I need to make dinner, (but/and) I need to make dessert.

TEACHER: Read the directions and questions in Part A and Part B to students. Guide students to complete each exercise, providing support as needed.

Name _____

> Simple sentences can be combined using a coordinating conjunction such as *and, or, but, yet,* or *so.* A comma is placed directly before the coordinating conjunction.
>
> The travelers were tired, <u>so</u> they walked slowly through the airport.

Read the simple sentences. Combine them into one sentence using a coordinating conjunction from the box. Write the new sentence on the line.

> yet   so   and   but   or

1. The children liked animals. They had fun at the farm.

    _____

2. We brought picnic food. We forgot to bring drinks.

    _____

3. He worked hard. He won an award.

    _____

4. Maynie visited the zoo. She visited the museum.

    _____

5. Katie lost the tennis match. She still felt good about trying her best.

    _____

Name _____

> Simple sentences can be combined using a coordinating conjunction such as *and, or, but, yet,* or *so.* A comma is placed directly before the coordinating conjunction.

Read the paragraphs. For each one, combine simple sentences using a coordinating conjunction. Use at least two coordinating conjunctions per paragraph.

1. The children liked animals. They had fun at the farm. One child liked the goats best. Another child liked the horses best.

   _____

   _____

   _____

2. The day was sunny. It was warm. We went to the park. We found a sunny spot to sit. We brought picnic food. We forgot to bring drinks.

   _____

   _____

   _____

3. Katie practiced hard. She played tennis every day. Then the day of the big tennis match came. Katie lost the tennis match. She still felt good. She knew she had done her best.

   _____

   _____

   _____

TEACHER: Read the directions and questions in Part A and Part B to students. Guide students to complete each exercise, providing support as needed.

Name _____

> **Complex sentences** contain an independent clause and a dependent clause. These are connected by a subordinating conjunction, such as: *after, although, as soon as, because, before, even though, if, until, when, where, while.*
>
> I study hard <u>because I want to learn.</u>
>
> <u>Because I want to learn,</u> I study hard.

A. Circle the subordinating conjunction in each sentence.

1. I help my brother walk because he's a baby.

2. I am happy when I go to the beach.

3. If you want to play outside, you must clean your room.

4. Even though it's cold, I will play outside.

B. Circle the correct subordinating conjunction in parentheses.

1. The cat ran up the tree (because, although) the dog chased it.

2. I will visit you (because, after) you invite me.

3. He likes to sing (while, although) he takes a shower.

Name _____

> **Complex sentences** contain an independent clause and a dependent clause. These are connected by a subordinating conjunction, such as: *after, although, as soon as, because, before, even though, if, until, when, where, while.*
>
> I study hard <u>because I want to learn.</u>
>
> <u>Because I want to learn</u>, I study hard.

Draw lines to connect the sentences.

1. I help my brother walk

2. If you want to play outside,

3. Sand gets in my hair

4. They wake up early every day

5. If you invite me,

6. The cat ran up the tree

a. even though they are tired.

b. when I go to the beach.

c. because the dog chased it.

d. because he's a baby.

e. you must clean your room first.

f. I will go to your party.

TEACHER: Read the directions and questions to students. Guide students to complete the exercise, providing support as needed.

Name _____

> **Complex sentences** contain an independent clause and a dependent clause. These can be connected by relative clauses, which often begin with: *who, whose, that, which, when,* and *where*.
>
> Minnesota, <u>where I live</u>, is cold in winter.
>
> The boots <u>that I'm wearing</u> are warm.

Draw lines to connect the sentences.

1. I have two brothers, _____ .

2. My sister, _____ , is younger than me.

3. The food _____ is avocado.

4. Oranges, _____ , are juicy.

5. After school is the time _____ .

6. I will miss my friend Kenji, _____ .

   a. which have a lot of vitamin C

   b. that I like best

   c. who is moving to Montana

   d. whose names are Clarence and Joshua

   e. whose name is Amina

   f. when I am most hungry.

TEACHER: Read the directions and questions to students. Guide students to complete the exercise, providing support as needed.

Grades 4-6   **425**

Name _____

> **Complex sentences** contain an independent clause and a dependent clause. These can be connected by relative clauses, which often begin with: *who, whose, that, which, when,* and *where.*

A. Draw lines to connect the sentences with their dependent clauses.

1. I have two brothers,_____ .   **a.** which have a lot of vitamin C

2. My sister, _____ , is younger   **b.** that I like best
   than me.

3. The food _____ is avocado.   **c.** who is moving to Montana

4. Oranges, _____ , are juicy.   **d.** whose names are Clarence
                                                 and Joshua

5. After school is the time _____ .   **e.** whose name is Amina

6. I will miss my friend Kenji, _____ . **f.** when I am most hungry

B. Write the word that begins the relative clause from each sentence on the lines.

1. _____

2. _____

3. _____

4. _____

5. _____

6. _____

TEACHER: Read the directions and questions to students. Guide students to complete the exercise, providing support as needed.

Name _____

When sentences are combined to form **compound subjects,** use the plural form of the verb:

Mike <u>plays</u> baseball. Anna <u>plays</u> baseball.   Mike and Anna <u>play</u> baseball.

When sentences are combined to form **compound predicates,** the verbs stay the same:

Anna <u>plays</u> baseball. Anna <u>watches</u> soccer.
Anna <u>plays</u> baseball and <u>watches</u> soccer.

Combine the sentences to form compound subjects or compound predicates. Write the correct words in the spaces.

1. Jen likes strawberries. Jan likes strawberries.

    _____ and _____ like _____ .

2. My sister is in high school. My brother is in high school.

    _____ and _____ _____ in high school.

3. The chicken smells good. The vegetables smell good.

    The _____ and _____ _____ good.

4. Miguel plays soccer on Saturdays. Miguel goes shopping on Sundays.

    Miguel _____ soccer on _____ and _____

    shopping on _____ .

5. I wrote on the chalkboard yesterday. I read a book today.

    I _____ _____ yesterday and

    _____ _____ today.

    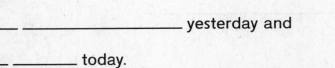

TEACHER: Read the directions and questions to students. Guide students to complete the exercise, providing support as needed.

Name _____

> When sentences are combined to form **compound subjects**, use the plural form of the verb:
>
> Mike <u>plays</u> baseball. Anna <u>plays</u> baseball.   Mike and Anna <u>play</u> baseball.
>
> When sentences are combined to form **compound predicates**, the verbs stay the same:
>
> Anna <u>plays</u> baseball. Anna <u>watches</u> soccer.
>
> Anna <u>plays</u> baseball and <u>watches</u> soccer.

Combine the sentences to form compound subjects or compound predicates. Write the correct words on the lines.

1. Jen likes strawberries. Jan likes strawberries.

    _____ and _____ like _____ .

2. My sister is in high school. My brother is in high school.

    _____ and _____ _____ in high school.

3. The chicken smells good. The vegetables smell good.

    _____ and _____ _____ _____ .

4. Miguel plays soccer on Saturdays. Miguel goes shopping on Sundays.

    Miguel _____ and _____ .

5. I wrote a letter yesterday. I read a story today.

    I _____ _____ _____ and _____ _____ _____ .

6. The new car looks good. The new car smells nice.

    The new car _____ .

TEACHER: Read the directions and questions to students. Guide students to complete the exercise, providing support as needed.

Name _____

> When sentences are combined to form **compound subjects**, use the plural form of the verb.
>
> When sentences are combined to form **compound predicates**, the verbs stay the same.

Combine the sentences to form compound subjects or compound predicates. Write the new sentence on the line.

1. Jen likes strawberries. Jan likes strawberries.

   _____

2. My sister is in high school. My brother is in high school.

   _____

3. The chicken smells good. The vegetables smell good.

   _____

4. Miguel plays soccer on Saturdays. Miguel goes shopping on Sundays.

   _____

5. I wrote a letter yesterday. I read a story today.

   _____

6. The new car looks good. The new car smells nice.

   _____

Name _____

Sentences that share elements can often be combined to form a single sentence.

I watched the children. They were happy. They ran quickly. They ran on the grass.

I watched the happy children run quickly on the grass.

Combine the sentences to form one sentence. Write the correct words in the spaces. Some sentences have more than one correct answer.

1. Alejandro wore boots and a coat. His boots were heavy.
    His coat was warm.

    Alejandro wore _____ boots and a _____ coat.

2. The teacher watched the students study. The teacher watched them closely. The students studied quietly.

    The teacher _____ watched the students study _____ .

3. The bird flew. It flew across the sky. It flew silently.

    The bird flew _____ .

4. I want to travel next summer. I want to travel by car.
    I want to travel to Canada.

    I want to travel next summer _____ .

5. Yoon saw the cat climb the tree. The cat was fast.
    The tree was tall.

    Yoon saw _____ cat climb _____ tree.

TEACHER: Read the directions and questions to students. Guide students to complete the exercise, providing support as needed.

Name _____

> Sentences that share elements can often be combined to form a single sentence.
>
> I watched the children. They were happy. They ran quickly.
> They ran on the grass.
>
> I watched the happy children run quickly on the grass.

Combine the sentences to form one sentence. Write the correct words in the spaces. Some sentences have more than one correct answer.

1. Alejandro wore boots and a coat. His boots were heavy. His coat was warm.

   Alejandro wore _____ and a _____.

2. The teacher watched the students study. The teacher watched them closely. The students studied quietly.

   The teacher _____ watched _____.

3. The bird flew. It flew across the sky. It flew silently.

   The bird _____.

4. I want to travel next summer. I want to travel by car. I want to travel to Canada.

   I want to travel _____.

5. Yoon saw the cat climb the tree. The cat was fast. The tree was tall.

   Yoon saw _____.

6. The student took the test. The test was difficult. The student took it slowly.

   The student _____.

Name _____

> Sentences that share elements can often be combined to form a single sentence.

Combine the sentences to form one sentence. Write the correct words in the spaces. Some sentences have more than one correct answer.

1. Alejandro wore boots and a coat. His boots were heavy. His coat was warm.

   _____.

2. The teacher watched the students study. The teacher watched them closely. The students studied quietly.

   _____.

3. The bird flew. It flew across the sky. It flew silently.

   _____.

4. I want to travel next summer. I want to travel by car. I want to travel to Canada.

   _____.

5. Yoon saw the cat climb the tree. The cat was fast. The tree was tall.

   _____.

6. The student took the test. The test was difficult. The student took it slowly.

   _____.

TEACHER: Read the directions and questions to students. Guide students to complete the exercise, providing support as needed.

Name _____

> We can combine sentences with these conjunctions:
>
> Tonight I will <u>either</u> read a book <u>or</u> write a letter. (I will do one or the other; not both.)
> Tonight I will <u>neither</u> read a book <u>nor</u> write a letter. (I will do neither.)
> Tonight I will <u>both</u> read a book <u>and</u> write a letter. (I will do both.)
> Tonight I will <u>not only</u> read a book <u>but also</u> write a letter. (I will do both.)

A. Circle the letter of the words that correctly combine the sentences. The combined sentence should keep the meaning of the original sentences.

1. I like cabbage. I like carrots. I like _____ cabbage _____ carrots.

   a. neither/nor   **b.** either/or   **c.** both/and

2. Sal doesn't like peas. Sal doesn't like carrots. Sal likes _____ peas _____ carrots.

   a. neither/nor   **b.** either/or   **c.** both/and

3. Ahmad reads books. Ahmad writes letters. Ahmad _____ reads books _____ writes letters.

   a. neither/nor   **b.** either/or   **c.** not only/but also

B. Circle the words that correctly combine the sentences. The combined sentence should have the same meaning of the original sentences.

1. Julia reads magazines. Talia reads magazines. _____ (Neither, Both) Julia _____ (nor, and) Talia read magazines.

2. I might go bowling. I might go to a movie. I will do one of these. I will _____ (neither, either) go bowling _____ (nor, or) go to a movie.

3. I will not go bowling. I will not go to a movie. I will _____ (neither, both) go bowling _____ (nor, and) go to a movie.

Name _____

> We can combine sentences with these conjunctions:
>
> Tonight I will <u>either</u> read a book <u>or</u> write a letter. (I will do one or the other; not both.)
> Tonight I will <u>neither</u> read a book <u>nor</u> write a letter. (I will do neither.)
> Tonight I will <u>both</u> read a book <u>and</u> write a letter. (I will do both.)
> Tonight I will <u>not only</u> read a book <u>but also</u> write a letter. (I will do both.)

Fill in the spaces with one of the correlative conjunctions from above.

1. I like peas. I like carrots. I like _____ peas _____ carrots.

2. Sal doesn't like peas. Sal doesn't like carrots. Sal likes _____ peas _____ carrots.

3. Ahmad reads books. Ahmad writes letters.

Ahmad _____ reads books _____ writes letters.

4. Julia reads magazines. Talia reads magazines.

_____ Julia _____ Talia read magazines.

5. I might go bowling. I might go to a movie. I will do one of these. I will _____ go bowling _____ go to a movie.

6. I will not go bowling. I will not go to a movie. I will _____ go bowling _____ go to a movie.

TEACHER: Read the directions and questions to students. Guide students to complete the exercise, providing support as needed.

Name _____

> We can combine sentences with these conjunctions:
>
> Tonight I will <u>either</u> read a book <u>or</u> write a letter. (I will do one or the other; not both.)
> Tonight I will <u>neither</u> read a book <u>nor</u> write a letter. (I will do neither.)
> Tonight I will <u>both</u> read a book <u>and</u> write a letter. (I will do both.)
> Tonight I will <u>not only</u> read a book <u>but also</u> write a letter. (I will do both.)

Combine the sentences using one set of the correlative conjunctions above. Write the new sentence on the line.

1. I like peas. I like carrots.

   _____

2. Sal doesn't like peas. Sal doesn't like carrots.

   _____

3. Ahmad reads books. Ahmad writes letters.

   _____

4. Julia reads magazines. Talia reads magazines.

   _____

5. I might go bowling. I might go to a movie. (I will do only one of these.)

   _____

6. I will not go bowling. I will not go to a movie.

   _____

TEACHER: Read the directions and questions to students. Guide students to complete the exercise, providing support as needed.

Grades 4–6   **435**

Name _____

> We can combine sentences with appositives. Appositives give more information about subjects or objects. They are placed next to the subject or object. They are set off by commas.
>
> Christina called Renee. Renee is her best friend.
> Christina called Renee, <u>her best friend</u>.

A. Choose the sentence that correctly combines the two sentences with an appositive.

1. That is our teacher. That is Mr. Smith.

   a. That is our teacher, Mr. Smith.

   b. Mr. Smith is our teacher.

2. The Tigers won the game. The Tigers are a hockey team.

   a. The Tigers hockey team won the game.

   b. The Tigers, a hockey team, won the game.

3. I went to the park. It is the nicest place in town.

   a. I went to the park, the nicest place in town.

   b. I went to the park, and the nicest place, in town.

B. Combine the sentences. Write the appositive on the line.

1. We watched the movie. It was a comedy.

   We watched the movie, _____.

2. George Washington was born in Virginia. George Washington was our first President.

   George Washington, _____, was born in Virginia.

3. My sister went to the library. It is the biggest building in Cedarville.

   My sister went to the library, _____

TEACHER: Read the directions and questions in Part A and Part B to students. Guide students to complete each exercise, providing support as needed.

Name _____

> We can combine sentences with appositives. Appositives give more information about subjects or objects. They are placed next to the subject or object. They are set off by commas.
>
> Christina called Renee. Renee is her best friend.
> Christina called Renee, <u>her best friend</u>.

A. Choose the sentence that correctly combines the two sentences with an appositive.

1. That is our teacher. That is Mr. Smith.

   a. That is our teacher, Mr. Smith.

   b. Mr. Smith is our teacher.

   c. Our teacher is Mr. Smith.

2. The Tigers won the game. The Tigers are a hockey team.

   a. The Tigers hockey team won the game.

   b. The Tigers, a hockey team, won the game.

   c. The hockey team won the game.

B. Combine the sentences with an appositive.

1. We watched the movie. It was a comedy.

   _____

2. George Washington was born in Virginia. George Washington was our first President.

   _____

3. My sister went to the library. It is the biggest building in Cedarville.

   _____

TEACHER: Read the directions and questions in Part A and Part B to students. Guide students to complete each exercise, providing support as needed.

Name _____

> We can combine sentences with appositives. Appositives give more information about subjects or objects. They are placed next to the subject or object. They are set off by commas.
>
> Christina called Renee. Renee is her best friend.
> Christina called Renee, <u>her best friend</u>.

Combine the sentences with an appositive.

1. That is our teacher. That is Mr. Smith.

   _____

2. The Tigers won the game. The Tigers are a hockey team.

   _____

3. I went to the park. It is the nicest place in town.

   _____

4. We watched the movie. It was a comedy.

   _____

5. George Washington was born in Virginia. George Washington was our first President.

   _____

6. My sister went to the library. It is the biggest building in Cedarville.

   _____

TEACHER: Read the directions and questions to students. Guide students to complete the exercise, providing support as needed.

Name _____

> A **noun phrase** is a group of words that act like a noun in a sentence. Replacing a pronoun with a specific noun and/or adding details to a noun creates a noun phrase. This is one way to expand a sentence.
>
> <u>It</u> is for sale.   <u>That little house</u> is for sale.
>
> <u>They</u> like <u>the principal</u>.   <u>All the students</u> like <u>the new principal</u>.

A. Underline the noun phrases.

1. My brother's pet turtle is cute.

2. Victor is playing the new piano.

3. The big, red car belongs to Mr. Lee.

4. My sister's friends came for the slumber party.

B. Add details to the noun to create a noun phrase. Write the phrase on the line.

1. teacher _____

2. students _____

3. school _____

TEACHER: Read the directions and questions in Part A and Part B to students. Guide students to complete each exercise, providing support as needed.   Grades 4–6   **439**

Name _____

> A **noun phrase** is a group of words that act like a noun in a sentence.
> Replacing a pronoun with a specific noun and/or adding details to a noun
> creates a noun phrase. This is one way to expand a sentence.
>
> <u>It</u> is for sale.   <u>That little house</u> is for sale.
>
> <u>They</u> like <u>the principal</u>.   <u>All the students</u> like <u>the new principal</u>.

A.   Rewrite the sentences adding details to the underlined noun phrases.

1.   <u>My turtle</u> lives in <u>a tank</u>.

_____

2.   <u>My friend</u> is playing <u>the piano</u>.

_____

3.   <u>The car</u> belongs to <u>his sister</u>.

_____

4.   <u>My friends</u> came for <u>the party</u>.

_____

B.   Add details to the noun to create a noun phrase.
     Then expand the noun phrase by adding articles,
     possessive pronouns, or determiners.

	Noun Phrase	**Expanded Noun Phrase**
1. teacher	_____	_____
2. students	_____	_____
3. school	_____	_____

**TEACHER: Read the directions and questions in Part A and Part B to students. Guide
students to complete each exercise, providing support as needed.**

Name _____

> A **noun phrase** is a group of words that act like a noun in a sentence. Replacing a pronoun with a specific noun and/or adding details to a noun creates a noun phrase. This is one way to expand a sentence.

A. Underline the noun phrases. Rewrite the sentences adding details to the underlined noun phrases.

1. My turtle lives in a tank.

   _____

2. My friend is playing the piano.

   _____

3. The car belongs to his sister.

   _____

4. My friends came for the party.

   _____

B. Change each pronoun or noun into a noun phrase.

1. She stood on the steps.

   _____

2. They walked to class.

   _____

Name _____

> A **noun phrase** is a group of words that act like a noun in a sentence. Adding details to a noun creates a noun phrase. Adding prepositions and adjective clauses, which usually come after the noun, is one way to expand a sentence.
>
> <u>It</u> is for sale.   <u>The house</u> is for sale.   <u>The house on the corner</u> is for sale.

Underline the noun phrases.

1. The dog with the curly tail is cute.

2. Victor is playing the piano that we bought yesterday.

3. The bike on the sidewalk belongs to Oscar.

4. The boy on the sofa was sleeping.

5. Eleanor played with the boy who was new to our school.

6. All the students who did their homework learned a new skill.

TEACHER: Read the directions and questions to students. Guide students to complete the exercise, providing support as needed.

Name _____

> A **noun phrase** is a group of words that act like a noun in a sentence. Adding details to a noun creates a noun phrase. Adding prepositions and adjective clauses, which usually come after the noun, is one way to expand a sentence.
>
> <u>It</u> is for sale.   <u>The house</u> is for sale.
>
> <u>The house on the corner</u> is for sale.

Expand the underlined noun phrase by adding details on the line.

1. <u>The dog</u> is cute.

    The dog _____ is cute.

2. Victor is playing <u>the piano</u>.

    Victor is playing <u>the piano</u>

    _____ .

3. <u>The bike</u> belongs to Oscar.

    The bike _____ belongs to Oscar.

4. <u>The boy</u> was sleeping.

    The boy _____ was sleeping.

5. Eleanor played with <u>the boy</u>.

    Eleanor played with <u>the boy</u>

    _____ .

6. <u>All the students</u> learned

    a new skill.

    <u>All the students</u>

    _____ a new skill.

TEACHER: Read the directions and questions to students. Guide students to complete the exercise, providing support as needed.

Name _____

> A **noun phrase** is a group of words that act like a noun in a sentence. Adding details to a noun creates a noun phrase. Adding prepositions and adjective clauses, which usually come after the noun, is one way to expand a sentence.

Expand each sentence by changing the nouns and pronouns to noun phrases. Add specific details before and after the nouns.

1. The dog is cute.

   _____.

2. Victor is playing piano.

   _____.

3. The bike belongs to him.

   _____.

4. The boy was sleeping.

   _____.

5. Eleanor played with the boy.

   _____.

6. The students learned a new skill.

   _____.

Copyright © McGraw-Hill Education

TEACHER: Read the directions and questions to students. Guide students to complete the exercise, providing support as needed.

Name _____

> Adjectives can help us expand sentences. Adjectives commonly appear before the nouns they modify:
>
> I like that <u>big</u>, <u>red</u> <u>hat</u>.
>
> But adjectives can also come after the nouns they modify, particularly in sentences with linking verbs, such as *is*:
>
> The <u>weather</u> is <u>hot</u> and <u>humid</u>.

A. **Choose the sentence that correctly expands the sentence using the adjectives in parentheses.**

1. Tomas is playing with a dog. (small, black)

    a. Tomas is playing with a dog small and black.

    b. Tomas is playing with a small, black dog.

2. That car belongs to Rico's family. (big, beautiful, new)

    a. That car big, beautiful, new belongs to Rico's family.

    b. That big, beautiful, new car belongs to Rico's family.

3. The Mississippi River is wide. (slow, powerful)

    a. The Mississippi River is wide, slow, and powerful.

    b. The Mississippi River is wide slow powerful.

B. **Expand each sentence using the adjectives in parentheses.**

1. We watched a movie. (long, funny)

    We watched _____ movie.

2. That bike is Sara's. (new, red)

    That _____ bike is Sara's.

3. My house is charming. (small, comfortable)

    My house is _____ charming.

Name _____

> Adjectives can help us expand sentences. Adjectives commonly appear before the nouns they modify.
>
> But adjectives can also come after the nouns they modify, particularly in sentences with linking verbs, such as *is*.

A. **Choose the sentence that correctly expands the original sentence using the adjectives in parentheses.**

1. Tomas is playing with a dog. (small, black)

   a. Tomas is playing with a dog small and black.

   b. Tomas is playing with a small, black dog.

   c. Tomas is playing with a small dog black.

2. That car belongs to Rico's family. (big, beautiful, new)

   a. That car belongs to Rico's big, beautiful, family new.

   b. That big, beautiful, new car belongs to Rico's family.

   c. That car beautiful belongs to Rico's big, new family.

B. **Expand each sentence using the adjectives in parentheses.**

1. We watched a movie. (long, funny)

   _____

2. That bike is Sara's. (new, red)

   _____

3. My house is charming. (small, comfortable)

   _____

TEACHER: Read the directions and questions in Part A and Part B to students. Guide students to complete each exercise, providing support as needed.

Name _____

> Adjectives can help us expand sentences. Adjectives commonly appear before the nouns they modify.
>
> But adjectives can also come after the nouns they modify, particularly in sentences with linking verbs, such as *is*.

Expand each sentence using the adjectives in parentheses.

1. Tomas is playing with a dog. (small, black)

   _____

2. That car belongs to Rico's family. (big, beautiful, new)

   _____

3. The Mississippi River is wide. (slow, powerful)

   _____

4. We watched a movie. (long, funny)

   _____

5. That bike is Sara's. (new, red)

   _____

6. My house is charming. (small, comfortable)

   _____

TEACHER: Read the directions and questions to students. Guide students to complete the exercise, providing support as needed.

Name _____

> Adjective phrases commonly include adverbs or prepositional phrases attached to adjectives.
>
> **Adverb + Adjective:** He is a <u>very nice</u> man.
>
> **Adjective + Prepositional Phrase:** He is <u>afraid of the dark</u>.

A. Choose the sentence that correctly expands the original sentence using the adjective phrase in parentheses.

1. That book is funny. (very)

   a. That book is very funny.   **b.** That book is funny very.

2. My family visited our kind grandparents. (extremely)

   a. My family visited our kind grandparents extremely.

   b. My family visited our extremely kind grandparents.

3. Becky is covered. (in mud)

   a. Becky is covered in mud.   **b.** Becky in mud is covered.

B. Expand the sentence using the adjective phrase in parentheses.

1. We watched a movie. (very funny)

   We watched a _____ .

2. Sara is bored. (with the movie)

   Sara is _____ .

3. This salad is delicious. (really)

   This salad is _____ .

TEACHER: Read the directions and questions in Part A and Part B to students. Guide students to complete each exercise, providing support as needed.

Name

You can add **adverbs** to a sentence to add information.

- We visited the fair.   Yesterday, we visited the fair. (when)
- The Ferris wheel rose.   The Ferris wheel rose upward. (where)
- People screamed.   People screamed happily. (how)

Underline the adverb. Write _when, where,_ or _how_ to tell what information it gives about the verb.

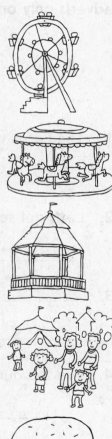

1. The Ferris wheel turns slowly. —————

2. Together we ride the carousel. —————

3. Tonight a band will play. —————

4. We see our friends everywhere. —————

5. Let's get some lunch soon. —————

TEACHER: Read the directions and questions to students. Guide students to complete the exercise, providing support as needed.

Name _____

You can add **adverbs** to a sentence to add information.

- We visited the fair.   <u>Yesterday</u>, we visited the fair. (when)
- The Ferris wheel rose.   The Ferris wheel rose <u>upward</u>. (where)
- People screamed.   People screamed <u>happily</u>. (how)

Complete each sentence by adding an adverb from the box that gives the information in parentheses. Then write the sentence on the line. Use each adverb only once.

slowly	tonight	everywhere	soon	together

1. The Ferris wheel turns _____ . (how)

_____

2. Let's get some lunch _____ . (when)

_____

3. _____ we ride the carousel. (how)

_____

4. We see our friends _____ . (where)

_____

5. _____ moonlight will light the fairgrounds. (when)

_____

TEACHER: Read the directions and questions to students. Guide students to complete the exercise, providing support as needed.

Name _____

> You can add **adverbs** to a sentence to add information.
>
> - We visited the fair.   <u>Yesterday,</u> we visited the fair. (when)
> - The Ferris wheel rose.   The Ferris wheel rose <u>upward</u>. (where)
> - People screamed.   People screamed <u>happily</u>. (how)

Add an adverb to each sentence that tells the information in parentheses.

1. The Ferris wheel turns. _____ . (how)

2. Let's get some lunch _____ . (when)

3. _____ we ride the carousel. (how)

4. We see our friends _____ . (where)

5. Look at the funhouse _____ ! (where)

6. _____ moonlight will light the fairgrounds. (when)

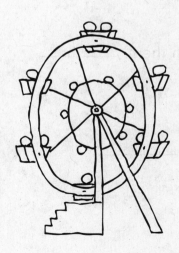

TEACHER: Read the directions and questions to students. Guide students to complete the exercise, providing support as needed.

Name _____

You can add **adverb phrases** to a sentence to add information.

- Two eggs hatched.   <u>On Monday</u>, two eggs hatched. (when)
- The bird landed.   The bird landed <u>in the nest</u>. (where)
- The baby birds chirped.   The baby birds chirped <u>with delight</u>. (how)

Underline the adverb phrase. Write *when, where,* **or** *how* **to tell what information it gives about the verb.**

1. One bird flies over the field. _____

2. The mother bird lands with ease. _____

3. After that, the babies eat lunch. _____

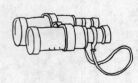

4. From our house, we watch them. _____

5. At night the nest is quiet. _____

TEACHER: Read the directions and questions to students. Guide students to complete the exercise, providing support as needed.

Name _____

> You can add **adverb phrases** to a sentence to add information.
>
> - Two eggs hatched.   <u>On Monday</u>, two eggs hatched. (when)
> - The bird landed.   The bird landed <u>in the nest</u>. (where)
> - The baby birds chirped. The baby birds chirped <u>with delight</u>. (how)

Complete each sentence by adding an adverb phrase from the box that gives the information in parentheses. Then write the sentence on the line. Use each adverb phrase only once.

> with ease   over the field   after that   from our house   on cool nights

1. One bird hunts flying insects _____ . (where)

   _____

2. The mother bird approaches and lands _____ . (how)

   _____

3. _____ the baby birds enjoy their lunch. (when)

   _____

4. We can observe the birds _____ . (where)

   _____

5. _____ the nest is quiet and safe. (when)

   _____

Name _____

> You can add **adverb phrases** to a sentence to add information.
>
> - Two eggs hatched.   <u>On Monday</u>, two eggs hatched. (when)
>
> - The bird landed.   The bird landed <u>in the nest</u>. (where)
>
> - The baby birds chirped.   The baby birds chirped <u>with delight</u>. (how)

Add an adverb phrase to each sentence. Make the adverb tell the information in parentheses. Choose from these prepositions: *after, in, on, under, over, from, to, during, at, with, for.*

1. One bird hunts flying insects _____ . (where)

2. The mother bird approaches and lands _____ . (how)

3. _____ the baby birds enjoy their lunch. (when)

4. We can observe the birds _____ . (where)

5. We watch the baby birds _____ . (how)

6. _____ the nest is quiet and safe. (when)

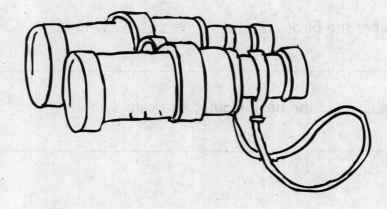

TEACHER: Read the directions and questions to students. Guide students to complete the exercise, providing support as needed.

Name _____

> You may **expand a sentence** using **prepositional phrases**. Adjective and adverb prepositional phrases add information to the sentence.
>
> Dad bought a new car.
>
> <u>In August</u>, Dad bought a new car <u>with a sunroof</u>.

A. Underline the two prepositional phrases in each sentence.

1. During long trips, we use the DVD player in the car.

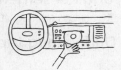

2. On the back doors, the car has safety locks for children.

3. At the dealership, I asked many questions about the car.

4. Dad drove a car with wire wheels around the lot.

B. For each sentence above, write the original sentence, leaving out the prepositional phrases.

1. _____

2. _____

3. _____

4. _____

TEACHER: Read the directions and questions in Part A and Part B to students. Guide students to complete each exercise, providing support as needed.

Name _____

> You may **expand a sentence** using **prepositional phrases**. Adjective
> and adverb prepositional phrases add information to the sentence.
>
> Dad bought a new car.
>
> In August, Dad bought a new car with a sunroof.

A. **Underline the two prepositional phrases in each sentence. Then write the original sentence on the line.**

1. During long trips we use the DVD player in the car.

   _____

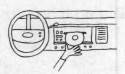

2. On the back doors, the car has safety locks for children.

   _____

3. At the dealership, I asked many questions about the car.

   _____

4. Dad drove a car with wire wheels around the lot.

   _____

B. **Write each prepositional phrase from the sentences above where it belongs.**

Adjective Phrases	Adverb Phrases
1. _____	_____
2. _____	_____
3. _____	_____
4. _____	_____

TEACHER: Read the directions and questions in Part A and Part B to students. Guide students to complete each exercise, providing support as needed.

Name _____

You may **expand a sentence** using **prepositional phrases**. Adjective and adverb prepositional phrases add information to the sentence.

Dad bought a new car.

<u>In August</u>, Dad bought a new car <u>with a sunroof</u>.

Underline any prepositional phrases you read in the story below. Then sort the phrases into the correct columns.

At the dealership, I asked many questions about our new car. It has several nice features for kids and adults. During long trips, we can watch the DVD player in the back. The radio on the dashboard gets stations from everywhere. For the first week, Dad drove with great care. He never accelerated above 30 miles an hour.

Adjective Phrases

1. _____

2. _____

3. _____

4. _____

5. _____

Adverb Phrases

6. _____

7. _____

8. _____

9. _____

10. _____

TEACHER: Read the directions and paragraph to students. Guide students to complete the exercise, providing support as needed.

Name _____

You may **expand a sentence** using **prepositional phrases.** Adjective and adverb prepositional phrases add information to the sentence.

    Original sentence: The band plays music.

    + **adjective phrase:**   The band plays music <u>by John Philip Sousa</u>.

    + **adverb phrase:**   <u>Before the game</u>, the band plays music.

A. **Add a phrase to expand each sentence. Start with the preposition in parentheses.**

1. The band rehearsed _____ .
                        (after)

2. Rico carried his trumpet _____ .
                        (in)

3. We played one song _____ .
                        (by)

4. Kara beat the drum _____ .
                        (with)

5. Is that your flute _____ ?
                        (under)

B. **Think of two phrases that could start with each preposition. Write your phrases on the lines.**

1. from _____   _____

2. across _____   _____

3. during _____   _____

TEACHER: Read the directions and questions in Part A and Part B to students. Guide students to complete each exercise, providing support as needed.

Name _____

> You may **expand a sentence** using **prepositional phrases.** Both adjective and adverb prepositional phrases add information to the sentence.
>
> | **Original sentence:** | The band plays music. |
> | **+ adjective phrase:** | The band plays music <u>by John Philip Sousa</u>. |
> | **+ adverb phrase:** | <u>Before the game</u>, the band plays music. |

A. Expand each sentence using one or more prepositional phrases. Write your new sentence on the line.

1. The band rehearsed.

   _____

2. Rico carried his trumpet.

   _____

3. Kara beat the drum.

   _____

4. Is that your flute?

   _____

B. Think of two phrases that could start with each listed preposition. Write your phrases on the lines.

1. below _____   _____

2. without _____   _____

3. toward _____   _____

TEACHER: Read the directions and questions in Part A and Part B to students. Guide students to complete each exercise, providing support as needed.

Name _____

You may **expand a sentence** using **prepositional phrases**. Both adjective and adverb prepositional phrases add information to the sentence.

Original sentence:	The band plays music.
+ adjective phrase:	The band plays music <u>by John Philip Sousa</u>.
+ adverb phrase:	<u>Before the game</u>, the band plays music.

Expand the sentences in this story by adding prepositional phrases that give information. Write your revised story on the lines.

1. The band rehearsed. Rico played his trumpet. Kara beat the drum. Our conductor raised her arm. We played one song. Everyone sounded great.

_____

_____

_____

_____

TEACHER: Read the directions and paragraph to students. Guide students to complete the exercise, providing support as needed.

Name _____

You can **combine sentences** to make ideas simpler and clearer.

The fox is in the yard. It is after my chickens.
The fox that is in the yard is after my chickens.

There is the barn. I keep my chickens there.
There is the barn where I keep my chickens.

A. Circle the letter of the sentence that best combines the original sentences.

1. I sell eggs. My chickens lay the eggs.

   a. I sell eggs and chickens.

   b. I sell the chickens who lay eggs.

   c. They are the chickens who lay sold eggs.

   d. I sell the eggs that my chickens lay.

2. There is the man. He buys my eggs.

   a. There is the man he buys my eggs.

   b. That man who buys my eggs.

   c. There is the man who buys my eggs.

   d. There is the egg man.

B. Read each sentence. Circle the word you would use to combine the sentence parts.

1. I met a woman (who, where) sells chickens.

2. She lives on a farm (that, where) Mott Road ends.

3. The farm has a large oak tree (that, who) shades the house.

4. I bought hens (they, that) lay eggs from her.

TEACHER: Read the directions and questions in Part A and Part B to students. Guide students to complete each exercise, providing support as needed.

Name _____

You can **combine sentences** to make ideas simpler and clearer.

The fox is in the yard. It is after my chickens.
The fox that is in the yard is after my chickens.

There is the barn. I keep my chickens there.
There is the barn where I keep my chickens.

A. Write *who, that,* or *where* in the blank to join the sentence parts.

1. I sell the eggs _____ my chickens lay.

2. There is the man _____ buys my eggs.

3. He lives on a farm _____ Mott Road ends.

B. Combine the sentence pairs using the word in parentheses. Write the new sentence on the line.

1. I met a woman. She sells chickens. (who)

_____

2. I bought some hens. They lay eggs. (that)

_____

3. There is the market. I sold some eggs there. (where)

_____

TEACHER: Read the directions and questions in Part A and Part B to students. Guide students to complete each exercise, providing support as needed.

Name _____

> You can **combine sentences** to make ideas simpler and clearer.
>
> The fox is in the yard. It is after my chickens.
> The fox that is in the yard is after my chickens.
>
> There is the barn. I keep my chickens there.
> There is the barn where I keep my chickens.

Use *who, that,* or *where* to combine the sentences. Write your new sentence on the line.

1. I met a woman. She sells chickens.

   _____

2. She lives in a farmhouse. It is at the place Mott Road ends.

   _____

3. The farm has a large oak tree. The oak tree shades the house.

   _____

4. I bought three hens. The hens lay eggs.

   _____

5. There is the market. I sold my eggs there.

   _____

TEACHER: Read the directions and questions to students. Guide students to complete the exercise, providing support as needed.

Name _____

You can **combine sentences** to make ideas clearer. Sometimes you must change some words before you can combine sentences.

<u>He was rude</u>. I did not like that.
I did not like <u>his rudeness</u>.

<u>He refused to help</u>. I was mad about that.
I was mad about <u>his refusal to help</u>.

A. Draw lines to match each adjective to a noun.

1. difficult   **a.** depth

2. different   **b.** difficulty

3. deep   **c.** departure

4. departed   **d.** difference

B. Circle the correct noun form for each verb or adjective.

1. discover   discovered   discovery

2. kind   kindness   kinder

3. act   action   actor

4. angry   angered   anger

TEACHER: Read the directions and questions in Part A and Part B to students. Guide students to complete each exercise, providing support as needed.

Name _____

> You can **combine sentences** to make ideas clearer. Sometimes you must change some words before you can combine sentences.
>
> <u>He was rude</u>. I did not like that.
> I did not like <u>his rudeness</u>.
>
> <u>He refused to help</u>. I was mad about that.
> I was mad about <u>his refusal to help</u>.

A. Circle the correct noun form for each adjective.

1. different   differ   difference

2. enjoyable   enjoyment   enjoyed

3. likable   likeability   likeliness

4. deep   deeper   depth

B. Write the noun form of the word in parentheses to complete each sentence.

1. We made an exciting _____ . (discover)

2. I enjoy the park's _____ . (beautiful)

3. Her gift shows her _____ . (kind)

4. I'm glad to bring her such _____ . (joyful)

Copyright © McGraw-Hill Education

Name _____

> You can **combine sentences** to make ideas clearer. Sometimes you must change some words before you can combine sentences.
>
> He was rude. I did not like that.
> I did not like his rudeness.
>
> He refused to help. I was mad about that.
> I was mad about his refusal to help.

Combine the sentences by using the noun form of the underlined adjective or verb. Write the new sentence on the line.

1. We did something exciting. We <u>discovered</u> something.

   _____

2. I can't wait to see Mom. I want to see how she will <u>react</u>.

   _____

3. She has a grin. It shows that she is <u>happy</u>.

   _____

4. She is so <u>joyful</u>. I am glad to cause it.

   _____

TEACHER: Read the directions and questions to students. Guide students to complete the exercise, providing support as needed.

Name _____

> **Antonyms** are words with opposite meanings. You can use antonyms to show contrast.
>
> The nicest apartments are <u>above</u> the first floor but <u>below</u> the fifth floor.

A. Draw lines to match the antonyms.

1. front   a. wet

2. open   b. back

3. weak   c. close

4. dry   d. strong

B. Circle the antonym for each word.

1. cruel   smart   mean   kind

2. huge   tiny   kiss   large

3. false   fake   true   pretend

4. heavy   light   weight   stone

TEACHER: Read the directions and questions in Part A and Part B to students. Guide students to complete each exercise, providing support as needed.

Grades 4-6   **469**

Name _____

Antonyms are words with opposite meanings. You can use antonyms to show contrast.

The nicest apartments are <u>above</u> the first floor but <u>below</u> the fifth floor.

A. Circle the letter of each sentence with antonyms. Then underline the antonyms.

1. **a.** Tim was a slow runner, but now he runs fast.

    b. I work out at the gym every day.

    c. Some exercises are difficult, but others are easy.

2. **a.** I lift weights to build my arm muscles.

    b. I start with a heavy weight and end with a light one.

    c. Then I lift it up and down several times.

B. Fill in the blank with an antonym for each underlined word. Then write the new sentence on the line.

1. The lifeguard sounds _____ , but she really is very <u>kind</u>.

    _____

    _____

2. When you <u>open</u> your locker, be sure to _____ it again.

    _____

    _____

TEACHER: Read the directions and questions in Part A and Part B to students. Guide students to complete each exercise, providing support as needed.

Name _____

Antonyms are words with opposite meanings. You can use antonyms to show contrast.

The nicest apartments are <u>above</u> the first floor but <u>below</u> the fifth floor.

Fill in the blank with an antonym for each underlined word. Then write the new sentence on the line.

1. Tim was a <u>slow</u> runner, but now he is a _____ runner.

_____

2. In yoga class, some exercises are _____, but others are <u>easy</u> to do.

_____

3. At the gym, Gina lifts a <u>heavy</u> weight and several _____ ones.

_____

4. I lift the weights _____ and <u>down</u> many times.

_____

5. After I <u>open</u> my locker, I remember to _____ it again.

_____

TEACHER: Read the directions and questions to students. Guide students to complete the exercise, providing support as needed.

Name _____

> **Synonyms** are words with the same or nearly the same meanings.
>
> Lucy will <u>carry</u> her heavy suitcase.
>
> Lucy will <u>lug</u> her heavy suitcase.

A. Draw lines to match the synonyms.

1. rear   **a.** boring

2. smart   **b.** back

3. end   **c.** finish

4. dull   **d.** clever

B. Circle the synonym for each word.

1. close   far   change   shut

2. odd   old   strange   great

3. sad   unhappy   angry   glad

4. lift   drop   raise   feel

TEACHER: Read the directions and questions in Part A and Part B to students. Guide students to complete each exercise, providing support as needed.

Name _____

> **Synonyms** are words with the same or nearly the same meanings.
>
> Lucy will <u>carry</u> her heavy suitcase.
>
> Lucy will <u>lug</u> her heavy suitcase.

Read each sentence and the words that follow. Circle the synonym for the underlined word in each sentence.

1. We could barely <u>shut</u> that suitcase.   close   wrap   lift

2. Dad put it in the <u>back</u> of the car.   seat   rear   foot

3. Lucy's vacation has <u>finished</u>.   covered   ended   begun

4. Soon school will <u>begin</u> again.   start   happen   learn

5. Lucy enjoyed the <u>beach</u>.   lake   seashore   country

6. She will be <u>happy</u> to see her friends.   sorry   unlucky   glad

7. She misses her <u>little</u> dogs, too.   friendly   good   tiny

8. We will all be home <u>shortly</u>.   soon   next   small

TEACHER: Read the directions and questions to students. Guide students to complete the exercise, providing support as needed.

Name _____

> **Synonyms** are words with the same or nearly the same meanings.
>
> Lucy will <u>carry</u> her heavy suitcase.
>
> Lucy will <u>lug</u> her heavy suitcase.

Replace the underlined word with a synonym. Then write your new sentence on the line.

1. We could barely <u>close</u> that suitcase.

   _____

2. Dad put it in the <u>rear</u> of the car.

   _____

3. Soon school will <u>begin</u> again.

   _____

4. Lucy will be <u>happy</u> to see her friends.

   _____

5. The <u>road</u> is crowded with cars heading home.

   _____

TEACHER: Read the directions and questions to students. Guide students to complete the exercise, providing support as needed.

Name _____

Sometimes, words that mean nearly the same thing have slight differences in their meanings. We call those differences **shades of meaning.**

WEAK: The stream <u>trickled</u> down.

STRONGER: The stream <u>flowed</u> down.

STRONGEST: The stream <u>gushed</u> down.

A. **Choose the strongest meaning to finish each sentence. Circle the letter of your answer.**

1. The water in the stream is _____.

   a. chilly   **b.** freezing   **c.** cold

2. Sunlight _____ on the water.

   a. glows   **b.** twinkles   **c.** flashes

3. A frog _____ into the air.

   a. leaps   **b.** hops   **c.** jumps

B. **Choose the word in parentheses that fits each sentence. Underline your answer.**

1. A dragonfly (flutters, trembles) its wings.

2. A (gentle, tender) breeze blows.

3. Turtles enjoy the warm (daylight, sunshine).

4. The pond is quiet and (nonviolent, peaceful).

TEACHER: Read the directions and questions in Part A and Part B to students. Guide students to complete each exercise, providing support as needed.

Name _____

Sometimes, words that mean nearly the same thing have slight differences in their meanings. We call those differences **shades of meaning.**

WEAK: The stream trickled down.

STRONGER: The stream flowed down.

STRONGEST: The stream gushed down.

A.   Circle the letter of the sentence with the strongest shade of meaning.

1.   **a.** The water in the stream is chilly.

     b. The water in the stream is icy.

     c. The water in the stream is cold.

2.   **a.** A small frog falls into the water.

     b. A small frog drops into the water.

     c. A small frog plummets into the water.

B.   Rewrite each sentence. Use a stronger shade of meaning for the underlined word.

1.   Those turtles seem to like the sunshine.

_____

2.   I feel the breeze tangle my hair.

_____

3.   The pond and stream are totally quiet.

_____

TEACHER: Read the directions and questions in Part A and Part B to students. Guide students to complete each exercise, providing support as needed.

Name _____

Sometimes, words that mean nearly the same thing have slight differences in their meanings. We call those differences **shades of meaning.**

WEAK:	The stream <u>trickled</u> down.
STRONGER:	The stream <u>flowed</u> down.
STRONGEST:	The stream <u>gushed</u> down.

Rewrite the paragraph. Replace the underlined words with more precise synonyms.

1. The pond was <u>mute</u>. Dragonflies <u>trembled</u> their wings. Turtles basked in the <u>daylight</u>. A <u>tender</u> breeze blew. I enjoyed the <u>nonviolent</u> scene.

_____

_____

_____

_____

_____

TEACHER: Read the directions and paragraph to students. Guide students to complete the exercise, providing support as needed.

Grades 4-6   **477**

Name _____

> Some words are spelled the same and pronounced the same, but have different meanings. Use context clues to decide which meaning of the word is correct.

A. Circle the letter of the word or phrase that has the same meaning as the underlined word in the sentence.

1. The boy went out to play in the <u>yard</u>.

   a. unit of measure   **b.** room   **c.** grassy area   **d.** wide road

2. There is not enough <u>space</u> in my suitcase for my clothes.

   a. empty area   **b.** universe   **c.** air   **d.** vehicle

3. We went on vacation in another <u>country</u>.

   a. farm   **b.** rural area   **c.** state   **d.** nation

B. Look at the picture. Circle the sentence if the meaning of the underlined word matches the picture.

1. We saw a <u>school</u> of fish.

2. The small <u>plant</u> grew into a large vine.

3. Don't <u>jar</u> the table and spill our drinks.

4. Why does the dog <u>bark</u>?

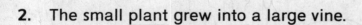

TEACHER: Read the directions and questions in Part A and Part B to students. Guide students to complete each exercise, providing support as needed.

Name _____

> Some words are spelled the same and pronounced the same, but have different meanings. Use context clues to decide which meaning of the word is correct.

A. Circle the sentences in which the underlined word matches the picture.

1. **a.** Don't <u>jar</u> the table and spill our drinks.

    b. Please open the <u>jar</u> of peanut butter.

    c. I put the pickles in a <u>jar</u>.

2. **a.** He was late for <u>school</u>.

    b. We saw a <u>school</u> of fish.

    c. <u>School</u> is closed for the holiday.

B. Write a new sentence using the underlined word. Your sentence should use the same meaning of the word.

1. The boy went out to play in the <u>yard</u>.

    _____

2. We went on vacation in another <u>country</u>.

    _____

3. Why does the dog <u>bark</u>?

    _____

TEACHER: Read the directions and questions in Part A and Part B to students. Guide students to complete each exercise, providing support as needed.

Name _____

Some words are spelled the same and pronounced the same, but have different meanings. Use context clues to decide which meaning of the word is correct.

A. Match the sentence with the word or phrase that has the same meaning as the underlined word.

1. The boy went out to play in the <u>yard</u>.   outer covering of a tree

2. We went on vacation in another <u>country</u>.   nation

3. The <u>bark</u> was used to make a canoe.   grassy area

4. There is not enough <u>space</u> in my suitcase for my clothes.   empty place

B. Circle the sentences in which the underlined word matches the picture.

1.   a. Don't <u>jar</u> the table and spill Mom's tea.

     b. Please open the <u>jar</u> of peanut butter.

     c. I put the pickles in a <u>jar</u>.

2.   a. He was late for <u>school</u>.

     b. We saw a <u>school</u> of fish.

     c. <u>School</u> was closed on the holiday.

TEACHER: Read the directions and questions in Part A and Part B to students. Guide students to complete each exercise, providing support as needed.

Name _____

Some words are spelled differently but pronounced the same. These words are **homophones**. Each spelling has its own meaning.

Choose the word that best completes each sentence.

1. The (cent, scent) of fresh bread filled the kitchen.

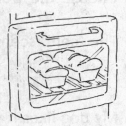

2. My dog likes it when I pet his (fir, fur).

3. She (blew, blue) out the candles.

4. The friends stopped at a park and (eight, ate) lunch before going to the water park.

5. There were (eight, ate) shoes in the closet.

TEACHER: Read the directions and questions to students. Guide students to complete the exercise, providing support as needed.

Name _____

Some words are spelled differently but pronounced the same. These words are **homophones**. Each spelling has its own meaning.

A. Choose the word that completes each sentence correctly.

1. The (cent, scent) of fresh bread filled the kitchen.

2. My dog likes it when I pet his (fir, fur).

3. She (blew, blue) out the candles.

4. The friends stopped at a park and (eight, ate) lunch before going to the water park.

B. Write a homophone to complete each sentence.

1. There were _____ shoes in the closet.

2. She has _____ eyes, like the color of the sky.

3. I only had one _____ left over after I bought the apple!

4. The _____ tree stays green all winter.

TEACHER: Read the directions and questions in Part A and Part B to students. Guide students to complete each exercise, providing support as needed.

Name _____

Some words are spelled differently but pronounced the same. These words are **homophones**. Each spelling has its own meaning.

A. Choose the word that completes each sentence correctly.

1. The (cent, scent) of fresh bread filled the kitchen.

2. My dog likes it when I pet his (fir, fur).

3. She (blew, blue) out the candles.

B. Write a homophone to complete each sentence.

1. There were _____ shoes in the closet.

2. She has _____ eyes, like the color of the sky.

3. I only had one _____ left over after I bought the apple!

C. Write a sentence that demonstrates the correct meaning of each word.

1. eight

    _____

2. ate

    _____

Name _____

Some words are pronounced differently but spelled the same. Each pronunciation has its own meaning. We call these words **homographs**.

A. Circle the letter of the word or phrase that has the same meaning as the underlined word in the sentence.

1. Don't get too <u>close</u> to the fire.

   a. shut **b.** near **c.** not open **d.** far away

2. We will <u>desert</u> the park when it starts to rain.

   a. dry place **b.** join **c.** sweet treat **d.** abandon

3. A single <u>tear</u> fell from the child's eye.

   a. pull apart **b.** mend **c.** drop of water **d.** hole

B. Look at the picture. Circle the sentence if the meaning of the underlined word matches the picture.

1. After you sing, please take a <u>bow</u>.

2. The store will <u>close</u> soon.

3. First, <u>tear</u> your paper into two pieces.

4. We visited the <u>desert</u>.

TEACHER: Read the directions and questions in Part A and Part B to students. Guide students to complete each exercise, providing support as needed.

Name _____

> Some words are pronounced differently but spelled the same. Each pronunciation has its own meaning. We call these words **homographs**.

A. Write *S* if the word in parentheses is a synonym (has the same meaning) of the underlined word. Write *X* if the word in parentheses is <u>not</u> a synonym of the underlined word.

1. Be careful! Don't get too <u>close</u> to the campfire. (near) _____

2. I read a book about a Civil War soldier who wanted to <u>desert</u> his army. (abandon) _____

3. A single <u>tear</u> fell from the child's eye. (rip) _____

B. Look at the picture. Circle the sentence if the meaning of the underlined word matches the picture.

1. After you perform your song, please take a <u>bow</u>.

2. Please finish shopping, because the store will <u>close</u> soon.

3. First, <u>tear</u> your paper into two pieces.

TEACHER: Read the directions and questions in Part A and Part B to students. Guide students to complete each exercise, providing support as needed.

Name _____

> Some words are pronounced differently but spelled the same. Each pronunciation has its own meaning. We call these words **homographs.**

A. Write _S_ if the word in parentheses is a synonym (has the same meaning) of the underlined word. Write _X_ if the word in parentheses is <u>not</u> a synonym of the underlined word.

1. Be careful! Don't get too <u>close</u> to the campfire. (near) _____

2. I read a book about a Civil War soldier who wanted to <u>desert</u> his army. (abandon) _____

3. A single <u>tear</u> fell from the child's eye. (rip) _____

B. Read the sentences. Circle the sentences if the meaning of the underlined words is the same.

1. After you perform your song, please take a <u>bow</u>.
   She had a <u>bow</u> in her hair.

2. Please finish shopping, because the store will <u>close</u> soon.
   We live <u>close</u> to the gas station.

3. First, <u>tear</u> your paper into two pieces.
   I will <u>tear</u> this page out of my notebook.

C. Write a definition for the underlined word.

1. We saw many cacti when we visited the <u>desert</u>.

   _____

2. Please <u>close</u> the refrigerator door.

   _____

TEACHER: Read the directions and questions in Part A, Part B, and Part C to students. Guide students to complete each exercise, providing support as needed.

Name _____

> An **idiom** is an expression that has a meaning that is different from the literal meaning of the words.

A. Circle the letter of the meaning of the idiom.

1. give it your best shot

   a. try as hard as you can   **c.** make a goal or basket

   b. use a bow and arrow   **d.** practice until you get better

2. down in the dumps

   a. works at the dump   **c.** in a low valley

   b. feels sad   **d.** wants to talk

3. down to earth

   a. very short   **c.** low to the ground

   b. enjoys gardening   **d.** keeps things simple

B. Choose the idiom that completes the sentence correctly.

1. Since his friend moved away, he's been (down to earth/ down in the dumps).

2. Don't worry about failing, just (give it your best shot/beat around the bush).

3. Josh never gets to the point. He just keeps (giving it his best shot/beating around the bush.

TEACHER: Read the directions and questions in Part A and Part B to students. Guide students to complete each exercise, providing support as needed.

Name _____

An **idiom** is an expression that has a meaning that is different from the literal meaning of the words.

A. Circle the idiom that completes the sentence correctly.

1. Since his friend moved away, he's been (down to earth/ down in the dumps).

2. Don't worry about failing, just (give it your best shot/ beat around the bush).

3. Josh never gets to the point. He just keeps (giving it his best shot/beating around the bush.

B. Write the meaning of the idiom.

1. give it your best shot

   _____

2. down in the dumps

   _____

3. down to earth

   _____

TEACHER: Read the directions and questions in Part A and Part B to students. Guide students to complete each exercise, providing support as needed.

Name _____

> An **idiom** is an expression that has a meaning that is different from the literal meaning of the words.

Rewrite the paragraphs using an idiom in place of the underlined words.

1. It was the day of the spelling bee. Sylvia was really nervous. Her mom said, "Don't worry about failing. Just <u>try as hard as you can</u>."

   _____

   _____

2. Josh's friend moved away. He was <u>feeling disappointed and sad</u>. We tried to cheer him up.

   _____

   _____

3. Ernesto keeps talking about some kind of surprise but won't say what it is. I wish he'd stop <u>avoiding the point</u>!

   _____

   _____

TEACHER: Read the directions and questions to students. Guide students to complete the exercise, providing support as needed.

Name _____

An **idiom** is an expression that has a meaning that is different from the literal meaning of the words.

A.   Circle the letter of the correct meaning of the idiom.

1.   go fly a kite

   a. go have fun   **c.** go away

   b. go do your work   **d.** go travel and see the world

2.   hold your horses

   a. good with animals   **c.** hold on to the reins

   b. try harder   **d.** be patient

3.   face the music

   a. see a concert   **c.** conduct an orchestra

   b. accept the consequences   **d.** turn toward the musicians

B.   Circle the idiom that completes the sentence correctly.

1.   She broke the rules, so now she has to
     (go fly a kite/face the music).

2.   My little brother is not so happy today because he (is walking
     around in a fog/got up on the wrong side of the bed)!

3.   I know roller coasters are exciting, but (hold your horses/
     go fly a kite)! Let's wait for Mom to come with us.

TEACHER: Read the directions and questions in Part A and Part B to students. Guide
students to complete each exercise, providing support as needed.

Name _____

> An **idiom** is an expression that has a meaning that is different from the literal meaning of the words.

A. Circle the idiom that completes the sentence correctly.

1. She broke the rules, so now she will have to (go fly a kite/ face the music).

2. My little brother is cranky because he (is walking around in a fog/got up on the wrong side of the bed)!

3. Carmen isn't feeling her best. She's really (facing the music/ walking around in a fog).

B. Write the meaning of the idiom.

1. go fly a kite

_____

2. hold your horses

_____

3. face the music

_____

TEACHER: Read the directions and questions in Part A and Part B to students. Guide students to complete each exercise, providing support as needed.

Name _____

> An **idiom** is an expression that has a meaning that is different from the literal meaning of the words.

A. Write the meaning of the idiom on the line.

1. go fly a kite _____

2. hold your horses _____

3. face the music _____

B. Circle the idiom that completes the sentence correctly.

1. My little brother is cranky because he (is walking around in a fog/got up on the wrong side of the bed)!

2. You want to play with friends now, but (hold your horses/go fly a kite)! Finish your homework first.

3. Jody isn't feeling well. She's really (facing the music/ walking around in a fog) today.

C. Use the idiom to write your own sentence. Include context clues, or details, to show the meaning of the idiom.

1. face the music

_____

_____

2. got up on the wrong side of the bed

_____

_____

TEACHER: Read the directions and questions in Part A, Part B, and Part C to students. Guide students to complete each exercise, providing support as needed.

Name _____

> A simile is one type of **figurative language**. In a simile, two unlike things are compared, using a word of comparison such as *like* or *as*.
>
> The clouds are <u>like</u> cotton balls.

Circle the word that best completes the simile. Then write the word.

1. My sweater is as soft as a kitten's _____.
    fur   claws

2. I was surprised, so I jumped like a _____.
    lion   kangaroo

3. The stars were shininig like _____.
    planets   diamonds

4. The crickets chirrped as loudly as a _____.
    wind   choir

5. He swims like a _____.
    fish   boat

6. The backpack is so big, the boy looks like a _____.
    student   snail

TEACHER: Read the directions and questions to students. Guide students to complete the exercise, providing support as needed.

Name _____

> A simile is one type of **figurative language**. In a simile, two unlike things are compared, using a word of comparison such as *like* or *as*.
>
> •   The clouds are <u>like</u> cotton balls.

A. Circle the word that best completes the simile.

1. The crickets chirped as loudly as a (choir/wind).

2. He swims like a (fish/boat).

3. The boy's backpack is so full, he looks like a (student/snail).

B. Write a word that completes the simile. Use the picture to help you.

1. My sweater is as soft as a kitten's _____.

2. I was startled, so I jumped like a _____.

3. The streetlights shined on us like _____ looking down.

TEACHER: Read the directions and questions in Part A and Part B to students. Guide students to complete each exercise, providing support as needed.

Name _____

> A simile is one type of **figurative language**. In a simile, two unlike things are compared, using a word of comparison such as *like* or *as*.
>
> The clouds are <u>like</u> cotton balls.

A. Circle the word that best completes the simile.

1. The crickets chirrped as loudly as a (choir/wind).

2. He swims like a (fish/boat).

3. The boy's backpack is so full, he looks like a (student/snail).

B. Write a word that completes the simile.

1. My sweater is as soft as a kitten's _____.

2. I was startled, so I jumped like a _____.

3. The streetlights shined on us like _____ looking down.

C. Use the words to write your own simile.

1. fuzzy   baby chick

   _____

2. hard   stone

   _____

TEACHER: Read the directions and questions in Part A, Part B, and Part C to students. Guide students to complete each exercise, providing support as needed. Grades 4-6 **495**

Name _____

> A metaphor is one type of **figurative language**. In a metaphor, two unlike things are compared **without** using a word of comparison. In a metaphor, one thing is said to **be** another.
>
> Her heart <u>was</u> a stone.
>
> The water in the lake <u>is</u> glass.

Circle the word that best completes the metaphor. Then write the word.

1. The applause was a(n) _____, sudden and loud.

   sunbeam   explosion

2. The sun is a curious _____, peeking out from the clouds.

   lamp   child

3. The food was a _____ in my mouth.

   fire   spicy

4. The fog is a soft _____, covering the ground.

   blanket   river

5. The music is _____ for my bad mood.

   medicine   melody

6. Traffic was a _____ of cars.

   lake   river

TEACHER: Read the directions and questions to students. Guide students to complete the exercise, providing support as needed.

Name _____

A metaphor is one type of **figurative language**. In a metaphor, two unlike things are compared **without** using a word of comparison. In a metaphor, one thing is said to **be** another.

Her heart <u>was</u> a stone.

The water in the lake <u>is</u> glass.

A. Circle the word that best completes the metaphor.

1. The applause was a(n) (sunbeam/explosion), sudden and loud.

2. The fog is a soft (blanket/river), covering the ground.

3. The music is (medicine/melody) for my bad mood.

B. Write a word to complete the metaphor. Use the picture to help you.

1. The sun is a curious _____, peeking out from the clouds.

2. The food was a _____ in my mouth.

3. Traffic was a _____ of cars.

TEACHER: Read the directions and questions in Part A and Part B to students. Guide students to complete each exercise, providing support as needed.

Grades 4-6   497

Name _____

A metaphor is one type of **figurative language**. In a metaphor, two unlike things are compared **without** using a word of comparison. In a metaphor, one thing is said to **be** another.

Her heart <u>was</u> a stone.

The water in the lake <u>is</u> glass.

A. Circle the word that best completes the metaphor.

1. The applause was a(n) (sunbeam/explosion), sudden and loud.

2. The fog is a soft (blanket/river), covering the ground.

3. The music is (medicine/melody) for my bad mood.

B. Write a word to complete the metaphor.

1. The sun is a curious _____, peeking out from the clouds.

2. The spicy food was a _____ in my mouth.

3. The cars were a _____, flowing along the highway.

C. Write a metaphor. Use the words provided, or make up your own.

1. darkness   robe

_____

2. air soup

_____

TEACHER: Read the directions and questions in Part A, Part B, and Part C to students. Guide students to complete each exercise, providing support as needed.

Name _____

The dictionary definition of a word is its **denotation**.

The emotions connected to a word are its **connotation**.

Write *D* if the sentence gives the underlined word's denotation. Write *C* if the sentence describes the underlined word's connotation.

1. If dishes are <u>delicate</u>, they are easily broken. _____

2. The material of that shirt is so <u>flimsy</u>, I feel that it will tear the first time I wear it. _____

3. The new mayor is a <u>powerful</u> woman and will get the job done right. _____

4. The <u>aroma</u> of the soup is how it smells. _____

5. I would not trust him because he is so <u>reckless</u>. _____

TEACHER: Read the directions and questions to students. Guide students to complete the exercise, providing support as needed.

Grades 4-6   **499**

Name _____

> The dictionary definition of a word is its **denotation**.
>
> The emotions connected to a word are its **connotation**.

A. Write *D* if the sentence gives the underlined word's denotation. Write *C* if the sentence describes the underlined word's connotation.

1. If dishes are <u>delicate</u>, they are easily broken._____

2. The material of that shirt is so <u>flimsy</u>, I feel that it will tear the first time I wear it. _____

3. The new mayor is a <u>powerful</u> woman and will get the job done right. _____

B. Use a dictionary to find the underlined word's denotation. Write it on the line. Then write if the word has a positive or negative connotation.

1. The soup gave off an <u>aroma</u> of oregano.

_____

2. The skateboarder is <u>reckless</u>.

_____

3. All the exercise has made her quite <u>fit</u>.

_____

TEACHER: Read the directions and questions in Part A and Part B to students. Guide students to complete each exercise, providing support as needed.

Name _____

> The dictionary definition of a word is its **denotation**.
>
> The emotions connected to a word are its **connotation**.

A. Write *D* if the sentence gives the underlined word's denotation. Write *C* if the sentence describes the underlined word's connotation.

1. If dishes are delicate, they are easily broken. _____

2. The material of that shirt is so flimsy, I feel that it will tear the first time I wear it. _____

3. The new mayor is a powerful woman and will get the job done right. _____

4. The aroma of the soup is how it smells. _____

5. I would not trust him because he is so reckless. _____

B. Choose two of the underlined words from the sentences above. Use them in two new sentences. Write if the words have connotations that are negative, positive, or neutral.

1. _____

   _____

   _____

2. _____

   _____

   _____

TEACHER: Read the directions and questions in Part A and Part B to students. Guide students to complete each exercise, providing support as needed.

Grades 4-6   **501**

Name _____

> The emotions connected to a word are its **connotation**. Connotations can be positive, negative, or neutral.
>
> **Positive:** The customer was <u>assertive</u>.
>
> **Negative:** The customer was <u>pushy</u>.

A. **Write + if the connotation of the word is positive. Write – if the connotation is negative.**

1. valuable _____

2. cheap _____

3. odd _____

4. curious _____

B. **The words in parentheses are synonyms. Circle the one that gives the sentence either a positive or negative meaning.**

1. **Negative:** Marianne wore her (fancy, gaudy) shoes.

2. **Negative:** He is a (stubborn, determined) student.

3. **Positive:** The performers wore (simple, plain) dresses for the show.

4. **Positive:** She (smirked, smiled) at his joke.

TEACHER: Read the directions and questions in Part A and Part B to students. Guide students to complete each exercise, providing support as needed.

Name _____

> The emotions connected to a word are its **connotation**. Connotations can be positive, negative, or neutral.
>
> **Positive:** The customer was <u>assertive</u>.
>
> **Negative:** The customer was <u>pushy</u>.

A. Write + if the connotation of the word is positive. Write – if it is negative.

1. valuable   _____

2. odd   _____

3. cheap   _____

4. curious   _____

B. Circle one of the words in parentheses. Then write <u>Positive</u> or <u>Negative</u> to show whether the word gives the sentence a positive or negative meaning.

1. Marianne wore her (fancy/gaudy) shoes.

_____

2. He is a (stubborn/determined) student.

_____

3. The school uniforms are very (simple/plain).

_____

4. She (smirked/smiled) at his joke.

_____

TEACHER: Read the directions and questions in Part A and Part B to students. Guide students to complete each exercise, providing support as needed.

Name _____

> The emotions connected to a word are its **connotation**. Connotations can be positive, negative, or neutral.
>
> **Positive:** The customer was <u>assertive</u>.
>
> **Negative:** The customer was <u>pushy</u>.

A. Write + if the connotation of the underlined word is positive. Write – if the connotation is negative.

1. He is a <u>valuable</u> employee.   _____

2. They have a very <u>odd</u> aunt.   _____

3. These shoes are <u>cheap</u>.   _____

B. The words in parentheses are synonyms. Circle one of the synonyms. Then write <u>Positive</u> or <u>Negative</u> to show whether the word gives the sentence a positive or negative meaning.

1. Marianne wore her (fancy/gaudy) shoes. _____

2. He is a (stubborn/determined) student. _____

3. The school uniforms are (simple/plain). _____

C. Think of a synonym for the underlined word. Write a new sentence using the synonym. Then tell how the new word's connotation is different from that of the original word.

1. The woman was <u>curious</u>. _____

    _____

2. She <u>smirked</u> at his joke. _____

    _____

TEACHER: Read the directions and questions in Part A, Part B, and Part C to students. Guide students to complete each exercise, providing support as needed.

Name _____

> A **nominalization** is a noun created from another word, such as *freedom* from *free*.
>
> careless → carelessness   different → difference
> refuse → refusal   intense → intensity
> live → life   react → reaction

A.   Read the words. Draw a line to match each word to its nominalization.

1.   difficult   **a.**   failure

2.   elect   **b.**   difficulty

3.   move   **c.**   election

4.   fail   **d.**   movement

B.   Circle the correct nominalization in parentheses.

1.   (Careless, Carelessness) can cause accidents.

2.   I love my (live, life)!

3.   There is a (difference, different) between snow and rain.

4.   We had a happy (react, reaction) to the good news.

TEACHER: Read the directions and questions in Part A and Part B to students. Guide students to complete each exercise, providing support as needed.

Name _____

> A **nominalization** is a noun created from another word, such as *freedom* from *free*.
>
> | | |
> |---|---|
> | careless → carelessness | different → difference |
> | refuse → refusal | intense → intensity |
> | live → life | react → reaction |

A. Circle the correct nominalization in parentheses.

1. (Careless, Carelessness) can cause accidents.

2. I love my (live, life)!

3. There is a (difference, different) between snow and rain.

B. Complete each sentence. Change the underlined words to a nominalization.

1. Jean is having a difficult time answering the questions.

   Jean is having _____.

2. Tomorrow is the day to elect our mayor.

   _____ for our mayor.

3. The way that fish moves is interesting.

   That fish's _____.

TEACHER: Read the directions and questions in Part A and Part B to students. Guide students to complete each exercise, providing support as needed.

Name _____

A **nominalization** is a noun created from another word, such as *freedom* from *free*.

careless → carelessness	different → difference
refuse → refusal	intense → intensity
live → life	react → reaction

Complete each sentence. Change the underlined words to a nominalization.

1. <u>Careless behavior</u> can cause accidents.

    _____ can cause accidents.

2. I love <u>to live</u>!

    I love _____!

3. Snow and rain <u>are different from each other</u>.

    There is a _____.

4. We <u>reacted happily</u> to the good news.

    We had a happy _____.

5. Jean is having <u>a difficult time</u> answering the questions.

    Jean is having _____

6. Tomorrow is <u>the day to elect</u> our mayor.

    Tomorrow _____ for our mayor.

Name _____

A **nominalization** is a noun created from another word. Some nominalizations have the same spelling and pronunciation, such as *change* and *change*. Some nominalizations have the same spellings but different pronunciations, such as **progress** and **progress**.

Same Spelling and Pronunciation: approach, dust, hope, increase, report, request, return, review

Same Spelling, Different Pronunciation: conduct, contest, duplicate, graduate, house, insert, insult, rebel, record, reject, use

Read each sentence. Circle the underlined word that is a nominalization (a noun).

1. The students who <u>graduate</u> are very proud.
   The <u>graduates</u> are very proud.

2. Heat creates a <u>change</u> in water.
   Heat makes water <u>change</u>.

3. Scientists must <u>record</u> all their work.
   Scientists must make a <u>record</u> of all their work.

4. We must learn how to <u>use</u> computers.
   We must learn the <u>use</u> of computers.

5. Stop at the <u>approach</u> to the canyon.
   Stop where the trail <u>approaches</u> the canyon.

TEACHER: Read the directions and questions to students. Guide students to complete the exercise, providing support as needed.

Name _____

A **nominalization** is a noun created from another word. Some nominalizations have the same spelling and pronunciation, such as *change* and *change*. Some nominalizations have the same spellings but different pronunciations, such as ***progress*** and ***progress***.

Same Spelling and Pronunciation: approach, dust, hope, increase, report, request, return, review

Same Spelling, Different Pronunciation: conduct, contest, duplicate, graduate, house, insert, insult, rebel, record, reject, use

Use the nominalization of the underlined word to create a sentence with the same meaning as the original.

1. The students who <u>graduate</u> are very proud.

_____ are very proud.

2. Heat causes the state of water to <u>change</u>.

Heat causes _____.

3. Scientists must <u>record</u> all their work.

Scientists must make _____.

4. The students learn computer programs to <u>use</u> computers.

The students learn computer programs to have

_____.

5. Stop where the trail <u>approaches</u> the canyon.

Stop at _____.

TEACHER: Read the directions and questions to students. Guide students to complete the exercise, providing support as needed.

Grades 4-6

Name _____

A **nominalization** is a noun created from another word. Some nominalizations have the same spelling and pronunciation, such as *change* and *change*. Some nominalizations have the same spellings but different pronunciations, such as *progress* and *progress*.

Same Spelling and Pronunciation: approach, dust, hope, increase, report, request, return, review

Same Spelling, Different Pronunciation: conduct, contest, duplicate, graduate, house, insert, insult, rebel, record, reject, use

---

Use the nominalization of the underlined word to create a sentence with the same meaning as the original.

1. The students who <u>graduate</u> are very proud.

   _____ are very proud.

2. Heat causes the state of water to <u>change</u>.

   Heat creates _____.

3. Scientists must <u>record</u> all their work.

   Scientists must make _____.

4. The students learn computer programs to <u>use</u> computers.

   The students learn computer programs to have

   _____.

5. Stop where the trail <u>approaches</u> the canyon.

   Stop at _____.

TEACHER: Read the directions and questions to students. Guide students to complete the exercise, providing support as needed.

Name _____

> **Prefixes** appear at the beginnings of words. Here are some common prefixes and their meanings:
>
> *un–*: not, against, *or* opposite   *mis–*: wrong *or* badly
>
> *dis–*: not *or* opposite of   *bi–*: two *or* twice
>
> *re–*: again *or* back

A. Circle the word that best completes each sentence. Then write the word on the line.

1. The cups have different sizes, so they are _____.

    equal   unequal

2. Two plus two does not equal five! This must be a

    _____.

    reprint   misprint

3. The TV is _____ from the electricity.

    connected   disconnected

4. This is not a _____ photo. It's black and white.

    color   discolor

5. I need more water. Please _____ my cup.

    fill   refill

B. Write the word with a prefix *un-, dis-, re-, mis-* or *bi-* that has the same meaning.

1. _____ afraid means "not afraid."

2. _____ behave means "to behave badly."

3. _____ cycle means "a cycle with two wheels."

TEACHER: Read the directions and questions in Part A and Part B to students. Guide students to complete each exercise, providing support as needed.

Name _____

> **Prefixes** appear at the beginnings of words. Here are some common prefixes and their meanings:
>
> *un–*: not, against, *or* opposite   *mis–*: wrong *or* badly
>
> *dis–*: not *or* opposite of   *bi–*: two *or* twice
>
> *re–*: again *or* back

A. Circle the word that best completes each sentence. Then write the word on the line.

1. The cups have different sizes, so they are _____.

   equal   unequal

2. Two plus two does not equal five! This must be a

   _____.

   reprint   misprint

3. This is not a _____ photo. It's black and

   white.   color   discolor

B. Write the word with a prefix *un-, dis-, re-, mis-* or *bi-* that has the same meaning.

1. _____ afraid means "not afraid."

2. _____ cycle means "a cycle with two wheels."

3. _____ fill means "to fill something again."

4. _____ connected means "not connected."

TEACHER: Read the directions and questions in Part A and Part B to students. Guide students to complete each exercise, providing support as needed.

Name _____

> **Prefixes** appear at the beginnings of words. Here are some common prefixes and their meanings:
>
> *un–*: not, against, *or* opposite   *mis–*: wrong *or* badly
>
> *dis–*: not *or* opposite of   *bi–*: two *or* twice
>
> *re–*: again *or* back

A. **Use the word in parentheses and the correct prefix from above to complete each sentence.**

1. The small box and the big box are _____. (equal)

2. A word in this book is spelled wrong. It must be a _____. (print)

3. This is a _____ photo. It's black and white. (color)

4. The TV won't work because it is _____ from the electricity. (connected)

5. I would like another cup of water. I'll ask for a _____. (fill)

B. **Write the word with a prefix *un-, dis-, re-, mis-* or *bi-* that has the same meaning.**

1. _____ means "not afraid."

2. _____ means "to behave badly."

3. _____ means "a cycle with two wheels."

4. _____ means "not healthy."

TEACHER: Read the directions and questions in Part A and Part B to students. Guide students to complete each exercise, providing support as needed.

Grades 4-6   **513**

Name _____

> **Prefixes** appear at the beginnings of words. Here are some common prefixes and their meanings:
>
> *im–*: not *or* without   *pre–*: before
>
> *in–*: not *or* without   *mini–*: small

A. **Circle the word that best completes each sentence. Then write the word on the line.**

1. The painting is nice but _____.

   imperfect   perfect

2. I'm almost done, but my report is still

   _____.

   complete   incomplete

3. Before school started, my parents

   _____ for my lunch.

   prepaid   paid

4. Talking during a movie is _____.

   polite   impolite

B. **Write the word with a prefix *im–, in–, pre–* or *mini–* that has the same meaning.**

1. _____ possible means "not possible."

2. _____ active means "not active."

3. _____ arranged means "arranged before."

TEACHER: Read the directions and questions in Part A and Part B to students. Guide students to complete each exercise, providing support as needed.

Name _____

> **Prefixes** appear at the beginnings of words. Here are some common prefixes and their meanings:
>
> _m–_: not _or_ without   _pre–_: before
>
> _in–_: not _or_ without   _mini–_: small

A.   Circle the word that best completes each sentence. Then write the word on the line.

1.   I'm almost done, but my report is still

_____.

incomplete   complete

2.   Before school started, my parents

_____ for my lunch.

prepaid   paid

3.   Talking during a movie is _____.

polite   impolite

B.   Write the word with a prefix _im–, in–, pre–_ or _mini–_ that has the same meaning.

1.   _____ possible means "not possible."

2.   _____ active means "not active."

3.   _____ arranged means "arranged before."

4.   _____ van means "a small van."

Name _____

> **Prefixes** appear at the beginnings of words. Here are some common prefixes and their meanings:
>
> *im–*: not *or* without   *pre–*: before
>
> *in–*: not *or* without   *mini–*: small

A. Use the word in parentheses and the correct prefix from above to complete each sentence.

1. I'm almost done, but my report is still _____. (complete)

2. I don't pay for my lunch daily. My family _____ for it. (paid)

3. Talking during a movie is _____. (polite)

4. This vase has a small crack in it. It is _____. (perfect)

B. Write the word with a prefix *im–, in–, pre–* or *mini–* that has the same meaning.

1. _____ means "not possible."

2. _____ means "not active."

3. _____ means "arranged before."

4. _____ means "cooked before."

TEACHER: Read the directions and questions in Part A and Part B to students. Guide students to complete each exercise, providing support as needed.

Name _____

> **Suffixes** appear at the ends of words. Here are some common suffixes and their meanings:
>
> _–able_: can be done _or_ giving   _–er_: person _or_ thing who
>
> _–ible_: not _or_ without   _–ful_: full of, having, _or_ giving

A. **Circle the word that best completes each sentence. Then write the word on the line.**

1. This soft shirt is very _____.

   comfortable   comfort

2. This jacket is _____. I can wear it inside out.

   reversible   reverse

3. The _____ made my dress.

   designer   design

4. Please be _____ when crossing the street.

   care   careful

5. Our music class is very _____.

   enjoy   enjoyable

B. **Write the word with a suffix _-able, -ible, -er_, or _-ful_ that has the same meaning.**

1. Collect _____ means "can be collected."

2. Lead _____ means "person who leads."

3. Use _____ means "having use."

TEACHER: Read the directions and questions in Part A and Part B to students. Guide students to complete each exercise, providing support as needed.

Name _____

> **Suffixes** appear at the ends of words. Here are some common suffixes and their meanings:
>
> *–able*: can be done *or* giving   *–er*: person *or* thing who
>
> *–ible*: not *or* without   *–ful*: full of, having, *or* giving

A. Circle the word that best completes each sentence. Then write the word on the line.

1. This jacket is _____. I can wear it inside out.

    reversible   reverse

2. Please be _____ when crossing the street.

    care   careful

3. Our music class is very _____.

    enjoy   enjoyable

B. Write the word with a suffix *-able, -ible, -er,* or *-ful* that has the same meaning.

1. Collect _____ means "can be collected."

2. Lead _____ means "person who leads."

3. Use _____ means "having use."

4. Design _____ means "someone who designs."

TEACHER: Read the directions and questions in Part A and Part B to students. Guide students to complete each exercise, providing support as needed.

Name _____

> **Suffixes** appear at the ends of words. Here are some common suffixes and their meanings:
>
> *–able*: can be done *or* giving   *–er*: person *or* thing who
>
> *–ible*: not *or* without   *–ful*: full of, having, *or* giving

A. **Use the word in parentheses and the correct prefix from above to complete each sentence.**

1. This soft shirt is very _____. (comfort)

2. This jacket is _____. I can wear it inside out (reverse)

3. The _____ made my dress. (design)

4. Please be _____ when crossing the street. (care)

5. Our music class is very _____. (enjoy)

B. **Write the word with a suffix *-able, -ible, -er,* or *-ful* that has the same meaning.**

1. _____ means "can be collected."

2. _____ means "person who leads."

3. _____ means "having use."

4. _____ means "machine that dries."

Name _____

> **Suffixes** appear at the ends of words. Here are some common suffixes and their meanings:
>
> –en: to cause *or* become   -less: without *or* missing
>
> –ward: in the direction of *or* moving toward

A. **Circle the word that best completes each sentence. Then write the word on the line.**

1. I need to _____ my pencil.
   sharper   sharpen

2. That car is moving _____.
   backward   downward

3. That circus performer is _____!
   fearless   useless

4. The sky will _____ when the sun goes down.
   darken   brighten

5. Getting a haircut is _____.
   painful   painless

B. **Write the word with a suffix -en, -less, or -ward that has the same meaning.**

1. Bright _____ means "to become brighter."

2. Sky _____ means "toward the sky."

3. Motion _____ means "without motion."

TEACHER: Read the directions and questions in Part A and Part B to students. Guide students to complete each exercise, providing support as needed.

Name _____

> **Suffixes** appear at the ends of words. Here are some common suffixes and their meanings:
>
> *–en*: to cause or become
>
> *–less*: without *or* missing
>
> *–ward*: in the direction of *or* moving toward

A. Circle the word that best completes each sentence. Then write the word on the line.

1. I need to _____ my pencil.

   sharper   sharpen

2. That circus performer is _____!

   fearless   useless

3. The sky will _____ when the sun goes
   down.   darken   brighten

B. Write the word with a suffix *-en, -less,* or *-ward* that has the same meaning.

1. Bright _____ means "to become brighter."

2. Sky _____ means "toward the sky."

3. Motion _____ means "without motion."

4. Flat _____ means "to become flat."

TEACHER: Read the directions and questions in Part A and Part B to students. Guide students to complete each exercise, providing support as needed.

Name _____

> **Suffixes** appear at the ends of words. Here are some common suffixes and their meanings:
>
> *–en*: to cause or become　　*–less*: without *or* missing　　*–ward*: in the direction of *or* moving toward

A. Use the word in parentheses and the correct prefix from above to complete each sentence.

1. I need to _____ my pencil. (sharp)

2. That mountain climber is _____! (fear)

3. The sky will _____ when the sun goes down. (dark)

4. That car is moving _____. (back)

5. Getting a haircut is _____. (pain)

B. Write the word with a suffix *-en, -less,* or *-ward* that has the same meaning.

1. _____ means "to become brighter."

2. _____ means "toward the sky."

3. _____ means "without motion."

4. _____ means "to become flat."

TEACHER: Read the directions and questions in Part A and Part B to students. Guide students to complete each exercise, providing support as needed.

Name _____

> **Once in a while** can appear at the beginning or at the end of a sentence: I eat pizza <u>once in a while</u>. <u>Once in a while</u> I eat pizza.
>
> **Never, occasionally, sometimes,** and **frequently** come before the main verb: I <u>sometimes</u> <u>eat</u> pizza. Or they come after a *be* verb: My dog <u>is</u> <u>frequently</u> hungry.

Circle the sentence that places the time word or words correctly.

1. My grandfather visits us <u>once in a while</u>.
   My grandfather <u>once in a while</u> visits us.

2. We eat <u>frequently</u> dinner at 6:00.
   We <u>frequently</u> eat dinner at 6:00.

3. Sara is <u>never</u> late for practice.
   Sara is late <u>never</u> for practice.

4. Our school <u>sometimes</u> is closed on holidays.
   Our school is <u>sometimes</u> closed on holidays.

5. I like to <u>once in a while</u> go bowling.
   I like to go bowling <u>once in a while</u>.

6. I <u>occasionally</u> go to the beach in the summer.
   I go <u>occasionally</u> to the beach in the summer.

TEACHER: Read the directions and questions to students. Guide students to complete the exercise, providing support as needed.

Name _____

> **Once in a while** can appear at the beginning or at the end of a sentence: I eat pizza <u>once in a while</u>. <u>Once in a while</u> I eat pizza.
>
> **Never, occasionally, sometimes,** and **frequently** come before the main verb: I <u>sometimes</u> <u>eat</u> pizza. Or they come after a *be* verb: My dog <u>is</u> <u>frequently</u> hungry.

Rewrite each sentence with the time words in the correct positions.

1. My grandfather visits us. (once in a while)

   _____

2. We eat dinner at 6:00. (frequently)

   _____

3. Sara is late for practice. (never)

   _____

4. Our school is closed on holidays. (sometimes)

   _____

5. I go to the beach in the summer. (occasionally)

   _____

TEACHER: Read the directions and questions to students. Guide students to complete the exercise, providing support as needed.

Name _____

> **Once in a while** can appear at the beginning or at the end of a
> sentence: I eat pizza <u>once in a while</u>. <u>Once in a while</u> I eat pizza.
>
> **Never, occasionally, sometimes,** and **frequently** come before the main
> verb: I <u>sometimes</u> <u>eat</u> pizza. Or they come after a *be* verb: My dog <u>is</u>
> <u>frequently</u> hungry.

**Read each sentence. Rewrite the sentence on the line. Place the words
in parentheses in the correct position.**

1. My grandfather visits us. (once in a while)

   _____

2. We eat dinner at 6:00. (frequently)

   _____

3. Sara is late for practice. (never)

   _____

4. Our school is closed on holidays. (sometimes)

   _____

5. I like to go bowling. (once in a while)

   _____

6. I go to the beach in the summer. (occasionally)

   _____

Name _____

> Time words can help readers understand when things happened.
>
> **First** comes at the beginning of a story or process. **Finally** comes at the end.
>
> **Next** and **then** come in the middle. They can be placed in any order.

Circle the word or word that complete each sentence correctly.

1. I am going to tell you about my weekend.

   _____, I went to my friend's house
        Next   First
   for pizza and a movie.

2. _____, on Saturday morning,
        Next   First
   I woke up early and went hiking with my mother.

3. _____, in the afternoon, I helped
        Finally   Then
   my father wash the car.

4. _____, we visited my grandparents
        After that   Finally
   and played board games.

5. _____, on Sunday morning,
        Then   First
   I worked on my homework.

6. _____, we celebrated my sister's
        First   Finally
   birthday with friends and family. It was a great weekend.

TEACHER: Read the directions and questions to students. Guide students to complete the exercise, providing support as needed.

Name _____

> Time words can help readers understand when things happened.
>
> **First** comes at the beginning of a story or process. **Finally** comes at the end.
>
> **Next** and **then** come in the middle. They can be placed in any order.

Complete the story by filling in the spaces with words from the box. Some of the words can be used more than once.

> Then   Finally   Next   First

1. I am going to tell you about my weekend. _____, I went to my friend's house for pizza and a movie.

2. _____, on Saturday morning, I woke up early and went hiking with my mother.

3. _____, in the afternoon, I helped my father wash the car.

4. _____, on Sunday morning, I worked on my homework.

5. _____, we celebrated my sister's birthday with friends and family. It was a great weekend.

Name _____

Time words can help readers understand when things happened.

First comes at the beginning of a story or process. **Finally** comes at the end.

Next and **then** come in the middle. They can be placed in any order.

Complete the story by filling in the spaces with time words from the instructions. Some of the words can be used more than once.

1. I am going to tell you about my weekend. _____, I went to my friend's house for pizza and a movie.

2. _____, on Saturday morning, I woke up early and went hiking with my mother.

3. _____, in the afternoon, I helped my father wash the car.

4. _____, we visited my grandparents and played board games.

5. _____, on Sunday morning, I worked on my homework.

6. _____, we celebrated my sister's birthday with friends and family. It was a great weekend.

TEACHER: Read the directions and questions to students. Guide students to complete the exercise, providing support as needed.

Name _____

> Many words look similar and have the same meanings in English and Spanish. These are called **cognates**. An example of a cognate is *car* in English and *carro* in Spanish.

Read each sentence. Then circle the Spanish word that has the same meaning as the underlined word.

1. I see an <u>insect</u> crawling on the wall.

   carro   insecto

2. Our teacher will not <u>accept</u> late homework.

   aceptar   actividades

3. Swimming is one of my favorite <u>activities</u>.

   carro   actividades

4. We are taking the <u>train</u> to New York City.

   tren   aceptar

5. I need a big <u>bottle</u> of water for my hike.

   botella   tren

TEACHER: Read the directions and questions to students. Guide students to complete the exercise, providing support as needed.

Name _____

Many words look similar and have the same meanings in English and Spanish. These are called **cognates**. An example of a cognate is *car* in English and *carro* in Spanish.

A. Read each sentence. Then circle the Spanish word that has the same meaning as the underlined word.

1. I see an <u>insect</u> crawling on the wall.

   a. carro

   b. insecto

   c. botella

2. Our teacher will not <u>accept</u> late homework.

   a. aceptar

   b. actividades

   c. botella

B. Read each sentence. Choose a Spanish word from the box with the same meaning as the underlined word. Write it on the line.

botella   actividades   insecto   carro   tren   aceptar

1. Swimming is one of my favorite <u>activities</u>. _____

2. We are taking the <u>train</u> to New York City. _____

3. I need a big <u>bottle</u> of water for my hike. _____

TEACHER: Read the directions and questions in Part A and Part B to students. Guide students to complete each exercise, providing support as needed.

Name _____

> Many words look similar and have the same meanings in English and
> Spanish. These are called **cognates**. An example of a cognate is *car* in
> English and *carro* in Spanish.

Read each sentence. Then write the Spanish cognate for the underlined word.

1. I see an <u>insect</u> crawling on the wall.

    _____

2. Our teacher will not <u>accept</u> late homework.

    _____

3. Swimming is one of my favorite <u>activities</u>.

    _____

4. We are taking the <u>train</u> to New York City.

    _____

5. I need a big <u>bottle</u> of water for my hike.

    _____

**TEACHER: Read the directions and questions to students. Guide students to complete
the exercise, providing support as needed.**

Name _____

Many words look similar and have the same meanings in English and Spanish. These are called **cognates**. An example of a cognate is *insect* in English and *insecto* in Spanish.

Read each sentence. Then circle the Spanish word that has the same meaning as the underlined word.

1. I helped my mother wash her <u>car</u> last weekend.

    carro   insecto

2. I saw a lizard in the <u>desert</u>.

    desierto   teatro

3. My brother is an <u>excellent</u> piano player.

    escuela   excelente

4. Mark Twain is a <u>famous</u> American writer.

    famoso   perfecto

5. The gymnast had a <u>perfect</u> score of 10.

    preferido   perfecto

TEACHER: Read the directions and questions to students. Guide students to complete the exercise, providing support as needed.

Name _____

> Many words look similar and have the same meanings in English and Spanish. These are called **cognates**. An example of a cognate is *insect* in English and *insecto* in Spanish.

A. **Read each sentence. Then circle the Spanish word that has the same meaning as the underlined word.**

1. I helped my mother wash her car last weekend.

    carro   perfecto   famoso

2. I saw a lizard in the desert.

    desierto   carro   insecto

3. My brother is an excellent piano player.

    desierto   excelente   escuela

B. **Write a sentence using the English cognate of the Spanish word provided.**

1. perfecto _____

    _____

    _____

2. famoso _____

    _____

    _____

TEACHER: Read the directions and questions in Part A and Part B to students. Guide students to complete each exercise, providing support as needed.

Grades 4-6   **533**

Name _____

> Many words look similar and have the same meanings in English and Spanish. These are called **cognates**. An example of a cognate is *insect* in English and *insecto* in Spanish.

Read each sentence. Then write the Spanish cognate for the underlined word.

1. I helped my mother wash her <u>car</u> last weekend.

   _____

2. I saw a lizard in the <u>desert</u>.

   _____

3. My brother is an <u>excellent</u> piano player.

   _____

4. Mark Twain is a <u>famous</u> American writer.

   _____

5. The gymnast had a <u>perfect</u> score of 10.

   _____

TEACHER: Read the directions and questions to students. Guide students to complete the exercise, providing support as needed.